Essays on the theory and practice of imperialism

Dan Wadada Nabudere was born in Uganda in 1932. He studied law at Lincoln's Inn, being called to the Bar in 1963. Until 1972 he was Advocate in the High Court of Uganda.

In the late sixties Nabudere was imprisoned by Milton Obote's civilian government for his activities as Chairman of the Uganda-Vietnam Solidarity Committee. Amin appointed him Chairman of the East African Railways Corporation, but in April 1973 he resigned in protest at the brutalities committed by the military regime against the Ugandan population, and in particular against the railway employees.

Exiled in Tanzania, he took up an appointment as senior lecturer in Dar es Salaam University's Faculty of Law, later becoming Associate Professor. Earlier this year Nabudere returned to Uganda to take up the post of Minister of Justice in the new Ugandan administration, later becoming Minister of Culture, Rehabilitation and Community Development.

Essays on the theory and practice of imperialism

D.Wadada Nabudere

onyx press

Essays on the Theory and Practice of Imperialism was first published by

Onyx Press Ltd.   and   Tanzania Publishing House
The Clerkenwell Workshops   P.O. Box 2138
27 Clerkenwell Close   Dar es Salaam
London EC1R 0AT   Tanzania

Distributed throughout Africa (except South Africa) by Tanzania Publishing House. Distributed elsewhere by Onyx Press.

ISBN 0 906383 02 1 (cased)
ISBN 0 906383 03 X (paper)

Printed by Russell Press Ltd., Nottingham.
Typesetting by H. Hems, The Malt House, Chilmark, Wilts.

CONTENTS

Preface   vi

1 The Political Economy of Imperialism — a theoretical outline   1

2 Finance Capital and the Transnational Corporation   45

3 Imperialism in the Contemporary World   65

4 Generalised Schemes of Preferences in World Trade   97

5 The Lomé Convention and the Consolidation of Neocolonialism 123

6 The World Economic Order — the old and the new   157

Bibliography   181

Index   184

PREFACE

These essays were written over a period of four years of my academic career in the Faculty of Law at the University of Dar es Salaam, where my main assignment as a teacher was in the field of international trade and investments (legal aspects). They were written as part of the need to clarify for myself the deep issues involved in today's international relations. In teaching and learning about these relations, the preoccupation in law teaching is with the rules, institutions and policies behind the institutions as 'law'. It became clear in the course of learning about these institutions with my students that they were incomprehensible outside a theory of imperialism. It occurred to us that unless such a theory was grasped, no real understanding of the practice behind these institutions was possible, and a lawyer taught in such narrow legalistic mould was no more than a parrot at the service of the exploiters and oppressors of our peoples and countries. These essays are the result of our effort to grapple with a theory of imperialism, based on the scientific method of Marxism-Leninism, and its implications for the practice of imperialism throughout the world but in particular in its impact on the third world countries.

The first essay is a summary of the thesis advanced in my book *The Political Economy of Imperialism* (London and Dar es Salaam, 1978), and was presented at the University of Dar es Salaam Economic Association meeting in October 1975. It is on this thesis that all the essays are based. Many of them were written for journals in East Africa, and some of them have appeared in print. Some were written for academic conferences and seminars. It was our feeling that these essays, although already circulated in the manner described, were nevertheless valuable as a publication in book form. My thanks go to the Faculty of Law—the Dean, my colleagues, and the students—as well as progressive opinion of the University of Dar es Salaam, for having generated the necessary intellectual atmosphere within which this work was possible, and for having assisted in one way or another in enabling these essays to come out in this intellectual fashion. To me they will remain a testimony to the vibrant intellectual atmosphere that has characterised the University of Dar es Salaam over the last few years, despite various reactionary efforts to stifle it, and to the democratic sentiments of the people of Tanzania and in particular the very enlightened leadership of Mwalimu Nyerere, despite the imperialist domination of the country which tends to negate democracy in general.

D. Wadada Nabudere
Dar es Salaam, August 1978

CHAPTER 1
THE POLITICAL ECONOMY OF IMPERIALISM—
A THEORETICAL OUTLINE

New and increasing interest is currently being witnessed in the study
and discussion of imperialism. This is not surprising. After Lenin's
booklet on imperialism appeared, a barrage of bourgeois criticism
emerged which was intended to demonstrate that Lenin's analysis was
one-sided, since it sought to explain imperialism 'solely' as an economic
phenomenon.[1] This criticism still continues in the same old way with
new emphasis. But in recent discussions among those who prefer to
identify themselves as Marxists, imperialism is being examined either to
show the correctness of Lenin's thesis, or to demonstrate its incorrect-
ness by calling to aid 'Marxist analysis'. This 'neo-Marxist' school can be
divided into two groups: the first, which seeks to examine monopoly
capital from the centre (the centrists), and the second, which seeks to
examine it from the periphery (the peripherists).

In this chapter we try to show in the first section the reasons why
renewed interest in imperialism has occurred. In the second we examine
the historical reasons why the bourgeoisie has never developed a
scientific philosophy which can explain modern imperialism. In the
third section we analyse in short the characteristics of mercantilist
imperialism and conditions leading to capitalist development. The
emergence of capitalism as a system and the laws of motion specific to
it are then examined in sections IV and V, thus laying the ground for
distinguishing 'free trade imperialism' from the modern finance
imperialism. We then present in section VI Lenin's thesis on modern
imperialism, examining the characteristics specific to this stage as the
highest stage of capitalist development. The developments of the inter-
war period are then briefly discussed, as a prelude to discussing multilateral imperialism of the post-war period in section VII, in which we
also present and refute arguments of the 'centre-periphery' ideologists
on imperialism.

I

In our view, at the back of the renewed interest in imperialism we
discern three major causes. The first is that for those who associate
imperialism with colonisation as such, the process of decolonisation
has been seen by them not to have put a stop to the imperialist
exploitation of the labour and resources of these countries.
The populism of the petty bourgeoisie and/or 'national bourgeoisie' has
never managed to conceal this major contradiction, and hence the claptrap about 'no political independence without economic independence'.
This is the reason there is agitation against imperialism in international
bodies like the UNO, GATT, IMF, and UNCTAD.

Secondly, open aggression against those forces still fighting for national liberation against colonialism and neocolonialism has been displayed by the imperialist camp, regardless of differences in details among the imperialist states. This has exposed the imperialist aim of maintaining colonialism and neocolonialism. Thus, Portuguese ultra-colonialism and its barbaric wars of repression were only possible with joint imperialist support through NATO etc. Equally, the US war of aggression in Indochina was a war of the entire imperialist camp against forces of national liberation. Their defeat in these areas sent shivers throughout the whole imperialist camp. In such circumstances of open conflict, efforts by imperialism to hide its aggressive and exploitative nature behind outworn catch-phrases like 'fighting to contain communist expansionism' sounded hollow to the people of the world, thus exposing imperialism even more. In this way the American working class and youth increasingly gained tremendous consciousness, and imperialism as a world system attracted wider interest in the US in particular, and throughout the world in general.

The third and last but not the least cause has been the growing forces of socialism opposed to imperialism. Since the Revolution of 1917 in the Soviet Union, the frontiers of imperialism have been shrinking slowly but surely. From one-sixth of the world's population in 1917, the socialist camp expanded to one-third in 1945, and grew to new heights in 1975—the year of Indochina. These growing forces of socialism have naturally helped focus world attention against imperialism. Although liberated, these countries have never escaped the harassment of imperialist reaction. From the interventionist wars against the young Soviet state; to the 'domino theory' aggression in Indochina intended to isolate the People's Republic of China, Vietnam and Korea; to the blockade of Cuba—all these are a catalogue of events that has increasingly exposed imperialism, thus creating new interest in literature and discussion. These three reasons are of course not exhaustive but in our view are the most important ones. The recent phenomenon of the rise of the transnational corporation has of course added to this interest but, as we shall see, that phenomenon is only the intensification of monopoly capitalism on a world scale in conditions of multilateral imperialism, and deserves no special attention as such.

II

Bourgeois ideologists, in their 'refutation' of the Marxist-Leninist theory of imperialism, have sought to show that political and psychological factors can and do in fact explain equally well why colonisation took place at different periods of time. This is because they associate imperialism solely with colonisation. The Marxist-Leninist explanation has sought to trace a true understanding of imperialism to the development of societies. Hence a study of imperialism to us is a study of *historical materialism,* the study of the development of human societies in their essentially contradictory movement. It also implies a study of *dialectical materialism,* which gives us the scientific tools for analysing these contradictory forces in nature and societies. These two constitute modern *materialist philosophy.* It also entails the study of *political economy,* for the development of man and his society is the development by man of his productive forces together with the corresponding production relations. All these help us to isolate laws of social development which then enable us to study the different *modes of production* and the laws of motion specific to them.

These three constitute Marxist-Leninist ideology and science; so that a Marxist-Leninist analysis of modern imperialism is both an ideology of the proletariat, and a *scientific exposition* of capitalism at a specific stage of its development. Bourgeois ideologists would smile at this statement for to them it is impossible for an ideology to be scientific. This is not surprising, for historically the bourgeoisie could not have advanced materialistic philosophy to a scientific level. When they emerged as a class still within the womb of feudalism, they counter-posed mechanical science to theology under the guise of 'natural philosophy'. They made a tremendous contribution to the rise of modern science, although instead of going further they then retrogressed.

From the Renaissance in the latter half of the fifteenth century interest in the philosophies of antiquity slowly shattered the dictator-ship of the church over men's minds, and with the Reformation Protestantism became the agent for change among the Germanic peoples. In Italy there was the work of Leonardo da Vinci who, like all great men of the period, took advantage of the new developments to travel widely, and in this way made valuable scientific observations in his travels. These discoveries pushed scientific knowledge forward. But perhaps one single development which created a new age in natural science was the great work of Copernicus. From that moment onwards natural science was liberated from theology, although up to this day the church still makes efforts to bring science within its confines. There is no doubt that from that day the bourgeoisie, who increasingly challenged the church, made rapid developments. The science which began with Kepler's discovery of the laws of planetary movement, was developed by Newton, who formulated the general laws of motion.

By the first part of the eighteenth century, however, although without doubt great advances had been achieved, natural science could no longer make any significant breakthrough in the general outlook on nature until the next century, by which time the bourgeoisie were rapidly becoming a reactionary force. No progress could be made so long as motion in all nature was restricted to the absolute *immutable laws* that mechanical science was able to elaborate at this time. All change and all development in nature were denied. As Engels commented,

Natural science, so revolutionary at the outset, suddenly found itself confronted by an out-and-out conservative nature, in which even today everything was as it had been from the beginning and in which—to the end of the world or for all eternity—everything would remain as it had been since the beginning.[2]

Here then we see that science, although it had challenged the church in the earlier phase, still remained deeply enmeshed in theology. 'Everywhere it sought and found the ultimate cause in an impulse from outside that was not to be explained from nature itself.'[3] It was only with philosophers beginning with Kant, Descartes, Dalton, etc., that the idea of the first impulse was done away with, establishing that the earth and the solar system had come into being in the course of time. Further scientific researches confirmed motion in nature linking organic and inorganic bodies through the laws of chemistry. But science even with this prop-up of philosophy was still 'predominantly a collecting science', a science of 'finished things'.[4] It could break out of this limbo to become a true science, concerned not with *collection* but with *systematising,* a science of the processes, of the origin, development and interconnection of all the processes into one coherent whole, only with the three great discoveries of the first half of the nineteenth century. These were: the discovery of the *cell* as the unit from which the whole plant and animal body develops, multiplies, and differentiates; the theory of *transformation of energy,* which demonstrated that all forces—heat, radiation, electricity, magnetism and chemical energy— are different forms of manifestation of universal motion; finally, there was the proof by Darwin that *all organic products* of nature, including man, are the result of a long process of *evolution* from a few originally unicellular germs, and that these arose from protoplasm or albumen which came into existence by *chemical means.* With these great discoveries a point was reached where it was possible to demonstrate the interconnection not only between the processes in nature in particular spheres, but also of those particular spheres on the whole, and present in an appropriately systematic form a comprehensive view of the interconnection in nature by means of the facts provided by empirical natural science itself.[5] On this basis the *dialectical* interconnection of nature as a 'system of nature' became possible.

But who was to bring about this science? The bourgeoisie by the 1830s were denying the very basis for developing such a scientific synthesis of knowledge. Every effort was made to deny philosophy any role in systematising the sciences. Auguste Comte put forward a 'new positive science' to 'put an end to metaphysical speculation'. In 1836 John Stuart Mill was hitting at the 'mistiness of what we find represented as preliminary and fundamental notions'. To him what were first principles were in truth last principles requiring proof:

Instead of being a fixed point from whence the chain of proof which supports all the rest of science hangs suspended, they are themselves the remotest links of the chain. Though presented as if all other truths were to be deduced from them, they are truths which are last arrived at.[6]

As we all know, the positivist movement began a chain of obscurantism with which today's bourgeois sociology is bewildered.[7]

It is for this reason that the historic mission to complete the scientific struggle ending with Darwin's work lay in the hands of a new class. It was no longer in the class interest of the bourgeoisie to develop philosophy and science together. They had attained what they desired and had abandoned their utilitarian moral philosophy with which they dragged the feudal aristocracy to the Bastille. They no longer saw the need for philosophy. Theology and obscurantism were sufficient. All they required were the natural sciences, since the development of capitalist production depended on them. The proletariat, who had a new vision of society arising out of capitalist contradictory development, saw the need for philosophy. But in order to confront the bourgeoisie as a class their philosophy had to be a scientific one arising out of the developments of natural science and philosophy in general. Their ideological representatives, Marx and Engels, were the people poised to carry out this mission.

Marxism thus emerged as the antithesis of bourgeois obscurantism. From German *philosophy,* English *political economy,* French *socialism,* they built materialist philosophy and scientific socialism. The materialist philosophy which they built up was no longer opposed to natural science; on the contrary, they merged into a coherent whole. Marxism had brought human knowledge to a point where Engels could finally state: 'The truth is the whole.' On the other hand, bourgeois 'science' remained and stagnated in the eighteenth century and never grew out of it. For instance, bourgeois economic 'science' stagnated essentially at 1776, for since Adam Smith's *Wealth of Nations* of that year, bourgeois political economy still retains as its basic thesis simple reproduction as constituting the rationale behind capitalist production. Ricardo never made any progress in this particular respect. Modern bourgeois economists, instead of moving forward, have stuck to this formulation, which presented simple reproduction of feudal commodity production as the basis of capitalist production and not expanded reproduction based on modern machinery. Bourgeois political economy therefore cannot comprehend the laws of motion leading to modern imperialism.

III

But armed with a scientific ideology Marxism-Leninism found no problem in explaining imperialism, or for that matter any social phenomenon. It did not claim to have absolute knowledge, for that would be nonsensical. On the contrary, it stated that given the scientific tools in our hands at present we are able to comprehend social reality around us, and with the method of historical and dialectical materialism, and with political economy, imperialism can be analysed scientifically.

To be sure, imperialism does not emerge only in our lifetime. It existed in antiquity, under feudalism, and does so under capitalism. Indeed as Lenin observed:

> Colonial policy and imperialism existed before the latest stage of capitalism, and even before capitalism; Rome, founded on slavery, pursued a colonial policy and practised imperialism. But 'general' disquisitions on imperialism, which ignore or put to the background the fundamental difference between socio-economic formations, inevitably turn into the most vapid banality bragging, like the comparison: 'Greater Rome and Greater Britain'. Even the capitalist colonial policy of *previous* stage of capitalism is essentially different from the colonial policy of finance capital.[8]

Thus, for us modern imperialism is a stage of development of capitalism at its highest level—that of monopoly capitalism *based on finance capital*. It was preceded by a mercantilist imperialism, based on *feudal merchant capital,* and the British free trade imperialism based on *industrial and loan capital*. All these are stages of the development of capital, the first within the womb of feudalism, the second on its own as a system propelled by its own laws of motion in its youthful age, and the third in its moribund, decadent old age. Therefore there cannot be any misconception as to what imperialism is. For us it has to be analysed in relation to the age and the stage of development of human society, looking at its material base, the productive forces that propel it, and the corresponding property relations and their interaction, hence the ideologies that sustain them.

When mercantilist imperialism emerges, it does so by erecting itself on the foundations of feudal 'natural economy' based on the lord/serf production relationship. The 'natural economy' is a self-sufficient one based essentially on agriculture and domestic handicraft industry. The product worked out of serf labour is distributed into two parts—one for the subsistence, maintenance and reproduction of the serf and his family, and the other, the surplus product, expropriated by the aristocrats of the manor through 'extra-economic means' for their consumption and the maintenance of their state hirelings.

The antagonism on which this production structure is erected soon led to developments in the productive forces—with the serf increasingly demanding to retain more of his product. The introduction of money and the trade that emerged with it enabled the slow but sure dissolution of feudal bonds. The rise of the towns intensified with long-distance trade, further exacerbating the property relations and the contradictions between country and town. The merchant class which thrived on this trade created the conditions for the plunder of other lands through a relationship of *unequal exchange.* Here merchant capital found its rationale.

Western feudalism, a distinct mode of production with more developed class relationships, entered into contact with other modes of production, at relatively lower levels of development, in Asia, Africa and South America. The products 'exchanged' between the two modes which merchants scrambled for were of unequal value. On the one side (Europe) there were *exchange values,* on the other (in the under-developed areas) there were merely *use values* not produced for exchange as such. As Marx observed:

> So long as merchant capital promotes the exchange of products between the underdeveloped societies, commercial profit not only appears as outbargaining and cheating but also largely originates from them. Apart from the fact that it exploits the differences between the prices of production of various countries (in this respect it tends to level and fix the values of commodities), those modes of production bring it about that merchant capital appropriates an overwhelming portion of the surplus product, partly as a mediator between communities which still substantially produce for use-value, or for that matter any scale of products as their value is of secondary importance; and partly, because under those modes of production the principal owners of the surplus product with whom the merchants deal represent the consuming wealth and luxury which the merchants seek to trap.[9]

Thus mercantalist imperialism was essentially based on and arose out of *trade* in products of unequal values in two or more different modes of production. This trade was quite distinct from free trade and trade under finance imperialism—both based on *capitalist production* at both ends, although stunted at the one end and not trade *qua* trade. As we shall see, one group of the 'centre-periphery' ideologists seeks to take us back to this level of conception of modern imperialism, by comparing today's trade between the 'centre' and the 'periphery' with the 'unequal exchange' of the earlier period.

IV

Primitive accumulation which arose out of merchant capital created the conditions for capitalist production and development. It is not that merchants turned into industrial entrepreneurs. On the contrary, only a small segment did so, and in course of time became real obstacles to it and declined with its development. The 'real revolutionary way' of capitalist development according to Marx occurred when a section of the producers themselves accumulated capital on their own account and, through trade, organised production on a capitalist basis away from guild restrictions.

This they did by deteriorating the conditions of the other direct producers, first through the 'putting-out system', and later by the direct employment of labour, absorbing their surplus labour on the basis of the feudal mode of production and transforming it in the interest of a wider market and greater profit. The process was of crucial importance to the new class. As Marx said, this process that clears the way for the capitalist system is no other than the system that separates the producers from their means of production, turning them into producers of surplus-value. It does so by taking away from the labourer's possession his means of subsistence and means of production and turning them into variable and constant capital, thus turning the direct producers into wage-labourers. The so-called primitive accumulation of capital is therefore nothing else than the historical process of divorcing the producers from the means of production: primitive because it forms the prehistoric stage of capital and the mode of production corresponding with it, just as the plunder, the enslavement, and entombment of aboriginal peoples are its result; and accumulation because it is the cumulative condition for future development. Poised in this manner, capitalist production historically comes to the scene, smashing through the barricades of feudal production and bringing along with it the productive forces and the new capitalist relations. With the development of modern machinery, the capitalist mode properly emerges with its own laws of motion, which become generalised. Under these laws of motion, specific to capitalist production, the capitalist and the proletariat confront one another as the new classes out of the old, one transient and the other historical, the capitalist fulfilling the transient but necessary role and the proletariat fulfilling the historical (i.e. revolutionary) role leading ultimately to a newer and higher mode of production—the socialist/communist.

The producer who was dispossessed becomes the new producer of capital and its antithesis. He produces value. Through the control of the objectified power (means of production) and state power the capitalist expropriates the major part of this value to himself (surplus-value) and pays to the proletariat that part of the value (wage) which enables him to subsist and reproduce more labour. This relation between the worker and capitalist constitutes the basic contradiction of capitalism which propels it on and finally brings it down, thus paving the way to the new.

Whence arises this contradiction that ultimately enables us to comprehend imperialism under capitalist production? In our view the origin of the contradiction lies in the necessary struggle that arises between living labour and dead labour as represented by the two classes. These two are necessary to capitalist production. The problem presents itself both historically as a general movement of capitalism as a whole, and specifically as a particular problem of an individual capitalist. The ideal situation for the worker is to apply his labour to his means of production, consuming a greater part and putting aside a part (seed, etc.) for production in the next period. This as we have seen was negated historically. The ideal situation for the capitalist is to apply dead labour to living labour such that he has the highest possible surplus-value, which enables him to accumulate and plough back some of the product as capital for further production without resistance from the labourer. This however is out of the question and production is possible only under given conditions, which are determined by the struggles between the two classes, hence the contradiction.

The capitalist will apply as much dead labour as is possible in his control. At first he uses this capital to apply it to living labour, requiring the worker to work the longest hours possible. Moreover, as the machinery becomes better and capable of being manipulated by child and female labour, the process is intensified against the whole family, who now work for much longer hours (four times if the family is four), for the same or slightly more wages compared to those which would have been worked by an adult breadwinner. In this way the capitalist has a higher rate of profit and surplus-value, which Marx called *absolute surplus-value*. This process not only produces more and better dead labour and consumer goods; it also produces a struggle for shorter working hours and against the employment of child and female labour, as the process intensifies. Here it becomes apparent that the worker is creating conditions for his exploitation amid conditions favouring his emancipation, because the capitalist soon uses the increased dead labour to raise the productivity of living labour, which as working hours are reduced reaps him a still higher surplus-value— Marx's *relative surplus-value*.[10] This solution of the capitalist momentarily continues production at higher levels, but at the same time creates more favourable material conditions for the struggle by the working class against him and his class.

As the capitalist is progressively forced to reduce working hours he increases machinery, doubles or trebles the turnover of labour into shifts and keeps his machinery working through day and night. This again helps him to fight what Marx calls the 'moral depreciation' of the machinery through non-use. Although it increases its wear and tear, it nevertheless produces sufficiently to replace itself with better machinery. The capitalist's ability to intensify the exploitation of labour through the increased application of machinery etc. is not, however, limitless. The process leads to higher organic composition of capital and soon winds itself into increasingly irreversible movements which as we shall see reflect the limits of capitalist production, expressed as crises, but indicating the highest contradiction between the classes.

The movement of the individual capital analysed above has a concomitant in the movement of the total social product, which Marx analyses in Book II, Part III, of *Capital* Volume II. Marx represents this movement in schema composed of two departments, again representing the two classes in production. For simplicity of analysis he closes the capitalist nation from the outside world, thus excluding foreign trade. He further assumes that the products in the two departments, including labour-power, exchange at their real value. Finally, he assumes that no technical changes or improvements in the skills of the workers take place. For him the fact that prices diverge from their values does not exert any influence on the movements of the social capital. On the whole there is the same exchange of the same quantities of products, although the individual capitalists are involved in value-relations no longer proportionate to their respective advances and to the quantities of surplus-value produced singly by every one of them.

Furthermore, the changes in technology and skills are merely changes in relative magnitudes of the proportions of value which function in the one or other capacity, because other values will have taken the places of the original ones. This is necessarily the case so long as the changes are universally and evenly distributed.

To the extent that they are not, however, it will mean that they represent divergences from unchanged value-relations, but once a law is proved according to which one portion of the value of the annual product replaces the constant capital and another portion the variable capital, any such divergencies would not alter anything in this law. As we shall see, Marx examines these changes and divergences etc. in *Capital* Volume III, thus bringing his analysis in the other two volumes down to the real world.

With this background Marx examines how the products in the two departments are exchanged—Department I (means of production) and Department II (means of consumption). He first examines the exchange under simple reproduction, i.e. reproduction on the same scale. This he again does to simplify the analysis, for once it is done expanded reproduction, which is always a part of it, can be examined separately as an actual factor of accumulation. In the exchange that takes place between the two departments, the workers' wages and that portion of the capitalists' surplus-value which they have to consume personally are exchanged with the product in the department producing means of consumption. There remains another portion of the surplus-value which is not utilised for personal consumption. This is the part that goes to the accumulation and ploughing back in the next period. This portion of the surplus-value is exchanged with the product in the department producing means of production. In so realising the surplus-value and wages in the industries which produce means of production, this exchange thereby realises the constant capital in the industries which produce articles of consumption. That part of the constant capital which is not realised in this manner is partially realised by part of the product going back to production in its natural form (e.g. used to produce more coal), and partly by exchange between individual capitalists in the same department (e.g. exchange of coal with iron).[11] In this way the 'capital for one becomes revenue for another'. This is proved by the fact that about 90 per cent of pig iron in the US is 'consumed' by the companies that produce it, and 50 per cent of the products of the steel industry is 'consumed' by the transportation industry.[12]

The analysis above is crucially important for the proper understanding of the debate on imperialism, which has tended to centre around the so-called *realisation problem.* This debate has its roots partly in classical political economy and partly in elements which have sought to accept the Marxist analysis, but which have vulgarised it in the process and thus tried to push Marx back into bourgeois classical political economy and its modern variants.

As we indicated earlier, bourgeois economics has never risen above Adam Smith's simple reproduction. To Adam Smith, capitalist production was essentially concerned with M-C-M, whereby the capitalist starts off with Money, turns it into Commodities, which he then realises in Money again. Here clearly the rationale for production is lacking, since the capitalist ends up as before! Although bourgeois classical political economy recognised that capitalist production could not go on on this basis, its theoretical formulations never went beyond it. Thus Adam Smith tells us that the total social product (revenue) is divided into two parts: wages and surplus-value (which is split into profit and rent). These are incomes which, according to him, enable production to go on. The incomes of the classes constitute total consumption and hence total production. Here classical political economy obscures one thing—that capitalist production involves more than production for personal consumption of the classes.

Marx's contribution lay in demonstrating that capitalist production is only possible on the basis of expanded reproduction. Instead of the individual product or the total social product being divided into two parts, as Adam Smith and his followers held (i.e. wages and surplus-value = wages + profit + rent), Marx showed that the product dissolved into three parts, namely constant capital, variable capital, and surplus-value. He showed that the rationale behind capitalist production was *accumulation.* The capitalist did not produce to get the same product. The rationale was to be found in M-C-M^{I}. It was from the latter expanded product that accumulation took place. Here Smith's division was shown to miss constant capital as a factor of accumulation which is not consumed personally but only productively.

It will be observed that to Proudhon and the Narodniks (Russian populists), as well as to Sismondi, capitalism was seen as being impossible precisely because of the basic error made by Adam Smith but solved for us by Marx. This was because, as we have seen, they stuck to the outworn Smithian simple reproduction dogma. They argued that in the long run surplus-value cannot be realised because social wealth cannot be expanded, that the foreign market must be resorted to because surplus-value cannot be realised in one country, and that capitalist crises occur because the product cannot be realised through consumption by the capitalists and workers alone.

This is the same error—in another form—that Rosa Luxemburg commits in her two books.[13] She takes Marx's reproduction schema in Volume II of *Capital* as her point of departure, and goes on to accuse Marx of not correctly approaching the problem of accumulation other than 'devising a few models' and 'merely suggesting an analysis'. According to her, the central question of capitalist production is the market. Although the capitalist is motivated by profit, he must have a 'steadily increasing possibility of selling the commodities'. This is important for keeping the accumulation as a continuous process. She attacks Marx for analysing the two departments assuming that only

two classes exist in the 'world' (which Marx never did). She blames
Marx too for excluding technical change and foreign market. The
result according to her is that Marx does not deal with 'total capital' in
the 'real world'.

Because Luxemburg did not understand Marx's method and his two
reproduction schema, she came to the wrong conclusion that realisation
on the basis of expanded reproduction in Marx's two departments is
impossible. In order to get out of the problem, she created a third
department. According to her, 'there must be more than the two big
portions of the social stock of commodities'.[14] This is because to her
constant capital is unrealisable in the two departments. Once it is
understood that for Luxemburg such realisation is impossible from the
incomes of the two classes, we shall appreciate why this third department is a prelude to her finding a 'third market' outside the capitalist
country—nay, outside capitalism. This third market which the
capitalists are forced to find must consist of 'other buyers who receive
their means of purchase from an independent source, and do not get it
out of the pocket of the capitalists'[15] or their collaborators like the
bureaucrats, clergy, etc. They have to be consumers who receive their
means of purchase on the basis of commodity exchange outside
capitalist commodity production. They must be producers whose
means of production are not to be seen as capital, and who belong to
neither of the two classes—capitalists or workers—but who have need
for capitalist commodities. This non-capitalist market may be inside
the capitalist country itself, but it is clear that it is to be found
increasingly in the 'agrarian' parts of the world outside Europe.

This Luxemburgist thesis as we shall see is at the back of today's
'centre-periphery' ideology. Moreover, it has significance for the topic
under discussion. For Luxemburg, imperialism is no more than the
struggle by the capitalist countries 'for what remains of the non-
capitalist world'. We shall come to this question again in Section VI.
What is of interest here is to show the extent of Luxemburg's
deviation from the Marxist thesis, which alone correctly explains to us
the essence of modern imperialism. There is no need to recapitulate
Marx as to the use of his schema. What we need to show here is how
Marx, having analysed expanded reproduction in his two departments
under those conditions, relates the results to the real world. This as we
indicated he does in Volume III of *Capital,* which he entitles: 'The
Process of Capitalist Production as a Whole'.

V

When we examined the production of an individual capital we noticed
a tendency towards increased organic composition of capital. This is
the result of the change in the technical composition of capital created
by the growth in the mass of the means of production, as compared
with the mass of labour-power that vivifies it. The same movement is
reflected in its value-composition by the increase in the constant

capital (dead labour) constituent. This movement of the individual capital is also reflected in the total social capital, and under conditions of increased technical change and skills the movement is exacerbated. Marx examined this tendency of the real world in Parts II and III of *Capital* Volume III. He shows how the value of commodities based on the labour theory of value (in Volume I) is transformed into prices of production. In his view there would be a tendency whereby prices of production (which diverge from values) equalled their value, because of the need for an equal rate of profit on capital, without which capital would tend to move from industries with a higher composition of capital to those with a lower composition, a process which would lead to an equalisation of the rate of profit.

There has been a heated debate on this so-called *transformation problem* initiated by Böhm-Bawerk, who saw this divergence as an unbridgeable contradiction in Marx's analysis. Today's 'centre-periphery ideology' too takes this issue as the point of departure in its economistic approach.[16] There can be no doubt, however, that values and prices of production do not stand in contradiction, on the contrary the latter are derived from the former and the latter cannot be examined outside the theory of value. Prices of production are derived from the conditions of production itself including remuneration for labour-power, and there is an interdependence between them.

For Marx the interrelationship is important. He pointed out that Adam Smith and Ricardo avoided the determination of the value of commodities by labour-time, preferring instead to use prices of production (which they called 'natural price', 'price of production' or 'cost of production') as centres around which market prices fluctuated. They did that, according to Marx, because the price of production

> is an utterly external and *prima facie* meaningless form of the value of commodities, a form as it appears in competition, therefore in the mind of the vulgar capitalist, and consequently in that of the vulgar economist.[17]

The transformation of values into prices of production is taken into account in Marx's formulation of the *law of the tendency of the rate of profit to fall*, which relates technical change and skills to production. Here Marx shows that the increasing organic composition of the individual capital develops into a general capitalist tendency. This is because the material growth of the constant capital implies a growth in its value and consequently in that of the total capital. This gradual growth of constant capital in relation to the variable capital (which declines) must necessarily lead to a gradual fall in the general rate of profit, so long as the rate of surplus-value, or the intensity of exploitation of labour by capital, remains the same. Said Marx:

> This is just another way of saying that owing to the distinctive methods of production developing in the capitalist system the same number of labourers...

operate, work and productively consume in the same time-span an ever-increasing quantity of means of labour, machinery, and fixed capital of all sorts, raw and auxiliary materials—and consequently to the total capital set in motion. This continual relative decrease in variable capital *vis-à-vis* the constant, and consequently the total capital, is identical with the progressively higher organic composition of the social capital in its average.[18]

Marx describes this law as *'the most important law of modern political economy, and the most essential for understanding the most difficult relations'.*[19] He pointed out that, in spite of this tendency, the productive forces had developed enormously, and that was because some counteracting influences were at work which crossed and annulled this general law, and which gave it merely the characteristic of a tendency. Among the counteracting influences he mentioned the increasing intensity of exploitation of labour, which is raised by lengthening the working day and intensifying labour; the depression of wages below the value of labour-power; the cheapening of the elements of constant capital by the same process that increases the mass of constant capital in relation to variable (which has the effect of reducing the value of constant capital), and finally but most importantly for our purposes *foreign trade* and consequently *colonial production.* Whereas for under-consumptionists the foreign market was important as a *market,* for Marx it was more so for purposes of *production.* We shall see that this distinction is important for the proper understanding of imperialism.

Whereas in his analysis of the reproduction schema, he excluded foreign trade as a factor, he now opens up the capitalist country to the world market where it belongs, since the foreign market is its product. Luxemburg's charge that Marx ignored the world market was a non-starter since for Marx:

> The industrialist always has a world market before him, he compares and must continually compare his cost price and those of the whole world, and not only with those of the home market.[20]

Thus foreign trade and colonial production were important to the capitalist because they partly 'cheapened the elements of constant capital and partly the necessitates of life for which the variable capital is exchanged'.[21] In this way such trade *'tended to raise the rate of profit by increasing the rate of surplus-value of constant capital'.* It generally did this by *'permitting an expansion of the scale of production',* and *thereby hastened the process of accumulation* and the shrinkage of the variable capital relative to the constant. While so doing it *also* opened up *'an ever-expanding market'* which the capitalist needed. The emphasis, which is added, is important.

In this way capitals invested in foreign trade yielded a higher rate of profit, because of the competition with commodities produced in other countries with inferior production facilities, so that the advanced one sold its commodities above their value, thus securing a 'surplus profit' which the capitalist class pocketed. Equally, capitals invested in a colonial country also yielded a higher rate of profit, for the same reason of backward development, and likewise the exploitation of labour, because of the use of slaves, coolies, etc.

But this trade and production had its opposite effect, since it expanded production at home and consequently tended to increase constant capital relative to variable, thus leading to over-production of capital in relation to foreign markets and hence tending to lower the rate of profit. This expressed itself in crises.

So long as capitalism operated at this competitive level, free trade imperialism ensured its development and expansion. Historically England, then the only 'workshop of the world' and free trade imperialist country, maintained its production on the basis of capitalist production at home, with the foreign and colonial trade playing its role. Thus British trade expanded quickest with those countries that produced the raw materials and other primary products that assisted her profitable production. *A market was established as a result and not before.* The production that arose in these areas—in colonial countries particularly—arose as capitalist production taking advantage of the backward conditions in these countries to reap a higher return, utilising slave labour or coolie labour. The consumers who arose as a result also provided a market using these capitalist incomes. Here capitalist production was providing a market for itself.

Thus in India, according to Marx, whereas the moneycracy had converted India into landed estates, the oligarchy had conquered it with its armies, and the millocracy had inundated it with their fabrics, with the industrial bourgeoisie the question was different. It was in the interest of the latter to create 'fresh productive powers' with capital, after India's textile industry had been ruined. He stated: 'You cannot continue to inundate a country with your manufactures, unless you enable it to give you some produce in return.'[21] Very soon after the 1830s India was turned into a producer of raw materials and primary products and into a new market. With the monopoly of the British India Company removed by 1833, Englishmen were encouraged to acquire land and enter into raw material and agricultural production. Exports of raw materials leapt up very rapidly. From 9 million pounds weight in 1813, cotton exports went up to 32 million in 1833, and 88 million in 1844; sheep's wool from 3.7 thousand pounds weight in 1833 to 2.7 million in 1844; linseed from 1,100 bushels in 1833 to 237,000 in 1844.[22] Exports of food grains also went up, principally wheat and rice, from £858,000 in 1849 to £3.8 million in 1858, £7.9 million in 1877 and £19.3 million in 1914. In Latin America, too, exports there were accompanied by the production of sugar, cotton, coffee, tobacco, grains, beef, mutton, and minerals. The trade with the USA increased even after its declaration of independence, mainly in

manufactured products from England and primary commodities from
the USA. Profitable production was being maintained on this basis.
British trade with the other European states was on the same basis.
Most of Europe was relatively underdeveloped. The ideology of the
British industrial bourgeoisie at that stage was 'free trade'. With this
face they confronted the landed interests in England, who were being
protected under the Corn Laws. The bourgeoisie set up an Anti-Corn
Law League in 1935 led by John Bright and David Cobden, to agitate
for the abolition of the laws. Why? Because the protection extended
to the landed interests tended to raise the price of food and hence
hastened the fall in profitability.[23] David Ricardo, the economic
ideologist of the bourgeoisie, had stated:

> If, therefore, by extension of free trade, or by improvements in machinery,
> the machinery, the food and necessaries can be brought to market at a
> reduced price, profits will rise. If instead of growing our own corn, or
> manufacturing the clothing and other necessaries of the labourer, we can
> supply ourselves with these commodities at cheaper prices, wages will fall
> and profits will rise.[24]

With this clear position that proved Marx's analysis, the bourgeoisie
finally obtained the abolition of the Corn Laws in 1846. Cobden went
on to Parliament and there negotiated a free trade treaty with France.
Under this, the Cobden-Chevalier Treaty of 1860, duties on French
wheat, brandy, etc. were reduced. In return, British manufactures were
admitted in France with reduced duty. The most-favoured-nation treatment, which was inaugurated in this treaty, was later generalised by
France and Britain by similar provisions in commercial treaties with
the other European states, signalling what came to be known as the
'golden age of free trade'. The 'golden age' of British free trade
imperialism, however, never went beyond 1871, being interrupted by
the Franco-German War and ultimately being ruled out by the rise of
monopoly capital and a new imperialism.

British relationships with Portugal which, beginning with treaties of
amity in the sixteenth century, had exposed Portugal to the exploitation of English merchants were under the new era of industrial capitalism subjected to the needs of industrial capital. British imports of
Portuguese wine became the means by which British textile production
was extended. Taking advantage of the French invasion of Portugal
during the Napoleonic Wars, Britain squeezed out of Portugal increasing
concessions, leading ultimately to her taking greater benefits from
Brazil and Portugal.[25] A contemporary Portuguese economist Das
Deves commented:

> The magical power of the steam engine, which has revolutionised mechanical
> arts within the last few years, has provided England with the means to produce
> manufactured goods so cheaply that nobody else can compete with them.[26]

British foreign trade was clearly the method by which her production at home expanded, while production overseas in the products she needed provided the means for creating a market for her products. It was not for nothing that the 'national economists' like List and Hamilton called for protection. The table below shows that Britain's import trade at this juncture comprised over 90 per cent imports of food and other primary products and less than 8 per cent manufactured goods. Her exports, on the other hand, which are not shown, were almost wholly manufactured goods. Here foreign trade was playing the exact role for Britain that Marx attributed to it.

UK IMPORTS STRUCTURE (%)

	1814-45	1854-60
Food and live animals	27.9	31.5
Primary products	64.4	61.2
Manufactures	7.7	7.3
	100.0	100.0

Her exports of capital also helped her to expand her market and production, particularly in her producer-goods industries like rails to Europe, Latin America and India. The rail facilities helped in turn to enlarge foreign trade. Her capital exports at this stage must however be distinguished from those under monopoly. The capital here was raised through the issue of stock and the industrial bourgeoisie did not have direct control of it. We shall see that under monopoly such control becomes a reality. As Jenks has correctly stated of this period: 'During 1851-1875 "imperialism" was not a prominent factor in the movement of British capital.'[27] Other distinguishing characteristics of free trade imperialism were (i) the role of the state in the economy was minimal; (ii) industrial enterprises were still small and hence competitive. The movement from this type of enterprise to the next was witnessed with crisis; (iii) the tariff policy was still utilised as a defensive weapon. In the next period this changed radically; and (iv) competitive capitalism was unable to control production directly in the colonial and informally colonial territories, hence the terms of trade were at this time still generally in favour of the primary producers.

The movement that negated the above characteristics of capitalism was not accidental. On the contrary, it arose from capitalist development itself. As we have seen, Marx scientifically noted that foreign trade, although it assisted in capitalist production, had its contradictory effect. By maintaining the rate of profit high, it tended to develop capitalism at home very rapidly and hence intensified the very tendency it tried to counteract. The organic composition of capital, which increasingly rose with foreign trade and colonial production, had the tendency of lowering the rate of profit again. Modern Luxemburgists like Paul Sweezy and Samir Amin express 'surprise' that imperialism should rely on the export of capital to other countries if the result is to create 'export of capital' in the opposite direction.[28] As we shall see, these gentlemen want to see imperialism without contradiction. As Bukharin correctly snubbed Luxemburg before he himself became a right-wing opportunist: 'Capitalist development is a process of the expanded reproduction of all the basic contradictions of capitalism.'[29] At this period it was developing in a contradictory way as it does today.

Capitalist development on this basis, however, soon geared into a crisis in view of its contradictory development. Expansion of production based on exploitation of labour at home and overseas, through foreign and colonial trade, gave impetus to new innovations and techniques. Soon, by the 1860s, a spate of new discoveries and innovations took place in what came to be known as the 'second industrial revolution'. Steel production through new processes was cheapened, leading to cheapening in the production of iron and coal. The discovery of electricity and chemicals added to the revolution in the technical composition of capital. All these led to a fall in prices of these products and other innumerable ones based on them. These developments increasingly led to higher and higher organic composition of capital arising from this changed technical composition, and implied a decline in the rate of profit and crisis. As Marx remarked generally: a decline in the rate of profit was identical with the fact that the already existing productive power was witnessed by a decline of that part of capital already produced which must be exchanged for immediate labour. This expressed itself in a great mass of products at low prices. These developments together at a certain stage 'suspend the self-realisation of capital instead of positing it'.[30]

Thus the expansion of production reaches a point where it outruns its profitability, when labour cannot be put to production without 'loss' to the capitalist or, what is but the same thing, when an increase in accumulation fails to lead to an increase in surplus-value or profits. At that point an *absolute* over-accumulation has occurred and the accumulation process comes to a halt, since no further production can take place. This is what constitutes the capitalist crisis. It represents an over-production of capital with respect to the degree of exploitation.[31] Marx added[32]:

> The growing incompatibility between the productive development of society and its hitherto existing relations of production expresses itself in bitter contradictions, crises, spasms.

What does this crisis imply for the capitalist class? For Marx, crisis is a 'danger signal' to the capitalists to adjust. The capitalist will do this by the 'suspension of labour and the annihilation of a great portion of capital'. He stated:

Since this decline of profit signifies the same as the decrease of immediate labour relative to the size of the objectified labour which it reproduces and newly posits, capital will attempt every means of checking the smallness of the relation of living labour to the size of the capital generally, hence also of the surplus-value, if expressed as profit, relative to the presupposed capital, by reducing the allotment made to necessary labour and by still more expanding the quantity of surplus labour with regard to the whole labour employed. Hence the highest development of productive power together with the greatest expansion of existing wealth will coincide with the depreciation of capital, degradation of the labourer, and the most straitened exhaustion of his vital powers. These contradictions lead to explosions, cataclysms, crises, in which by momentaneous suspension of labour and annihilation of a great portion of capital, the latter is violently reduced to the point where it can go on. . . fully employing its productive powers without committing suicide.

A clear understanding of how this crisis originates, how it propels on production, and how it veers into an irreversible contradictory movement as analysed above, is vitally important for correctly comprehending the historical rise of monopoly capitalism and hence the new imperialism that characterise the next stage. Marx went on to say that the crisis will be delayed where possible by the creation of new branches of production in which more direct labour in relation to capital is needed, or where the productive power of labour (i.e. of capital) is not yet developed. It will 'likewise' do so by 'monopolies'. This latter point is vital for the understanding of the rise of modern imperialism, and clearly fixes Lenin's analysis into Marx's *Capital,* from where it is creatively developed by him. The point is elaborated in analysing the capitalists' actions in readjusting capital and labour to enable them to 'go on' with production after the crisis.

Since this crisis arises historically out of the conditions of competition of small enterprises, the solution to the crisis lies in creating limits to free competition of enterprises and hence giving further impetus to concentration, which manifests itself in the higher organic composition of capital. Firstly, the capitalist will begin by destroying, either through non-use or abandonment, part of the constant capital which is least profitable. This will help him to reduce the relation between this capital and labour, helping to increase the latter, and at the same time helping to increase the surplus labour force, which will further help in depressing wages and hence help to increase surplus-value. This step will have to be taken with supporting measures, and so the capitalist will endeavour to restructure production towards greater concentration of production. The crisis will have sorted out the weaker competitive capitals, which will have been thrown out of the competitive game. Their place will be taken over by those that survive and hence help the restructuring towards greater concentration which, when combined with the destruction of the least profitable plant, puts capital increasingly on its feet. These steps reflect the intensified struggle between the two classes at this stage of development. The shifting of

labour in this process of restructuring is only possible because the
capitalists, through their control of objectified labour (means of
production) and the state machine, are in a position to force labour to
accept a rearrangement of the two capitals—variable and constant—in
such manner described that will enable production to continue at new
profitable levels, making it possible for expansion of production to
take place.

Against this analysis of the causes of crisis and their dissolution are
counterposed two other 'theories' of capitalist crisis. One such theory,
the *disproportionality theory,* holds that capitalist crisis arises because
of the lack of control and management of the 'correct' proportions in
the exchange between the two departments of reproduction. The
theory springs from a vulgarisation of Marx's reproduction schema in
Volume II of *Capital.* This theory was mainly propounded by the
'Legal Marxists' in Russia, led by Tugan Baranowski. The other theory—
the *under-consumptionist theory*—holds that capitalist crisis occurs
because of the lack of market that arises from the inherent tendency
towards increased accumulation and lower wages. This thesis has its
support from the views of Rosa Luxemburg, as we have seen, and has
its roots in bourgeois classical political economy (particularly in
Malthus).[33] Its current proponents include all the 'neo-Marxists' like
Sweezy, Amin, etc.

These theories have their weakness in abstracting one element out of
Marx's analysis and turning it into a 'theory'. The approach of the two
groups is one-sided, ahistorical and hence eclectic, and has nothing in
common with Marx's method. Marx saw the principal contradiction in
capitalist production as being the contradiction between increasing
socialisation of production and the increasing private appropriation of
the product. This was reflected in the struggle between the two classes
at the factory level and not in the market-place. If capitalism could
successfully control the proportions of exchange between the two
departments, it would no longer be capitalism, it would be a planned
economy, which is only possible under socialism. Moreover, the
proportionality thesis recognised the problem at a very formal level,
ignoring the essence of capitalist production.

The under-consumptionists also overlooked the fact that capitalist
production created its own market, and the fact that it was not the
overproduction of commodities that created a crisis but the over-
production of capital itself, where capital became its own limit. Moreover, the under-consumptionists' error lay in their identifying
realisation with personal consumption, a mistake which Sismondi
committed. As Lenin observed:

> The identification of realisation with *personal* consumption naturally leads to
> the doctrine that it is *surplus-value* that the capitalists cannot realise, because
> of the two parts of the social product, wages are realised through workers'
> consumption. . . Lastly, this same doctrine that national revenue and national

production are identical led to Sismondi's theory of crisis. His theory that
production must conform to revenue naturally led to the view that crises are
the result of an excess of production over consumption.[34]

Contrary to what the under-consumptionists imagined, capitalist
crisis occurred at that very moment when workers' wages were higher
than before the crisis. Marx was clear on this when he said:

> But if we were to attempt to give this tautology the semblance of a profounder
> justification by saying that the working class receives too small a portion of its
> own product and that the evil would be remedied as soon as it receives a
> larger share of it and its wages in consequence, one could only remark that
> crises are always prepared by precisely a period in which wages rise generally
> and the working class gets a larger share of that part of the annual product
> which is intended for consumption.[35]

But the restructuring by the capitalists to enable production to go
on does not solve the contradiction in capitalist production once for
all. For Marx these regularly recurring catastrophes lead to their
repetition on a higher scale, and finally to capitalist overthrow.[36] But
such overthrow would arise out of the acute struggle between the
classes, whereby the working class overthrows the capitalists, and not
through the collapse of capitalism as such.

VI

This restructuring and rearrangement of capitalist production which
historically took place after the Great Depression of 1873 signalled the
arrival of a new epoch of capitalist development. The restructuring was
characterised by the rise of monopolies—trusts, syndicates and cartels
first in Germany and the USA, followed by 'free trade' England and
other capitalist states. This is the stage where Lenin took over from
Marx in analysing contemporary capitalism. His analysis of imperialism
as the highest stage of capitalism[37] brought Marxist-Leninist science
and ideology to new heights. His point of departure was the bourgeois
reformist under-consumptionism of John A. Hobson who, in his book
Imperialism,[38] correctly pointed out that imperialism manifested itself
in the political struggle for and the absorption of territories occupied
by the 'lower races'. Its 'economic tap root' lay in the need of advanced
capitalism to find markets for its capital which could not be used at
home. He, however, believed naively that Britain could do without
opening up 'new' foreign markets. According to him the home market
was capable of indefinite expansion. 'Whatever is produced in England
can be consumed in England, provided that the "income", or power to
demand commodities, is properly distributed. He attributed
imperialism to the 'unwholesome specialisation' which emphasised
certain 'manufacturing trades' for the purpose of effecting foreign sales.

He believed that reforms could take Britain out of this drive for expansion outside its borders.

Lenin, although acknowledging Hobson's contribution and placing him above the Kautskyite revisionists, at the same time called Hobson's solutions reformist. Further drawing on the analysis of the Marxist Hilferding, who had published a book on finance capital, Lenin wrote out a popular synthesis, a truly Marxist analysis of imperialism. In his analysis Lenin argued that the bourgeoisie had tried to ignore and create silence over Marx's work: 'Half a century ago', he wrote,

> when Marx was writing *Capital,* free competition appeared to the overwhelming majority of economists to be a natural law. Official science tried, by a conspiracy of silence, to kill the work of Marx, who by a theoretical and historical analysis of capitalism had proved that free competition gives rise to the concentration of production, which in turn, at a certain stage of development, leads to monopoly. Today, monopoly has become a fact. Economists are writing mountains of books in which they describe the diverse manifestations of monopoly, and continue to declare in a chorus that Marx is refuted. But facts are stubborn things, as the English proverb says, and they have to be reckoned with, whether we like it or not. The facts show that differences between capitalist countries, e.g. in the matter of protection of free trade, only give rise to insignificant variations in the form of monopoly or in the movement of their appearance; and that the rise of monopolies as the result of the concentration of production is a 'general and fundamental law of the present stage of the development of capitalism'.[39]

We have seen what form and content this concentration took. We observed that the tendency in capitalist production—through the accumulation process—leads to higher and higher organic composition of capital. This arises out of two similar tendencies. Firstly, the tendency for the constant capital to increase relative to the variable capital. Secondly, the tendency for the fixed portion of the constant capital (e.g. buildings, machinery, etc.) to increase relative to the raw, processed, and auxiliary materials. Both these movements lead to the rise in the average size of the production unit, first through evolution and finally through a leap created by the crisis of falling profitability. This is why the law of the tendency of the rate of profit to fall is central to the Marxist-Leninist analysis of imperialism as a stage of the development of capitalism at its highest level, for monopoly, although it does not completely do away with competition, cannot be replaced by any other form of capitalism. The socialisation of production that monopoly capitalism brings about only signals the necessity for the socialisation of the means of production themselves and hence their appropriation, which is only possible on the basis of the monopoly bourgeoisie being overthrown and the working class establishing a socialist system.

Marx drew a distinction between two forms of monopoly— *concentration* and *centralisation.* The former occurred when individual capitalist accumulation successfully resulted in the quantity of capital under his control increasing, making it possible for him to expand production on a larger scale, while at the same time eliminating the competitors. The latter occurred when capital already in existence combined, thus creating a change in the distribution of capital already 'at hand and functioning'. Its sphere was not therefore limited by the absolute growth of social wealth and accumulation. It was gained in one hand and lost in the other. The former consisted in the *concentration* through production and the latter in *centralisation* through the credit system—the banks, investment houses, security, and the stock markets, etc. Marx observed that without the centralisation of capital, railway constructions would never have taken place.

As we have seen, the historical origin of monopolies was around the 1870s. Lenin based his conclusions on this issue on Levy's work, and pointed to the following principal stages in the evaluation of monopolies: (i) 1860-70, the highest stage, the apex of the development of free competition, monopoly was still in embryonic stage; (ii) 1873-90s, after the crisis, a lengthy period of development of cartels—monopoly still exceptional not durable; (iii) 1900-3, with the boom at the end of the century, cartels become one of the foundations of the whole economic life. 'Capitalism has been transformed into monopoly.'

It has been argued by academic 'Marxists' that Lenin's periodisation for all the capitalist countries 'does not fit the facts', on the grounds that British expansion of territory and capital occurred simultaneously in the 1880s and French in the 1870-90s, while German territorial expansion 'preceded' her capital exports.[40] Whereas it is true that for Britain monopoly came later, a fact that Lenin acknowledged, at the same time it would be highly pedantic to read exact dates for epochs. When Lenin used the words 'precisely that period' in relation to 1860-70, he was doing so in relation to the boom in capital expansion in a global sense, and in relation to this period as the 'apex of the development of free competition'. So no problem arises in Lenin's analysis of this issue. Indeed, he himself remarked in the same study that:

> Needless to say, of course, all boundaries in nature and in society are conventional and changeable, and it would be absurd to argue, for example, about the particular year or decade in which imperialism definitely became established.[41]

There is no doubt, however, that the crisis of the 1870s signalled a turning point which by the 1880s was already noticeable: a new imperialism, based on finance capital.

What were the advantages of monopoly? Hilferding pointed out that, firstly, 'combinations' levelled out the 'fluctuations' of trade and assured the monopoly a stable rate of profit; secondly, and because of the above, it had the effect of eliminating trade among the combined enterprises; thirdly, it enabled technical improvements and hence assured higher profit than that obtained by the smaller competitive firms; and, finally, it strengthened the position of the monopoly as opposed to the competitive firms in periods of depression, when the fall in the prices of raw materials did not keep pace with those of manufactured goods. This competitive advantage of a monopoly arose because it had attained control of a sector of the industry, whereby it was able to restrict supply at will and in this way fix prices above costs of production, which under competitive conditions would have normally included the average profit. Monopoly in other words seeks to reap a maximum profit—over and above the actual costs of production—which under purely competitive conditions would be impossible. Thus, whereas competitive capitalism historically comes into life with the dispossession of the producers, turning them into workers, monopoly capitalism ushers itself in by dispossessing the small capitalists and turning them into a middle class—a petty bourgeoisie and proletariat to service it.

The same movement that characterises concentration of production and capital resulting in industrial monopolies also characterises the *centralisation* of capital through the banks. We observed that, in the period associated with free trade imperialism, the industrial bourgeoisie as a group had no control over the banks and the process of the centralisation of capital itself. In the era of monopoly capitalism this changes, and the creation of bank trusts goes hand in hand with monopolisation of industrial production. Thus the original function of banks as that of a middleman in the making of payments, of turning inactive money into active and making profit in the process, is turned into that of control of production. This took place very rapidly at the period of the crisis and after.

In the process the smaller banks were swallowed up by the bigger banks, as small industrial enterprises were swallowed up too. The two processes assisted one another. The banks, through intimate knowledge of the financial position of the enterprises, could extend credit on conditions. In this way the banks began to influence them, by extending credit or restricting it; and determining their income by depriving them of capital or extending it. They increasingly assumed the role of stock exchange. Moreover, through these methods they established control by requiring a certain amount of representation in the enterprise they financed. This led to an interlocking directorship being established over the major part of industrial production. The banks began to take more than casual interest in the profitability of the enterprises in which they had an interest. Through their representation on the boards of directors they acquired a voice in production. Hence we notice the emergence of a new type of capital which Hilferding called *finance capital*, a concept which Lenin developed further.

Whereas for Hilferding finance capital was capital controlled by the banks and utilised by the industrialists, for Lenin the concept of finance capital was more all-embracing. Criticising Hilferding's definition, Lenin stated:

> This definition is incomplete in so far as it is silent on one extremely important fact—on the increase of concentration of production and of capital to such extent that concentration is leading and has led to monopoly. . . The concentration of production, the monopoly. . . arising therefrom, the merging and coalescence of the banks with industry, such is the history of the rise of finance capital and such is the content of the concept.[42]

Thus, for Lenin finance capital as a concept is the interrelated development of monopolies and the merger and coalescence between bank and industrial capital.

In this way, finance capital emerges with a new bourgeoisie which Lenin called the *financial oligarchy*. Through the mechanism of the 'holding company' this financial oligarchy acquired the power of centralising capital and controlling production of other enterprises. Here the separation of ownership and application of capital to production reaches vast proportions:

> The supremacy of finance capital over all other forms of capital means the predominance of the rentier and of the financial oligarchy; it means that a small number of financially 'powerful' states stand out among all the rest.[43]

A further characteristic of imperialism under monopoly capitalism was the shift in emphasis from the export of goods to the export of capital. This inevitably arose out of the contradiction which led to capitalist crisis. Here, export of 'surplus' capital took place not because such capital could not be utilised at home, as Lenin pointed out. It took place because of insatiable greed by the monopolists for maximum profits. Marx had also commented:

> If capital is sent to foreign countries, it is done not because there is absolutely no employment to be had for it at home. It is done because of a higher rate of profit in a foreign country.[44]

In the foreign country, and in particular in the colonies, the capital was utilised in the production of raw materials and other primary and auxiliary materials on which a profit could be made on the operation. The more crucial point, however, was that these products were sent to the monopoly enterprises at home where they cheapened partly the components of the constant capital, and partly the necessities on which wages were spent, in order to maintain high profitability there. Hence the law of the tendency of the rate of profit to fall also explained the export of finance capital in this way.

This point requires emphasis because, as we shall see later, it has come under attack in diverse ways by modern Luxemburgists—the 'neo-Marxist', 'centre-periphery' ideologists. Professor Cairncross, in his book on British investments, shows that in the period 1907-14 Britain provided £600 million for the construction of railways in countries supplying her with foodstuffs and raw materials: 'At a time when the population was increasing rapidly it was vital that foodstuffs should be obtained as cheaply as possible.'[45] This was true of the other imperialist states. Other critics of Lenin have tried to argue that

> in order to sustain the Marxist thesis, which relates colonial expansion to openings of surplus capital, as well as surplus goods, it would be necessary to show that the direction of capital exports was to the colonies.[46]

The above is not Lenin's point, but is attributed to him by his critics in order to argue against it. Lenin, or for that matter any Marxist worth that name, could not have put forward that rubbish attributed to Marx. It is clear that when Lenin spoke of export of capital to 'backward countries' and colonies, he had more countries in mind than the critics suppose. When he stated the 'principal sphere of British capital' as being the colonies, he included here informal colonies as well as 'dominions'. He clearly showed that French investment was invested mainly in Europe, and Russia in particular, hence its being called by him 'usury imperialism'. He went further to show how 'finance capital literally. . . spread its net over *all* countries of the world'.[47]

It was in connection with this that Lenin put forward his final characteristics of modern imperialism, namely the *actual* division of the world among monopolistic capitalist associations, cartels, syndicates and trusts; and finally among the great powers. The monopolies first divided the home market among themselves and then the foreign market which was bound up with it, which capitalism had created.[48] The division was on the basis of *international cartel agreements,* which during the period 1900-40 were numerous. According to Raymond Vernon, they were developed in

> practically every important processed metal, in most important chemical products, in key pharmaceuticals, and in a variety of miscellaneous manufacture running the alphabetical gamut from alkalis to zinc.

The object of these agreements was 'generally the same as that of similar agreements in raw materials industry; to take uncertainties out of the market'. They fixed prices above costs and prevented a competitor 'stealing a technological march on the others'.[49] The penalties for not complying with these agreements were serious and included heavy fines and possible boycotts.

For Lenin, however, the main characteristic distinguishing modern imperialism from the old was that for the first time in history the *whole* world was divided up among the financial oligarchy of the powerful states, so that in the future *only* a redivision was possible.

Hence, we are living in a peculiar epoch of world colonial policy, which is most closely connected with the latest stage in the development of capitalism, with finance capital.[50]

This development was important, for it signalled an end to the possibilities of colonial and semi-colonial countries developing a fully fledged capitalist economy. It meant that all the colonised countries were henceforth to be either outright colonies, informal colonies, or neocolonies.

For Lenin[51], modern imperialism was not to be associated with colonisation as such, although it was part of it. Imperialism was a world system. It is for this reason that he spoke of 'a number of *transitional forms of state dependence*', and of countries which, 'politically, are formally independent but in fact are enmeshed in the net of financial and diplomatic dependence'. Thus Portugal, and 'especially Argentina', were such countries subjected to similar exploitation: 'Portugal is an independent sovereign state, but actually, for more than two hundred years, since the war of the Spanish succession (1701-14), it has been a British protectorate.' Today, as we know, there are more Portugals under US hegemony, in this 'system of divide the world', than in Lenin's time and hence the 'arguments' of our 'neo-Marxist' gentlemen on this issue must fall to the ground.

One other characteristic explaining imperialist expansion which needs to be mentioned for completeness is the problem associated with the dual monopolisation of all land in the imperialist metropole by a landlord class. The *natural monopoly* by the landlord class enables the landlords to reap an *absolute rent* which will normally be a price above the price of production. Furthermore, the landlords' *property monopoly* over these lands will ensure the landlords a *differential rent*. This latter rent will be collected from those capitalist farmers producing on the most fertile (or accessible) land, under conditions of an 'empty market', since under these conditions the product on the least fertile (or least accessible land) will determine the market price. This price will then greatly exceed the price of production on the more profitable land, enabling it to realise a super-profit. Thus the landlords reap a rent from this super-profit which tends to increase industrial costs of production, and hence give rise to a fall in the rate of profit. Moreover, the differential rent which the landlords reap does not enter into the general equalisation of the average rate of profit because of this monopoly, which further complicates conditions for the industrial bourgeoisie. No wonder therefore that Ricardo, speaking for the industrial bourgeoisie, insisted on the need to nationalise all land. Thus, the financial oligarchy under conditions of monopoly will find an additional reason to go to the colonies and other countries, where they will directly control, through the power of finance capital, production of raw materials, etc.

In this new imperialism, the tariff acquired a new significance. From a defensive weapon under free trade imperialism, it took on a new offensive function of penetrating other countries' markets, apart from protecting one's own. 'Protecting one's own' meant the monopolies charged prices above cost in the home market, which in turn enabled them to export and sell overseas at 'dumping prices' below costs. Moreover, tariffs tended to assist a country's capital exports, by establishing a protective barrier to assist the mother country's monopoly enterprises in the colonies and at home. Capital exports too tended to raise the rate of profit at home by reducing the available capital, and hence increasing the price for its demand. The tariff mania that arose in the inter-war years was concerned essentially with this struggle for raw material sources and outlets for capital exports. Lenin summarised modern imperialism as having the following five characteristics:

> 1) Concentration of production and capital has developed to such a high stage that it has created monopolies which play a decisive role in economic life; 2) the merging of bank capital with industrial capital, and the creation, on the basis of finance capital, of a financial oligarchy; 3) the export of capital as distinguished from the export of commodities acquires exceptional importance; 4) the formation of international monopolist capitalist associations which share the world among themselves; and 5) the territorial division of the whole world among the biggest capitalist powers is completed.

Many 'neo-Marxists' have tried to add and others to subtract from these major characteristics of imperialism which Lenin's scientific summary reveals to us. It contains the basic elements of today's contradiction, reflecting the latest stage of the development of capitalism.

This scientific thesis of Lenin was far superior to those which were advanced by the bourgeoisie, who sought to explain imperialism solely on political or psychological grounds. It was also superior to theses advanced by those on the left like Luxemburg who sought to see imperialism as the struggle by the imperialist states 'for what remains of non-capitalist markets', and by revisionists like Kautsky who saw imperialism as 'the striving of every industrial capitalist nation to bring under its control or annex all large areas of *agrarian* territory, irrespective of what nations inhabit it'. Moreover, Lenin's thesis was confirmed by actual historical experience. The struggle for the redivision of the world led to the two imperialist wars. The first socialist state was born out of these struggles and hence the revolts of colonial peoples against imperialism for the first time became part of the proletarian struggle. The victories of colonial and semi-colonial struggles since then have confirmed this thesis. The struggle of the proletariat in the imperialist countries went forward, but was increasingly betrayed by petty-bourgeois elements and a small upper crust of labour aristocrats.

In spite of accusations that Lenin's analysis of imperialism was 'economistic', a careful reading of his thesis reveals that Lenin was conscious of the influence of other factors which contributed to an imperialist policy. In a passage that is usually ignored by his critics he pointed out that the 'non-economic superstructure which grows upon the basis of finance capital, its politics, and its ideology, stimulates the striving for colonial conquest'. He then quoted a certain 'French bourgeois writer', who wrote that social causes should be added to the economic causes of modern colonial policy. Moreover, after summarising the five basic features, Lenin observed:

> We shall see later that imperialism can and must be defined differently if we bear in mind not only the basic, purely economic concepts—to which the above definition is limited—but also the historical place of this stage of capitalism in relation to capitalism in general or the relation between imperialism and the two main trends in the working class movement. *The thing to be noted at this point is that imperialism as interpreted above, undoubtedly represents a special stage in the development of capitalism.*[66] [Emphasis added]

Thus Lenin's analysis, as the subtitle to his booklet indicated, was intended to prove, in refutation of 'vapid banalities' of comparisons like 'Greater Rome—Great Britain', that modern imperialism was the highest stage of capitalism and that it was not just imperialism 'in *general*'. This had first to be done by seeking the explanation, in accord with the Marxist science, in the economic base itself. While he admitted the five characteristics as being *economic,* his analysis cannot by any stretch of imagination be referred to as 'economistic'.

VII

Imperialism emerged from the second imperialist war badly bruised. Its sphere of exploitation had shrunk by another one-sixth. The socialist camp was expanding at the expense of imperialism. Europe in particular was in bad shape. It needed bandaging. The US in the meantime, having taken advantage of the war to consolidate itself against its 'allies', came out of the war in better shape. Its production had risen by 100 per cent in only five years between 1939 and 1944. Its gold reserves rose from $1.4 billion in 1936 to around $4.7 billion in 1940. Profitability of the monopolies had jumped from $3,300 million in 1938 (10.3 per cent of the GNP) to $107,400 million in 1945 (23.8 per cent of the GNP). Poised in this way, it was in a position to impose conditions for any aid it was obliged to extend to its imperialist partners. Thus, the Marshall Plan became the instrument by which the US imposed its redivision of what remained of the world on the basis of the open-door policy. Working right throughout the war, it drummed up a series of plans to reactivate monopoly capitalism on the basis of *multilateral imperialism.* A number of institutions, the so-called Bretton-Woods System, were organised for this purpose.

The first of these institutions was the International Trade Organisation (ITO), which was to be based on a charter of world trade. Writing of the work on this charter—which came to be known as the Havana Charter—Clayton, a US official, recalled that the European recovery programme and the trade charter went together. Both were parts of a common policy:

> If we were not to ease the burdens of Europe. . . our chances of reducing barriers to trade would not be good. . . If we do not reduce barriers to world trade and thus make possible a great expansion in the production, distribution, and consumption of goods throughout the world, there is little hope that the aid we are extending. . . will accomplish its purpose. . . The trade programme must take over where the recovery programme leaves off.[52]

In the charter the US called for the removal of preferential (colonial) markets held by Europe. This was because, as Gardner pointed out, 'closed trade areas controlled by imperial powers were held to deny other countries their natural rights *[sic!]* to the vital raw materials, markets and investment outlets'.[53] As it happened, the ITO never took off and another organisation—the General Agreement on Trade and Tariffs (GATT)—incorporating similar basic aims and objectives, took its place. Under it, multilateral trade based on the non-conditional most-favoured-nation principle was inaugurated.

The second institution, the International Monetary Fund (IMF), was to take care of the monetary and current policy intended to establish a multilateral system of payments and capital transfers and to ensure free convertibility thereof. This was to assist the multilateral trade system under the GATT. The third, the International Bank for Reconstruction and Development (IBRD), was to ensure the multilateral free flow of private investible capital under US hegemony. As it has turned out, the Bank has been the agent in internationalising the centralisation of capital for the global aims of the financial oligarchy in the US and other imperialist states.

Thus, under the multilateral imperialism dictated by the US monopoly groups, Europe and Japan became the junior partners in their struggle against the socialist camp, 'to contain communism' and to suppress any liberation movements in the neocolonial world that would interfere with the new imperialist system. A warfare machine was built up to bolster multilateral imperialism, both in the imperialist centre and in the neocolonial periphery. A programme of 'aid' and military assistance was built up to reinforce puppet regimes throughout the world.

But this change in the balance of forces in the world necessarily implied a change in the strategy of monopolies for production and distribution on a world scale. The progressive dismantling of colonial markets on the insistence of US monopolies implied the struggle by the monopolies on a changed basis. Moreover, the international cartel agreements that the earlier form of monopoly production implied had proved inadequate by the forties. They collapsed one after the other. A multilateral market implied movement away from this, and from production based on separate units, to production based on a global strategy of 'complex units of production with closely articulated and integrated labour processes (integrated production) with its various establishments spread over several countries'.[54] The rise of the transnational corporation was therefore no more than monopoly organised in different form. Monopolies under this arrangement went in for direct investments, setting up units of production all over the imperialist globe, all directed from the centre of the imperialist country.

The rearrangement of imperialism in the post-war period has received a reinterpretation by those who claim to be 'Marxists'. This re-interpretation has resulted in more confusion than clarity. We refer here to the recent literature by 'neo-Marxist' elements in the US and Europe as well as in the 'periphery', which we earlier referred to as the 'centre-periphery ideology'. The first group of those ideologists is the Monthly Review group, which has tended to put forward a 'centrist' position. In their book *Monopoly Capital,* which came out in 1966, Baran and Sweezy sought to show that monopoly capitalism no longer operates under the basic laws of capitalist production. According to them monopoly capitalism has negated the competitive model on which Marx's *Capital* was based. We refer to their analysis because it has a fundamental bearing on our understanding of modern imperialism. Baran and Sweezy point out that since price competition is no longer operative, and since monopolies fix their prices above cost, and with the ever-increasing efforts to cut costs of production, it is 'inescapable that surplus must have a strong and persistent tendency to rise'.

From this they draw a conclusion which leads them to revise what Marx, as we have seen, had called *'the most important law of political economy from a historical point of view',* namely the *law of the tendency of the rate of profit to fall,* which as we have shown is fundamental to the whole understanding of imperialism. Baran and Sweezy substitute this law with their own, which they call the *law of rising surplus:*

> By substituting the law of rising surplus for the law of falling profit, we are therefore not rejecting or revising a time-honoured theorem of political economy *[sic!]* : we are simply taking account of the undoubted fact that the structure of the capitalist economy has undergone a fundamental change since that theorem *[sic!]* was formulated.[55]

In actual fact, Baran and Sweezy 'simply' revise the law, for they go further to show how the monopolists, confronted with this 'increasing surplus', are forced to 'absorb' it into 'wasteful' expenditure like the military, the bureaucracy, and the so-called sales effort.

This 'confusion' of Baran and Sweezy is bound to arise, since their concept of 'surplus' has nothing in common with Marx's surplus-value. For the 'economic surplus' is defined as:

the difference between what a society produces and the costs of producing it. The size of the surplus is an index of productivity and wealth, of how much freedom a society has to accomplish whatever goals it may set for itself. The composition of the surplus shows how it uses that freedom: how much. . . it consumes. . . how much it wastes and in what ways.[56]

Thus, for them 'surplus' includes surplus-value plus government and other 'wasteful' expenditure, when in fact these so-called expenditures are themselves part of the surplus-value. Barratt-Brown, although his 'economics' does not take us very far from eclecticism, has nevertheless correctly pointed out the mistake of Baran and Sweezy. He has shown that what had in fact steadily increased was not surplus-value but government expenditure: 'The surplus not taken by the government remained remarkably stable as a proportion of the GNP.'[57]

If Baran and Sweezy's analysis looks too contrived for us to believe, it is because it does not explain to us why the monopolists should bother to wage interventionist wars throughout the world if the 'surplus' increases so amazingly. Here Baran and Sweezy take the problem to be the solution and invert the reality, as in the *camera obscura.* It is quite clear that imperialism cannot reap any 'surplus' without a bureaucracy at its disposal, without war and without the 'sales effort'. For them these are the solutions to the 'increasing surplus', when in fact they are the prerequisites. Moreover, Baran and Sweezy go so far as to suggest that exports of capital are in the reverse. Taking New Jersey, which in 1962 paid approximately 40 per cent of dividends mainly from profits from foreign operations, they conclude: 'In a word, Standard Oil of New Jersey is a very large and consistent *importer* of capital.'[58] Here clearly they confuse earnings on capital with capital. They themselves have shown that 40 per cent of this 'capital' imported went to shareholders, and so cannot be regarded as capital. The Marxist concept of capital as that part which is ploughed for productive application is apparently abandoned. To compound the confusion Samir Amin comes to the aid of Baran and Sweezy to defend their thesis, while at the same time maintaining that Marx's law of the falling rate of profit is still operative under monopoly capitalism.

This confusion is soon cleared when it turns out that Baran and Sweezy, as well as Amin, are under-consumptionists, for throughout their analyses they maintain the *primacy of the market over production.* Amin, for instance, states:

It is the contradiction between the capacity to produce and the capacity to consume, constantly arising and constantly being overcome—the essential law of capitalist accumulation—which accounts for the inherent tendency for the extension of markets and for the international movement of capital.[59]

Baran and Sweezy also see the wasteful expenditure under monopoly capitalism as intended to stimulate 'demand' as such: 'The stimulation of demand—the creation and extension of markets—thus becomes. . . the leitmotif of business and government policies under monopoly capitalism.'[60] And again: *the market* is the thing, the 'leitmotif' of production under monopoly capitalism, and not vice versa.

Whilst it is true that under monopoly the law of value and hence the law of the falling profit are increasingly challenged, it would be wrong to conclude therefrom that under monopoly capitalism these laws are no longer operative. To do so is to try to remove the very essence of Marxist political economy. The monopoly capitalist does not do away with the two classes in capitalist production. The two classes remain, and the laws of motion of production based on property relations of these two classes remain as well. The monopolist will fix his prices *above* costs of production, which are determined under the law of value. In other words, the law of value remains the guideline to the monopolists in fixing prices *above* the average based on value. This is because the laws of motion of production based on the two classes still operate, but are increasingly challenged by monopoly. It is the same as saying, as Lenin did, that monopoly capitalism and hence imperialism are 'the eve of the socialist revolution'. This increasing challenge by monopoly of the basic laws of motion of capitalism is the historic call for their abolition through the socialist revolution.

Another 'neo-Marxist' who has tried to show fundamental changes in monopoly capitalism is Pierre Jalée, who in his recent book *Imperialism in the Seventies* has asserted that since the second world war the relationship between 'finance capital' and 'industrial capital' has 'undergone radical change'. The result, according to him, is that

> industrial capital is now a self-starting enterprise, the hegemony of finance capital is no longer as absolute as it once was. Finance capital is defending its position. Industrial capital meanwhile is breaking through old barriers pushing its way into the investment business and engaging in banking and financial activities. Ultimately, the two are merging and becoming largely inter-dependent. The financial oligarchy remains and, through this pincer move-ment, grows stronger as it unifies its functions. It begins to be a financial and industrial oligarchy.[61]

The only evidence which Jalée puts forward for this profound discovery is three pieces of statistics covering single years, and at most three years. He does not tell us when and why the 'pincer' battles emerged between the two capitals, apart from the bare assertion that this is the case 'since the second world war'. No historical movement in capital itself is established for this rupture in the two capitals. Jalée's statement, for it does not amount to anything more than that, also demonstrates a certain amount of confusion. He appears to assert that 'finance

capital' is the same thing as 'bank capital'. Jalée is not alone in this misconception and it can be said with certainty that a great majority of
'neo-Marxists' hold this position. Sweezy, for instance, in his 1942
book,[62] holds to the 'self-financing' ideology. The bourgeois academics
do the same.

As we have shown above, Lenin's concept of *finance capital* was one
in which the concentration of production and capital led to monopoly;
bank capital and industrial capital merged and coalesced. Lenin's
concept explains the development under monopoly whereby the
objectified power of finance capital expresses itself through a financial
oligarchy and the state in which the oligarchy acquires the power to
centralise all other capitals and savings of the working class, and put
them to production on its terms. It is the same objectified power of
finance capital that divides the world, the same power which we call
imperialism. Menshikov, in his study of US finance capital and the
financial oligarchy, has shown the 'self-financing' ideology to be false.
He produces scientific data ranging over thirty-five years, including
those from the US Department of Commerce, to show that in fact,
except for the years 1930-39 and to a lesser extent 1946-50, external
sources on long-term operations were on the average 22 per cent.
Using statistics by S. Kuznets which give the share of external sources
in the financing of large corporations in the manufacturing industry,
he shows that this was 33 per cent in 1946-53, 40 per cent in 1915-19,
and 30 per cent in 1900-10. In comparison, the internal shares in the
total expenditure of all corporations was 56 per cent in 1900-9,
60 per cent in 1910-19, 55 per cent in 1920-29, and 61 per cent in
1946-56. In subsequent years it never exceeded 70 per cent, and 'most
often was about 60 per cent'. He concludes: 'Thus the thesis about the
wane of external financing does not correspond to the facts.'[63]

Jalée further attempts to show that today's mergers are of the
'conglomerate type'. He shows that 43 per cent of the group assets in a
German monopoly are industrial and invested in banks and financing.
He then concludes that a number of these holding companies 'are
taking a path diametrically opposed to the one Lenin described', for
according to him 'instead of being taken over by banks, they are
becoming like banks, themselves'! Jalée then produces evidence from
the US House of Representatives Committee in 1968, which proves
Lenin's thesis! He quotes the committee as stating that because of the
widespread distribution of capital, 5 per cent capital interest by a
bank in enterprises is enough to control many boards of directors.
He goes on:

> The report adds that 49 banks control 5 per cent or more of capital of the 147
> largest industrial companies as well as 5 per cent or more of the capital of the
> 17 important merchandising companies and the 17 biggest transport
> companies.

Lenin had argued that through the 'holding company' technique a handful of monopolists was able to acquire controlling interests in subsidiaries ('daughter companies') which in turn controlled other subsidiaries
('granddaughter companies'). He had given 40 per cent as enough to
obtain such control. Jalée brings evidence to show that today, in the
US at least, 5 per cent is enough to effect control. This, contrary to
what Jalée is trying to hold out, is the objectified power of finance
capital exercised by the financial oligarchy which shows that, in
conditions of increasing socialisation of production on a world scale,
an increasingly smaller financial oligarchy is exercising greater and
greater control over capital and production throughout the imperialist
world.

Capital exports have offered a fertile ground for 'neo-Marxist' critics
of the thesis by Lenin. According to their view, capital exports were
more pronounced in the period before monopoly. This argument is put
up by Barratt-Brown in relation to England. We do not wish to go into
the argument here because we have already shown that it is associated
with the periodisation question which merely looks at quantities and
not the quality of the capitals and their historical conditions. But the
more recent argument is the one trying to show that capital exports
of the 'old imperialism' of Lenin are quite different from those of the
'new imperialism', in which capital exports are replaced by exports of
technology, skills, etc. This position, put forward by Hamza Alavi,
maintains that monopolies are increasingly interested in extending their
markets for the manufactures from the metropole and are 'setting in
motion a stream of payments by way of royalties and fees for "technical
services", use of patents and brand names'.[65] The weakness of Alavi's
argument is that it regards exports of technology and know-how as
opposed to capital exports. In fact, such technological exports are part
and parcel of the package in the export of capital. A UN Report of the
Group of Eminent Persons on Multinationals has referred to technology
as 'an essential input for production' which is bought and sold in the
following forms:

> (a) embodied in physical assets as, for example, plant, machinery, equipment
> and sometimes intermediate products; (b) as services of skilled and often
> highly specialised manpower; (c) as information, whether of a technical or
> commercial nature.[66]

Thus technology, skills, etc. are part of the package of capital exports,
all intended to be put to production and maintenance of markets.

The second group of the 'centre-periphery' ideologists is the
peripherist one, represented by the so-called third world ideologists.
The central figure of this group is Samir Amin. He is buttressed by a
number of others, and the real central thesis of their ideology is
'unequal exchange'. For this reason Arghiri Emmanuel's thesis is
crucial. The Latin American group led by Gundar Frank falls on the

other side of the same ideology, namely in their ahistorical treatment of imperialism. The danger of this ideology is that it leads to wrong prescriptions for the struggle against imperialism. This is where the two currents converge. One of the central points of unity for all 'neo-Marxists' is that they start from a petty-bourgeois dogmatic standpoint against Marx. Thus it is a characteristic necessity for them in order to show that they are making a contribution to start off by showing 'flaws' in either the 'Marxist model' or the 'Leninist model'.

Emmanuel's analysis, for instance, begins with a refutation of Lenin's thesis on imperialism. Emmanuel charges that the thesis on 'financial' imperialism which is 'supposed to be different from mercantilist imperialism of the seventeenth and eighteenth centuries' was 'put to severe trial' with the 'break-up' of the huge colonial empires 'without proportionate violence and without any marked impoverishment of the great imperial parent states.'[67] Hence, according to Emmanuel, neocolonialism is an unsatisfactory concept which was 'devised for argument's sake, in the face of an unexpected situation'.[68] Lenin's work is described by him as 'a marginal work which never had any scientific pretensions, and which was written rapidly in difficult conditions of exile with no other documentary to hand but the Bern library'. Anybody who has looked at Lenin's notebooks of this work, now published as Volume 39 of his *Collected Works,* will see that Emmanuel's criticism of Lenin's thesis has no foundation. The notebooks show that he consulted a wide range of literature and authorities, ranging over 146 volumes, and a mass of statistical data.

But for us this is an important background to the proper understanding of Emmanuel's thesis on *Unequal Exchange.* It is clear for him, as it is for the others who saw decolonisation an 'end to empire', that it also spelled an 'end to imperialism'. This wrong conception of history is at the back of his unscientific thesis that trade and exchange as such are the basis of the relationship between the 'centre' and the 'periphery'.

In this way Emmanuel embarks on his task of proving unequal exchange as the basis of exploitation of the periphery by eclectically using Marx's formula for calculating 'prices of production' into their values. As we know, this formula is based on the organic composition of capital in different industries within a country. Emmanuel utilises the formula and applies it to countries, where the organic composition differences would not be the same as between industries within a capitalist country. Using this formula, he arrives at an unequal exchange 'in the general sense'. His second analysis of unequal exchange, which he calls unequal exchange 'in the strict sense', is based on wage differentials instead of differences in organic composition of capital. He concentrates his analysis on the second sense and comes to the conclusion that this unequal exchange takes place through differences in *prices* which arise out of wage differences. According to him the different levels of wages do not 'vary in dependence upon prices but

prices vary in dependence on wages', wages being an 'independent
variable'. He states:

> By transferring, through non-equivalent exports, a large part of its surplus to
> the rich countries, it (the periphery) deprives itself of the means of accumula-
> tion and growth. The narrowness and stagnancy of the market discourage
> capital, which flees from it, so that despite the low organic composition and
> the low wages a substantial proportion of labour force is unable to find
> employment.

As a result of these 'unequal' relationships 'wealth begets wealth' and
'poverty begets poverty'.

These revolutionary-sounding formulations of Emmanuel's are,
however, of no scientific content. First, they do away with history, as
we have seen. They see the relationships between the centre and the
periphery as emerging from nowhere, although they pretend to give
their analysis a 'historic' content, which unfortunately is one of ideas.
Emmanuel's analysis also does away with scientific concepts like
'finance capital' and 'financial oligarchy', which represent reality.
Today's neocolonialism and multilateral imperialism cannot be comprehended outside these concepts. In our view the neocolonial world is not
exploited because it exchanges 'its' products below value (although that
is formally true), but because the objectified power of *finance capital*
dictates that type of relationship whereby labour in the periphery is
exploited, taking advantage of relative backwardness which in turn
dictates low wages. Hence a true understanding of these 'unequal
relationships' lies in a clear historical conception of how finance capital
operates in different countries and the forces which are behind this
objectified power. There is no doubt whatsoever that any scientific
analysis of these forces will reveal that the third world does not produce the commodities sold on the world market with its own capital. It
is clear that all production of any significance in these countries is
activated and dominated by finance capital as defined by Lenin. The
power of the financial oligarchy to centralise all capitals and savings in
the metropole also operates in the neocolony, so that all 'national
capital' comes under its domination, in the sense that such capital can
only be used for the production of raw materials and other resources
the financial oligarchy requires in its global strategy of production and
accumulation. To the extent that the 'national capital' goes to no
other production than raw materials (as well as to dictated import
substitution), it is part and parcel of finance capital, which fact
demonstrates the power of the financial oligarchy globally. Thus
finance capital exploits labour in the neocolony, just as it does in the
centre. It does so by taking advantage of, and bending to its needs, the
backward conditions in the neocolony, and thereby blocking any
possibilities of development outside those needs. In the centre it does
it by intensifying the exploitation of labour through increased

machinery. In such circumstances it is unscientific to talk of 'low wages' or 'low prices' in the neocolony, as if these are things in themselves, since they are products of the objectified power of finance capital over production in the neocolony. Equally, to talk of 'unequal exchange' is really to talk of unequal exchange between finance capital itself.

Samir Amin puts the same thesis in defence of Emmanuel, when he too speaks of 'hidden transfers'.[69] Having attacked Lenin's thesis as concerned with accumulation in the 'centre', and having poked his finger in Marx's eye for not paying 'attention to our problem'(!) (i.e. of underdevelopment through unequal exchange), he boldly comes forward to provide us with his theory of accumulation on a world scale. He fails miserably. With his under-consumptionism he cannot comprehend the laws of motion of capitalist development and consequently cannot provide us with a true understanding of accumulation on a world scale. For Amin, like all Keynesian underconsumptionists, 'the essential law of accumulation' is the extension of markets. We have already quoted him as suggesting that it is the contradiction between the capacity to produce and consume which accounts both for the inherent tendency for the extension of markets and for the international movement of capital. This position follows naturally from his ahistorical and unscientific approach to the question of accumulation.

Amin becomes the arch-ideologist of the peripherists when he additionally builds his theory of *social formations* which he counterposes to the capitalist mode of production, when in fact these formations are caricatured and stunted by the laws of motion specific to the capitalist mode. In this ahistorical manner Amin tries to establish, by equating his social formations with the precapitalist mode of production, that primitive accumulation of the mercantilist period is still continuing to this period between the centres and the peripheries. Although he recognises that the 'pre-monopoly' forms of international division of labour are different from those under imperialism, he nevertheless reverts to the dogma by stating that:

> Nevertheless both these stages of international specificisation depend upon mechanisms of *primitive accumulation* for they are for the benefit of the centre; that these mechanisms cannot be grasped only in the context of analysis confined to the capitalist mode of production.

Thus Amin tries to build another theory in support of Emmanuel's unequal exchange, and his Luxemburgist bent is evident in the above formulation, for he credits her for being 'the first Marxist' who pointed out the 'present-day mechanisms' of primitive accumulation—of plunder of the third world. It will be recalled that Luxemburg's attempt to find a 'third non-capitalist market' was to provide her with an explanation for the realisation of constant capital within capitalist production. Amin tries to extend this analysis and explain this accumulation in his non-capitalist social formations. In our view this 'non-capitalist' connection of imperialism cannot be idealised and absolutised. A true understanding of accumulation on a world scale lies in grasping its many-sided contradictions, of which the production and accumulation in the 'periphery' are part. Capitalist production emerges on the basis of a world market. It is therefore important to see this movement historically, and imperialism must be understood in its dialectical development based on the laws of motion of capitalist development, which leaves no peripheries to be examined outside the general movement of these laws. In short, it is Marx's analysis of expanded reproduction which, brought to the real world through the laws of the tendency of the rate of profit to fall—through foreign trade and colonial production—and based on a correct understanding of Lenin's concept of financial capital in the monopoly era, can correctly explain to us accumulation on a world scale—that is, capitalist production in the centre and the periphery as a world system. The centrist and peripherist explanations do not bring us to this scientific understanding of modern imperialism, nor do they give us a strategy for struggle against it, and here lies their real weakness.

The danger that the 'centre-periphery' ideology poses is indeed in the struggle against imperialism. The ideology tends to fan populist sentiments and 'solutions' to imperialist exploitation. The populists look to improvements in *terms of trade* as the answer to the imperialist exploitation. This is encouraged by the peripherists. Indeed, Emmanuel urges as a solution the increase of wages in the periphery, leading to an increase in prices, and hence to better terms of trade. He also advocates that the periphery should 'tax exports' and transfer this excess surplus-value to the state in order to diversify production from export production sectors, to replace import sectors.[70] In other words, the solution of the national democratic revolution is to be sought in the market-place, and not in the class struggle on the basis of a revolutionary united front, which does away with the production relationships dictated by international finance capital—a struggle which joins up with the struggle of the working class in the centre, for they too are exploited by the same class of the financial oligarchy, the monopolist bourgeoisie.

Further, the peripherists, in their concept of unequal exchange, try to pit the working class in the centre against the working class in the periphery by showing that the former exploits the latter. Indeed, Amin almost says as much when he states: 'Consequently in relative terms, the proletariat of the periphery suffers an increasing degree of exploitation as compared with the proletariat of the centre.'[71] Mandel suggests somewhat the same position in this formulation:

> It [i.e. imperialism] also creates the possibility, on the basis of its monopoly productivity, of ensuring the workers of the metropolitan countries standards of living higher than those of the colonies.[72]

Whilst these statements can be justified in more ways than one, at the same time they create a negative impression that in fact monopoly capital and imperialism are in the interest of the working class in these countries. What the workers are able to wrest from the monopoly bourgeoisie in the form of higher wages is through struggle. Moreover, this is only a small part of the product which they produce. The exploitation of the workers is a function of the application of machinery to labour. It is therefore unscientific to say or imply that the workers of the centre exploit those in the colonies. To say so as Bettelheim has shown, would be to hold that such workers in the centre have 'ceased to be exploited themselves, which must mean that *their labour is no longer a source of surplus-value'.* In reality, he continues,

> These workers are, in general, *more exploited* (in the strict sense of the word) than the workers in the poor countries: Marx emphasised this, noting that, owing to a high level of intensity and productivity of labour *in the rich countries,* the wages of the workers in these countries, *though nominally higher,* and (to a lesser extent) *higher in purchasing powers than in the poor countries,* generally correspond to a smaller proportion of the value these workers produce.[73] *[Emphases in original]*

Related to the question of the struggle against imperialism is the question of strategies and tactics that must be worked out if victory is to be achieved. What is the character of the revolution that must be waged in the periphery against imperialism? The theory advanced by Gundar Frank in his two books[74] and a series of articles has relevance to this question. Frank, going to the other side of the peripherists, puts forward a centrist solution to the struggle against imperialism in Latin America, by showing that Latin America is poised for a socialist revolution. What leads him to this wrong strategic and tactical position is his ahistorical analysis of the developments in this part of the world from the sixteenth century. Whilst the Amins argue that primitive accumulation is still continuing to date, Frank goes to the other extreme to 'prove' that Latin America has been under capitalist development since then. He argues that the internal contradictions in Chile and Brazil are the expropriation of the 'economic surplus'. Furthermore, the polarisation of the capitalist system into metropolitan centres and peripheral satellites, and the continuity of the fundamental structure of the capitalist system throughout the history of expansions and transformation of capitalism, are due to the persistence or recreation of these contradictions everywhere and at all times'.[75] Thus Frank, like his friends, sees no qualitative difference in mercantile capitalist plunder from capitalist exploitation under free trade, and exploitation under monopoly capitalism. Nor does he see the difference in strategies for struggle in the centre and the periphery. Laclau[76] correctly points out this error in Frank's theory, although he himself does not address his mind to the issue of the solution which

Frank puts forward. Armed with this wrong theoretical base, it is not surprising that Frank ends up by prescribing a wrong solution to the struggle, namely a socialist solution in a situation in which the national democratic revolution was arrested by imperialism and remains to be completed. In our view this struggle can only succeed when the proletariat in these countries can provide a leadership which unites all the democratic forces opposed to imperialism, on the basis of the national democratic revolution. This strategy would lead to the defeat of imperialism, and thus establish a basis for a socialist revolution. A socialist solution is clearly presented to the proletariat in the metropolitan countries. Nevertheless, the national democratic revolution in the neocolonial world is interlinked, as Lenin pointed out after 1917, to the proletarian socialist revolution in the metropolitan centres. Historical experience has proved this thesis to be correct. The victory over imperialism in Indochina has demonstrated that it is only on the basis of unity of the working class in the metropoles and material support from the socialist countries that the national democratic revolution can succeed in the neocolonies.

The petty-bourgeois ideology which is at the base of the centre-periphery ideology weakens the working class in both the metropole and the neocolonial countries. It blames the working class in the metropole for 'exploiting' the working class in the neocolony, while the working class in the neocolony is accused of exploiting the peasantry, whose alliance the working class must seek. Thus it has been shown that the centre-periphery ideology is a danger to the struggle against imperialism in the world, and that Lenin's thesis on the national question and on the 'new democracy', as developed by Stalin[77] and Mao Tse Tung,[78] is the scientific thesis of the working class throughout the world in its struggle against imperialism.

NOTES

1. See, for instance, Robinson, R.E. & Gallagher, J.A., London, 1961; *Africa and the Victorians;* Schumpeter, J.A.: *Imperialism and Social Classes,* 1972; Fieldhouse, D.K.: *The Theory of Capitalist Imperialism;* London, 1967; Barratt-Brown, M.: *After Imperialism;* London, 1963.
2. Engels, F.: *Dialectics of Nature,* p. 24; Moscow, 1969.
3. *Ibid.,* p. 25.
4. Engels, F.: 'Feuerbach and the End of Classical German Philosophy' in Marx and Engels: *Selected Works* Vol. 3, pp. 363-5; Moscow, 1969.
5. *Ibid.*
6. Mill, J.S., in Nagel, E.: *J.S. Mill's Philosophy of Scientific Method,* pp. 408-9; 1950.
7. E.g. Gouldner, A., *The Coming Crisis in Western Sociology,* New York, 1965.
8. Lenin, V.I.: *Imperialism, the Highest Stage of Capitalism,* p. 79; Moscow, 1970.
9. Marx, K.: *Capital* Vol. III, pp. 330-1; Moscow, 1971.

10. Marx, K.: *Capital* Vol. I, Parts III-IV; Moscow, 1968.
11. Lenin, V.I.: 'A Characterisation of Economic Romanticism' in *Collected Works* Vol. 2, pp. 153-4; Moscow, 1970.
12. Dunayevskaya, R.: *Concerning the So-Called Market Question;* Chicago.
13. Luxemburg, Rosa: *The Accumulation of Capital* and *The Accumulation of Capital. An Anti-critique;* London, 1951.
14. *Ibid. (Anti-critique),* p. 56.
15. *Ibid.,* p. 76.
16. For instance, Emmanuel, A.: *Unequal Exchange;* London, 1972.
17. Marx, K.: *Capital* Vol. III, *op. cit.,* p. 198.
18. *Ibid.,* p. 212.
19. Marx, K.: *Grundrisse,* p. 748. Harmondsworth, 1973.
20. Marx, K.: *Capital* Vol. III, *op. cit.,* p. 396.
21. *Ibid.,* pp. 237-40.
22. Marx, K.: 'Capital, The East India Company, Its History and Results' in Marx & Engels: *On Britain,* pp. 180-1; Moscow, 1971.
22. Dutt, Palme: *India Today,* p. 131; London, 1940.
23. Semmell, B.: *The Rise of Free Trade Imperialism,* p. 111; Cambridge, 1970.
24. Ricardo, D.: *Principles of Political Economy and Taxation,* p. 115; Harmondsworth, 1971.
25. See Sideri: *Trade and Power: Informal Colonialism in Anglo-Portuguese Relations;* Rotterdam, 1970.
26. Quoted in *ibid.,* p. 47.
27. Jenks, L.H.: *The Migration of British Capital to 1875,* p. 131; New York, 1927.
28. See Baran, P.A. & Sweezy, P.M.: *Monopoly Capital;* Harmondsworth, 1968; Amin, Samir: *Accumulation on a World Scale;* New York, 1974.
29. Bukharin, N.: 'Accumulation of Capital and Imperialism' in Tarbuck, K.J. (ed.): *Introduction to Rosa Luxemburg and N. Bukharin, Imperialism and the Accumulation of Capital,* p. 265; London, 1972.
30. Marx, K.: *Grundrisse, op. cit.,* pp. 748-9.
31. Yaffe, D.S.: 'The Marxian Theory of Crisis, Capital and the State' in *Economy and Society* Vol. 2 No. 2, May, 1973, p. 204.
32. Marx, K.: *op. cit.,* p. 749-50.
33. See Sweezy, P.M.: *The Theory of Capitalist Development,* pp. 190-234; New York, 1942; see also Yaffe, D.S.: *op. cit.,* pp. 207-16.
34. Lenin, V.I.: 'A Characterisation of Economic Romanticism', *op. cit.*
35. Marx, K.: *Capital* Vol. II; pp. 410-1; Moscow, 1971.
36. Marx, K.: *Grundrisse, op. cit.,* p. 750.
37. Lenin, V.I.: *Imperialism, op. cit.*
38. Hobson, J.A.: *Imperialism: A Study;* London, 1902.
39. Lenin, V.I.: *op. cit.,* pp. 18-22.
40. Barratt-Brown, M.: *Economics of Imperialism,* p. 184; Harmondsworth, 1974.
41. Lenin, V.I.: *op. cit.*

42. *Ibid.*, p. 46.
43. *Ibid.*
44. Marx, K.: *Capital* Vol. III, *op. cit.*, p. 195.
45. Cairncross, A.K.: *Home and Foreign Investments, 1870-1913,* p. 197; Cambridge, 1953.
46. Barratt-Brown, M.: *op. cit.,* p. 184.
47. Lenin, V.I.: *op. cit.,* pp. 62-5.
48. *Ibid.,* p. 86.
49. Vernon, Raymond: *Sovereignty at Bay,* p. 87; Harmondsworth, 1971.
50. Lenin, V.I.: *op. cit.,* p. 74.
51. The quotes that follow are all from Lenin, *ibid.,* pp. 82-6.
52. Clayton, W.L.: in *Foreword* to Wilcox, C.: *A Charter for World Trade;* New York, 1972.
53. Gardner, R.: *Sterling Dollar Diplomacy,* pp. 817-8; New York, 1969.
54. Poulantzas, N.: 'Internationalisation of Capitalist Relations and the Nation-State' in *Economy and Society* Vol. 3 No. 2, 1974, p. 157.
55. Baran & Sweezy, *op. cit.,* pp. 86-7.
56. *Ibid.,* p. 23.
57. Barratt-Brown, M.: *op. cit.,* p. 216.
58. Baran & Sweezy, *op. cit.,* p. 194.
59. Amin, S.: *op. cit.,* p. 91.
60. Baran & Sweezy, *op. cit.,* pp. 115-6.
61. Jalée, P.: *Imperialism in the Seventies,* pp. 134-5; New York, 1974.
62. Sweezy, P.M., *op. cit.,* p. 267.
63. Menshikov, S.: *Millionaires and Managers,* pp. 192-3; Moscow, 1969.
64. Jalée, P., *op. cit.,* pp. 128-9.
65. Alavi, H.: 'Imperialism Old and New' in *Socialist Register;* London, 1964.
66. UNO: *The Impact of Multinational Corporations on Development and International Relations;* New York, 1974.
67. Emmanuel, A.: 'White-Settler Colonialism and the Myth of Investment Imperialism' in *New Left Review* No. 73, 1972, p. 34. See also his *Unequal Exchange,* pp. 124-92.
68. This and the following quotes are from Emmanuel, A.: *Unequal Exchange;* London, 1972.
69. This and the following quotes are from Amin, S., *op. cit.*
70. Emmanuel, A., *op. cit.,* p. 267.
71. Amin, S., *op. cit.,* p. 25.
72. Mandel, E.: *Marxist Economic Theory,* p. 479; London, 1971.
73. Bettelheim, C.: 'Appendix I: Theoretical Comments' in Emmanuel, *op. cit.,* pp. 299-300.
74. Frank, A.G.: *Capitalism and Underdevelopment in Latin America;* Harmondsworth, 1971; see also *Latin America, Underdevelopment or Revolution;* New York, 1971.
75. Frank, A.G.: *Capitalism and Underdevelopment in Latin America,* pp. 27-38, 249-305.
76. Laclau, E.: 'Feudalism and Capitalism in Latin America' in *New Left Review* No. 67, 1970, pp. 19-39.

77.   Stalin, J.V.: 'The October Revolution and the National Question' in *Works* Vol. IV, pp. 169-70; 'The National Question Once Again, in *Works* Vol. VII, pp. 225-7.

78.   Mao Tse Tung, 'The Chinese Revolution and the Chinese Communist Party' and 'On New Democracy' in *Selected Works* Vol. II, pp. 305-84; Peking, 1954.

CHAPTER 2

FINANCE CAPITAL AND THE TRANSNATIONAL CORPORATION*

Recent literature on the subject of the transnational corporation has tended to evaluate these giants as a new phenomenon emerging on the world scene. 'Marxist' literature has also been taken in by this rather superficial approach, as we have seen, and emphasis has been placed on the economistic appearances of the transnational corporation by 'neo-Marxist' literature. The purpose of this chapter is to present a broad methodological outline within which a more detailed research methodology can be worked out on the phenomenon of the transnational corporation and its impact on society both in the imperialist centre and the neocolonial hinterland.

The starting point of our analysis is capital itself. In our view a proper understanding of the transnational corporation must start from the scientific proposition that this strategy is a historical product of capitalist development. It must then proceed to show the historical epoch in which the phenomenon arises and its causes, and then concretely specify the forms monopoly has taken. Hence its real essence must be traced in the historical movement of capital as a product of society, as discussed in the previous chapter.

What are the contemporary characteristics of this phenomenon which confirm our thesis? According to Raymond Vernon, a prominent bourgeois economist who has conducted and supervised university research at Harvard on the transnational corporation, there are three main characteristics of US transnational corporations.[1]

The *first* he regards as the 'sheer size of the enterprise concerned'. He shows that most US transnationals have to establish and maintain a network of subsidiaries and branches in foreign countries. This is an undertaking very few small enterprises can manage to engage in. Taking a list of the 500 largest US corporations listed by *Fortune* in 1964, and breaking them down by degree of involvement in foreign markets, he showed that those that had *manufacturing* facilities in six countries or more outside of the US numbered 460 assessed by sales, and 470 assessed by assets. He also showed that the 460 employed 29,000 employees, as compared to 7,000 for the 160 'national' enterprises. He then concludes: 'By and large, a multinational spread goes hand in hand with giant size.'

The *second* characteristic, according to Vernon, is that the size of the enterprise is *even more pronounced* for US-based enterprises whose subsidiaries and branches are founded in the neocolonial

---

*This chapter is derived from a paper prepared for presentation at the African Association of Political Science, Panel on Multinational Corporations, held in Lagos, 4th-8th April 1976.

hinterland:

> Indeed, the newer and more remote the country appears from the United States viewpoint, the more likely it is to harbour the largest of the United States-based multinational enterprises.

He cites data which shows that the number of enterprises operating in the developed capitalist world have fewer average worldwide sales than those operating in the third world:

> Large size and extensive geographical reach, therefore, are two major characteristics of United States-based multinational enterprises whose subsidiaries are located in developing countries.

But Vernon also gives a *third* characteristic. This, which reinforces the other two, shows that US-based enterprises that establish subsidiaries overseas are found mainly in industries which are highly concentrated *in structure*—'that is to say, industries which are dominated by relatively few firms'. This means that US-based industries that operate overseas and particularly in third world countries are those that are highly integrated both vertically and horizontally. He cites US aggregate investments in developing countries for 1970 as amounting to $21 billion, of which 39 per cent went to petroleum, and 12 per cent to mining and smelting. Most of the mining was concentrated in the copper and aluminium industries, and to a lesser extent in iron ore and a variety of non-ferrous metals. In manufacturing the areas of interest were chemicals, food, machinery, and transport equipment. Once it is realised how important these investments are to the monopolies and their interconnection with other industries, then the role of the corporations in these countries becomes obvious.

What is the significance of Vernon's evidence? In our view it confirms a number of characteristics which Lenin showed as being fundamental to monopoly enterprises. The evidence proves Lenin's characteristics (1) and (5),   as we have shown. But our thesis is that the corporations dominate production in our countries through exports of finance capital. Vernon obscures this, and in fact only touches on it incidentally. Our next task is to demonstrate the interweaving of bank and industrial capital on the basis of which finance capital has its way in transnational enterprise, and to go further to show how this affects production, and hence how the transnational enterprise is based on exports of finance capital in various forms, as the only way of maintaining profitability.

To begin with, concentration and centralisation of capital have continued unabated in the post-war period. The best illustrative example of this is the position of the US. The concentration and expansion of US capital, without which the US cannot maintain its lead, have been facilitated by her banks. Such multilateral agencies as

the World Bank and its affiliates like the International Development
Association (IDA) and IFC, as well as national institutions like the US
Import-Export Investment Bank, are important channels. But of more
importance are the US banking and financial institutions. This is
evidenced by the fact that the biggest growth in US banking, according
to *Fortune* magazine, is not in the US but overseas, thus 'creating the
first truly international network of banks'.[2] This coincides with
Vernon's evidence of US monopolies in production being sited
overseas.

If further evidence is required of the increasing role of banks as a
means of concentrating capital and hence production both at home and
overseas, the *US News & World Report* of 25th March 1974 is worth
noting. Writing under the heading: 'Are the Nation's Banks Getting
Too Powerful', the magazine reported that: 'Buying billions of stock in
the nation's industries, branching into all sorts of business, opening
offices around the world—that's the picture of big US banks that is
arousing concern in the government and elsewhere.' For instance, the
paper reported, the Bank of America

> has literally spread across the nation, and around the world, with more than
> 1,000 offices. It recently acquired General Acceptance Corporation, giving
> it another 317 finance-company Loan Offices in the East and Middle
> West.

The magazine reported that the National City Corporation, 'only
second to Bank America in assets', had more than five hundred domestic
and foreign offices. They engaged in activities 'from finance to insurance,
from computer services and management advice to armoured cars'.
Statistics showed that the trust departments of the big banks holding
pension funds, etc., used them to control industrial concerns. For
instance, Morgan Guaranty, with the biggest trustee department, had
close to $23.6 billion under 'investment management'. Of these,
employee benefit funds totalled $16 billion, i.e. more than 70 per cent
and growing at $859 million per year. They had full discretion as to
how these funds were invested.

Also, according to the report, 'interlocking directorships' were the
order of the day. A survey of 49 banks in ten major cities found more
than 8,000 cases, involving 6,500 firms, in which officials of banks
surveyed acted as directors of other companies and vice versa. For
instance, of the 23 directors of the Central Penn Company, 16 were
also directors of 19 banks. Among the 30 of the company's top
stockholders, with an aggregate of 22 per cent of the stock, were 17
bank trust departments. Many of these banks had made loans to the
'ailing corporation'. Some of the directors involved in both loans and
trust stock-holdings were those with interlocking directorships. The
report also reproduced the assets of the fifteen biggest US banks,
which make the budgets of most petty-bourgeois 'banana republics' a
laughing stock!

An example of how capital is centralised by the US financial oligarchy is the case of interlocking commercial, industrial and banking companies grouped around Sears, Roebuck and Company, a US monopoly (see Figure A). The picture that this figure illustrates is most instructive in understanding how transnational enterprise operates. The power to centralise capital and earnings of the entire population which the monopoly then utilises for its global strategy also operates in other capitalist countries, as well as in the neocolonial hinterland. As can be seen from the figure, this monopoly has centralised even workers' pensions, and is linked to 'non-profit foundations' through which further capital is tapped. In this way the monopoly is both *vertically* and *horizontally* integrated, with direct access to its own industries and markets.

In a publication intended to show an opposite opinion, Jalée cites evidence from a US House of Representatives Committee of 1968 which shows that large US banks 'are unaffected by the anti-trust legislation', and that they control $607 billion in assets, 'or 60 per cent of the total institutional investment'. Insurance companies, the second largest source of investment after banks, only possess $162 billion in assets. He continues:

> The report adds that 49 banks control 5 per cent or more capital of the 147 largest industrial companies as well as 5 per cent or more of the capital of the 17 most important merchandising companies and the 17 biggest transport companies.[3]

He quotes the committee as concluding that because of the widespread distribution of capital, these 5 per cent interests are enough to control many boards of directors in industry.

All this data which Jalée quotes supports Lenin's thesis of the inter-locking character and merger of bank capital and industrial capital. *These two monopoly situations are what Lenin calls finance capital and the financial oligarchy.* Contrary to Jalée's thesis, industrial capital cannot free itself from finance capital because it is part of finance capital, which is a merger of bank and industrial capital, both of which are under the control of the financial oligarchy. This became a historical reality by the turn of the century, and it was on the basis of this change in the control of capital and production that monopoly of modern imperialism, the basis of current economic relationships, developed. Henceforth colonial production came under the command of finance capital put to use by the financial oligarchy. To the extent that neocolonialism is an extension in new form of the exploitative relationships between the imperialist centre and cheap labour in the neocolonial country, the same power of finance capital reigns over production, distribution and exchange in the third world. And the transnational corporation is the vehicle that has arisen in the inter-war

Figure A

Interlocking of Commercial, Industrial and Banking Companies Grouped around Sears, Roebuck and Company.

(Figures indicate assets at the end of 1965 in million dollars)

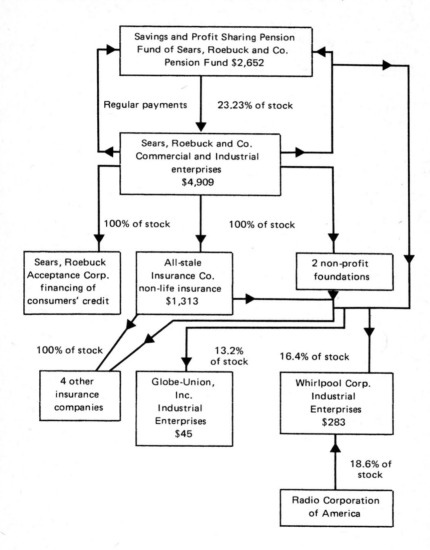

years, as we have shown, to perpetuate these exploitative links, through exports of finance capital.

We have already cited Vernon as showing that the transnational corporation pours most of its capital into petroleum, mining and other raw materials. It also invests in manufacturing. It is our thesis that these investments aim to tap cheap labour in production and maintain markets, all for the sole purpose of maintaining global profitability. A document of the United Nations Economic Commission for Africa indicates that in its production of raw material resources the transnational corporation is geared

> either to selling the product on the world market directly or to using the raw material as an input for its own internationally integrated processing operations, as in the case of palm products, copper and bauxite.[4]

In manufacturing, the document states that the corporation goes for light consumer goods, 'demanding relatively simple and accessible technology',[5] some of which are for the domestic market in the neocolony and others for export. In many cases, if not all, investment in raw material production is intended to assist the maintenance of a market for monopoly products, whether produced locally or overseas, and investment in manufacturing is aimed at securing and bringing under control raw material bases. The sources of finance capital in this respect may come directly from the transnational corporation and/or from multilateral or state agencies. They all have the same aim ultimately, as we have argued. Thus, finance capital may be brought into the following activities: (i) production in peasant-grown cash crops; (ii) estate or plantation products which are normally on a large scale; (iii) petroleum and mining; (iv) processing and semi-processing of above; (v) manufacturing; (vi) marketing and distribution, including transportation.

Finance capital in these and other activities will take diverse forms. Indeed, a recent UN Report has shown that private direct investment through the transnational corporation provides from a single source a package of inputs which includes capital, technology, managerial skills and other services.[6] All these are monopolised 'property' and are 'sold' together, actually forming part and parcel of capital exports for the sole purpose of exploiting cheap labour production and captive markets. The fact that finance capital is dominant and in many places the sole activator of production is today broadcast by any popular international magazine with such advertisements as: 'This is your bank!' or 'Our-man-on-the-spot—The Bank of America world-wide service!' The one reproduced below is characteristic:

> Not far from Kuala Lumpur, Malaysia, grow valuable red merenti trees. Helping this lumber get to markets around the world is our-man-on-the-spot there. . . For lumber concerns around the world, Bank of America is a

primary source of every kind of routine financing and assistance. . . For example, we can handle receivables and payables, equipment leasing, search out new customers and new sources of supply, and arrange for foreign exchange management through our International Finance Centers in London, Singapore and Panama. And because we are a global network, your international transactions are handled swiftly and effectively.

This advertisement expresses in a nutshell the role of finance capital and international banks in US monopoly capitalism. They are a source of *primary financing* in 'every kind of routine' activity. They handle investment in *production* of trees, and handle their marketing the world over, including finding customers. They even help to beat the 'foreign-exchange man' in Kuala Lumpur or wherever he may be! Their role is characteristic of Lenin's analysis of the role of banks in the export of capital in the early twentieth century. Today their role is even more pronounced: they directly engage in financial and industrial activities overseas.

To show concretely the involvement of finance capital in third world countries, we discuss below in general the four main types of productive activities. We shall then illustrate this involvement with a number of agreements signed between a third world country and transnational corporations and/or multilateral institution by which finance capital is given access to cheap labour and surplus-value extraction.

To begin with, the *first* type of products which is characteristic is the peasant cash-crops like cotton, coffee, tropical food products, etc. The capital needed to back the production of these crops in one way or another, including the provision of insecticides, fertilisers, hoes, tractors, improved seeds, as well as the finance required for their transportation, marketing and distribution, is raised by aid, loans, grants or actual private investment from the corporations or multilateral or imperialist state agencies. Under the first Yaoundé Convention, for instance, the EEC provided aid and loans amounting to $104 million for 'structural and improvement in crop growing' alone. All these types of financing require a certain return of a surplus-value to be extracted. To the extent that most of the financing is external, the question of surplus-value syphoning becomes a reality of everyday life, and to that extent the products become products of finance capital, since the inputs have the first charge on the proceeds. Any 'national capital' utilised in the production of these crops is put to use on the account of monopolies who 'purchase' them.

The *second* type of production is the one which comes from capitalist estates and plantations in typical 'plantation economies'. Here the product comes out of a capitalist enterprise, sometimes a monopoly like Brooke Bond or United Fruit Co., which invests private capital, exploits the cheap labour in these countries in producing surplus-value, and then exports the products to the imperialist centres. Products of this more direct and brazen exploitation by giant corporations, which Beckford has described in his study of 'plantation economies',[7] cannot by any stretch of imagination be called 'our products'. They are clearly products of finance capital. The immediate interest is clearly profit and no development of any kind is, or indeed could be, left behind in the third world. As Beckford has correctly said:

> Once metropolitan corporate enterprise got involved in plantation production the stage was set for subsequent cumulative growth of these enterprises without any significant corresponding growth of plantation economy. . . However, because metropolitan plantation enterprises are normally multinational in character, the benefits of these economies do not accrue as much to any single country as to the firm itself. . . Everywhere in the plantation world proper, we find that metropolitan enterprise is predominant in production and trade.

In this way, according to Beckford, British enterprises account for the bulk of West Indian sugar production and trade; US enterprises for the bulk of sugar output and trade in Puerto Rico, the Dominican Republic, Haiti and the Philippines; US rubber companies in Liberia; US companies for almost all the banana output and trade in the Central American republics; Australian companies for all raw sugar in Fiji; and US, British, Dutch and other European companies for most of the rubber, tea, and oil palm and for the trade in Sri Lanka and South-East Asia. The fact that some of these plantation enterprises get nationalised makes very little difference, since the finance capital and monopoly world markets are owned by the metropolitan financial oligarchies. Beckford observes that

> Some of the names of these enterprises are better known to the people of plantation society in many countries than the names of their government prime ministers or presidents.

The *third* type of product is minerals and petroleum. Here, whether the enterprise is nationalised or n t, its successful operation depends to a large extent on the capital investments and technology from the monopolies. The royalties or profits accruing to the third world states are negligible compared to surplus-value extracted by the monopolies either through profits, dividends on its equity shares, and royalties on technology, or through other mechanisms of exploitation. Here clearly the product, just like the peasant cash product, is 'our product' in juridical terms only. The real owners are the owners of finance capital.

The *fourth* type of products is the semi-processed products. These may be processed from peasant crops, or crops from 'plantation enterprises'. Whoever the 'owner', the semi-processing to a large measure will be dependent on a technology possessed by a monopoly; and through this means the monopoly is guaranteed control of the raw material source. To quote Beckford again:

> Metropolitan firms engaged in the processing or marketing of plantation pro-
> ducts first get involved in plantation raw material suppliers in order to control
> or influence input prices for metropolitan processing, or because market
> restrictions on further expansion of processed output limit investment
> opportunities at the processing level. In either event, the enterprise is induced
> to engage in this activity by the prospect of greater profits in the long run
> and/or less variability of profit in the short run. Once the enterprise embarks
> on plantation production a chain of events follow, leading to further
> expansion.

The same can be said of peasant economies inasmuch as processing
can be under circumstances which compel reliance on external capital
inputs. All these production relations reveal a fundamental point, and
that is that in all these situations imperialist finance capital is king,
whilst cheap neocolonial labour is its servant. The products that are
created by the cheap labour are appropriated by the capital precisely
because their value has to be realised in order to 'service' it. This is
because the cheap labour exploited in this way helps the monopolists
to cheapen the consumer goods on which metropolitan labour spends
its incomes and hence helps the monopolist to keep wages down and
maintain a higher rate of profitability than without it. Equally the
cheap raw materials cheapen the components of constant capital,
which too helps to improve the profitability of the monopoly. In this
way monopoly capitalism and imperialism are given an extended life.
It follows that so long as finance capital is the initiator of such
production, and the appropriator of the surplus-value therefrom, the
'ownership' of these products by the neocolonial state can be in
juridical form only, to the extent that we claim to be 'nations' trading
with other nations. In actual fact this is not the case.

Fifthly, in manufacturing finance capital takes the form of investment in import-substituted luxury goods production. Finance capital
may take the form of direct investment of actual capital, or may be
tied to technology (patents, trade marks, designs, etc.) and skilled
personnel, who will ensure the interests of the transnational corporation in the joint venture. Sometimes technology may be converted into
equity share in order to afford the monopoly a place on the board of
directors, or vice versa. Through a number of agreements—management,
technical, consultancy, marketing, financial, etc.—the transnational
corporation is able to assert, through restrictions, its objective power
over production and its captive markets. These restrictions will arise
out of the use of its patents, trade marks, etc. Thus the transnational
will normally restrict the volume of exports outside the geographical
area, which is intended to protect its other markets; or where it allows
a certain amount of exports, it will insist on the right to market the
product itself; and finally it will restrict the sources from which
machinery and other intermediate goods may be purchased. Other

'tie-in' clauses may be inserted in the agreement, requiring purchases of equipment from the monopoly itself, or its agent or principal. In this way monopoly both over production and over the neocolonial market is controlled and maintained, and in this way too its control over raw materials is assured.

II

A few concrete examples as to how the above activities in a neocolony are dominated by imperialist finance capital, and how cheap labour and 'national capital' is put at the service of finance capital, will help further clarify our thesis. We have already stated that finance capital takes diverse forms and comes through various channels. Whether it comes in as aid, loan, private investment, or by way of technology and skills as a package deal is of very little importance from this point of view. It all has the same aim: to facilitate monopoly capitalist production, distribution and exchange in the neocolony as part of the global strategy of finance capital. Furthermore, whether it comes from the transnational corporation directly, in the form of direct investment in raw material or manufacturing production, or it comes in from the World Bank, IFC or IDA, and/or from imperialist state institutions (US Import-Export Bank, USAID, CIDA, SIDA, Arab Development Bank) is of very little consequence, since all of it has the same ultimate aim.

The first concrete example is a financial deal made between the World Bank's sister institution, the IDA, and the Tanzania National Development Credit Agency (NDCA) and two other parastatals involved in production, marketing and processing of tobacco. As is well known, the multilateral institution IDA is an intermediary of the imperialist states which wish to back up 'social projects' in third world countries. The loans are supposed to be 'government to government' and are given on 'soft terms', that is, with very low interest rates (no more than three-quarters of 1 per cent) in many cases and longer grace periods. The loan agreement (Credit No. 217 TA) was signed in October 1970. Under the agreement the IDA 'agreed to assist in the financing of a flue-cured tobacco production project' by making available to the borrowers an amount in various currencies equivalent to $9 million on a number of conditions, some of which are given below. It was stipulated by the Project Agreement that the NDCA should carry out the project with

> due diligence and efficiency and shall at all times conduct its operation and affairs in accordance with sound administrative, financial, agricultural and economic practices, under the supervision of experienced and competent management. *[Art 11:2.01]*.

The NDCA was required to make loans according to the 'operating policies and procedures' to co-operative societies for on-lending to

village farmers as seasonal, medium-term and long-term loans, to
enable purchase of seasonal 'on-farm inputs' and equipment needed for
carrying out and continuing the planting programme approved by the
IDA. *[Art 11:2.03]* Particular covenants extracted from the tobacco
parastatals required them to employ a Chief Marketing Officer, Chief
Executive Officer and a Chief Accountant acceptable to the IDA; and
the Tanzania Tobacco Board (TTB) was required additionally to
continue its marketing arrangements until agreement based on a study
demanded by the IDA was approved. It was to continue after the
introduction of 'auction floor arrangement, to purchase flue-cured
tobacco leaf and to make arrangements satisfactory to the IDA to
manage the auction floor' to be established in accordance with
Part B to the Project. *[Art 11:204]*

The operating policies and procedures of the NDCA in respect of
the loan were spelt out in a schedule, which were to be followed by the
NDCA in making loans. Under these policies and procedures, the NDCA
was to give seasonal and medium-term loans to 'all co-operative
societies and such other co-operative societies as may have been joined
by any farmers in any villages with the agreement of the Association',
i.e. IDA. *[Sec: 1]*

The NDCA was then to make *seasonal loans* to each eligible co-
operative society of up to (Tanzania) Shs. 450 for each acre of flue-
cured tobacco expected to be planted in any of the villages by farmer-
members in any year, to cover costs of seasonal inputs such as barn-
flue pipes and fertiliser for maize production, which was to be produced to meet their subsistence as well for export. A *medium loan*
of up to Shs. 1,300 for each farmer-member was to be advanced to
meet the costs of constructing three curing barns and one grading shed
and of purchasing equipment such as a watering can, a soil-injector gun
and a barn thermometer needed for the 'efficient cultivation and
curing of flue-cured tobacco'. Further *long-term loans* to the two
parastatals (TTB and TTPC) were to be made as appropriate from this
loan to finance the Marketing and Processing Study and the construction or extension of auction floor, storage and processing facilities
included in the Project. *[Secs: 2-4]*

The seasonal loans were to fall due under the agreement not later
than September 30 in the year in which the crop for which the loans
were made was to be harvested, and medium-term loans were to be
repayable in four annual instalments to fall due not later than
September 30 of the year of the first crop, and thereafter every
September 30. Long-term loans were for a period of twelve years
with a grace period of two years. The rate of interest was to be 8½ per
cent. These loans were to be made on the signing of agreements with
societies, who were obliged to allow the NDCA and the IDA to visit
the cultivated land. The society was required to deduct the debt
servicing of the capital loaned first before paying members, and the
TTB was required to do the same in respect of the societies, such

deductions to amount to 75 per cent 'of the value of any payments that would otherwise have been made to any of the co-operative societies until its debt service obligation has been fully met for that season'. *[Secs: 5-13]* There were other obligations imposed on the TTB, the TTPC, and the NDCA to approve loan applications, examine accounts, issue Liability Certificates etc., etc. *[Secs: 14-15]*

In this single transaction cheap labour on a co-operative basis is exploited by finance capital (represented by a multilateral institution). The finance comes from a financial oligarchy or taxes of an imperialist state. Whatever the source, the function is the same. The neocolonial state officials and parastatal officials, or the so-called 'bureaucratic bourgeoisie', are involved to the detail in carrying out the project on behalf of finance capital. In this way 'national resources and capital' are put to use by this loan to obtain the crop. The neocolonial state exports the crop and earns 'foreign exchange' and imposes levies and taxes to maintain the state apparatus. The peasantry obtains 'employment' which finance capital exploits directly. Here finance capital finds no need for 'merchant capital' as a mediator between producers and monopolies, as 'neo-Marxism' would seem to imagine.

These provisions are quoted *in extenso* to show the power of finance capital not only over production, distribution and marketing, but also over the neocolonial state. It has been estimated that under this loan scheme altogether 15,000 peasants were settled in tobacco villages. Tobacco production trebled in tons over nine years and particularly rose from 11,066 tons in 1966 to 18,011 tons in 1971. It is not a dramatic increase nor are the amounts involved too great, but the production relation is clear. The estimated income of Shs. 2,075 average per year from the crop in 1973/74 was distributed as follows: Shs. 770 cost of inputs, Shs. 72 society levy, Shs. 116 interest on loan, Shs. 1,117 income to the family for the year. This Shs. 1,117 is for a five-month growing season of intensive work for an average family of 1.7 adult workers, resulting in a wage of Shs. 653 per adult per year or Shs. 54 per month[8], below the 'national level' by about Shs. 200 per month.

Not that all the tobacco is exported. A quantity remains to be used as raw material by the 'national industry'. Here too finance capital is on the spot to exploit its production and distribution. The British-American Tobacco Company Tanzania Limited (BAT)—a 'nationalised' company—for a period of seven years operated under the management and technical consultancy of the transnational BAT Co. Ltd. Under the Management Agreement and through control of technology and markets they exercised considerable control over production and reaped considerable surplus-value. Under a new agreement signed in 1974 the role of the managing agent was terminated, but their role of technical consultants was retained, which for the transnational is sufficient to exercise the same if not greater control, and their share in the product as fees for consultancy and patents and skilled manpower is not

negligible, as the following figures will show: (i) 0.65% of the net turnover (i.e., ex-factory price less excise and sales tax); [Note: and not all
other costs.] (ii) Shs. 28,000 per month consultancy fee;
(iii) Shs. 11,500 per month from 1st January to 30th June 1975;
(iv) Shs. 5,000 per month net of tax to each staff member seconded by
the transnational plus all fringe benefits. Although under the agreement
a number of trade marks were transferred to the Tanzania company,
patents remained the transnational's sole property.

Finally, another type of agreement to close our discussion on this
issue. Here the activity is a processing one and, like elsewhere, finance
capital is the activator of production. Under an agreement entered into
in 1975 between Cordemex S.A. de C.V., of Mexico (a monopoly with
obvious links with British finance capital), and the Tanzania Sisal
Corporation (TSC), it was agreed between the two parties that a new
company—Tanzamex—be incorporated in Tanzania with the two
parties as the sole shareholders in proportions of 40 per cent and 60
per cent, the majority shareholding being in favour of TSC. The
principal object of the company was to establish and operate a sisal
rope and twine factory on the estate of TSC at Ngombezi, Korogwe,
where a lot of sisal is produced on co-operative and small-farm basis. It
was further provided that immediately upon the incorporation of the
company the promoters of the new company would undertake to cause
the new company to enter into two other agreements, one with a
finance company for the supply of machinery on the terms negotiated
beforehand, and one with Cordemex for marketing the product. It was
then stipulated that James Mackie & Sons Ltd., of Belfast, would
supply the machinery on which Cordemex had already made a 'down
payment', which 'down payment' was to be utilised to purchase
Cordemex a share in the new company. The Finance Agreement was
entered into in accordance with the provision above with Brandts
Export Finance Ltd., of UK. The agreement gave TSC a right to buy
off the 40 per cent share held by Cordemex, but this would only be
possible after the tenth anniversary of the 'commissioning of the
factory', upon six months notice, and upon liquidation of any
indebtedness due under the finance agreement. Thus it can be inferred
from this provision that Cordemex is prepared to promote the new
company so long as it has the protection of participation in the venture
for at least ten years, and so long as the finance capital is assured of
security of exploitation over that period. Cordemex moreover plays the
role as guarantor of the capital lent by Brandts.

Under the agreement TSC undertook to supply the company sisal
fibre for the factory at prices, terms and conditions not less favourable
than those applicable to local spinners. It also undertook to provide
land for the factory and other buildings on a lease of not less than
twenty years. In return, Cordemex promised not to engage or promote
old or new ventures in Tanzania, Kenya and Uganda which would
compete with the new company. Cordemex was to provide a General

Manager and Plant Engineer on conditions and terms to be agreed, who were to supervise the construction of the factory and installation of machinery and to provide know-how and partly manage the company. These provisions are understandable since under the agreement Cordemex is also expected to provide, at prices to be agreed, five pieces of machinery under the Mexican Patent No. 12188 to supplement the machinery to be supplied from Ireland.

The Marketing Agency Agreement between the new company and Cordemex 'requests' Cordemex to market the product and Cordemex 'agrees' to do so on condition that they sell the products at the 'most favourable prices obtainable'. The company must however manufacture the products in accordance with the technical procedures and standards of quality as indicated by Cordemex, and they must bear a Cordemex symbol. For this service they may pay themselves 2½ per cent of the proceeds of the marketed product FOB.

To sum up, this agreement, like the first one, assures the monopoly control under finance capital in the production of rope and twine, the market of the product, and lastly the security of the raw material base, which is available with cheap labour in Tanzania.

These few examples are a minute sampling of the involvement of finance capital in production, distribution and exchange in Tanzania, but they give an insight into the operation and global strategy of the transnational corporation. The diverse forms of finance capital have not all been indicated but the few examples do indicate on a small scale the diverse methods of control and exploitation. Tanzania entered into at least thirty-four such agreements after the Arusha Declaration in 1967, but these have increased and are bound to increase with any new venture and/or old ones. Thus finance capital still seeks to enter into each and every type of activity in production, distribution and exchange. If the activities of the East African Community are added, the catalogue grows bigger. The hold of finance capital has increased since the Declaration, which was supposed to be the watershed en route to self-reliance. To quote a recent paper on the subject:

> The Bank's lending operations have accelerated sharply over the last few years. While the cumulative total of approved IBRD and IDA loans to Tanzania stood at Shs. 822 million ($114.9 million) by June 1970, it had increased to Shs. 2,623 million ($366.8 million) by June 1975. In fiscal year 1974/5 alone Shs. 656 million ($91.7 million) worth of loans were approved, making Tanzania the sixth largest country by loans in Africa. Adjusting for differences of population, Tanzania ranks tenth in per capita loans in 1974/75 out of the forty African countries currently borrowing from the Bank: Shs. 188 ($26.3) was borrowed per Tanzanian citizen in 1974/75.[9]

And all this objective power of finance capital springs from the most powerful states of Europe, USA and Japan subjugating and exploiting the peoples of Africa, Asia and Latin America.

III

We must now conclude and suggest the best way of approach in researching the transnational corporation. We have established our main thesis by tracing the movement of capitalist production historically and the laws of motion that finally compelled the financial oligarchies into a monopolistic position. We have seen that in order for a capitalist to survive the profitability crisis which occurs historically around the 1870s, he had to operate on a monopolistic basis if he expected to operate in a basic sector of the economy or to participate in the international, colonial and neocolonial markets. But this monopolistic power was a function of its tie-up with monopolistic banks and other financial institutions, which gave the industrial bourgeoisie greater availability of finance capital to enable research and development, in order to tap overseas production and markets. We have also shown some of the diverse forms of exports of finance capital and the institutions involved in its export, based on a few studies to illustrate the objective power of finance capital in one third world country.

Hence it seems obvious to us that the best way of approach in any research is to assume the involvement of monopoly control in all major projects in which a transnational corporation in a third world country is a participant. It should also be assumed where multilateral finance is involved. This should be taken as given, unless the contrary is clearly the case. The enquiry must then proceed to establish the form or type of finance capital exported and utilised by the corporation to achieve its purpose. Although the purpose here will be the attainment of a profit higher than average and a high rate of surplus-value, it will nevertheless be useful to establish whether the corporation is really interested in the profit on the project as such without anything more, or whether it seeks some access to additional advantages, e.g. to raw material bases, or markets (existing or new). This will be easy to establish if in fact some of the raw materials and other products produced are actually exported to the monopoly itself. This is in addition to the fact that the raw material or other product produced would go to one or other monopoly in the imperialist countries in any case. It nevertheless would be an important fact to establish if the particular monopoly is itself interested in the product. The same will apply to the market question.

Furthermore, the study must then proceed to show whether the corporation is, through the project or venture, availing itself of local or 'national capital'. This it will achieve in various ways, either by requiring the local capital as a necessary component to its operations, or by being exempted from taxes, levies or other assessments or by obtaining certain services below price or service charge. These are quantifiable cost advantages that are borne by local consumers of similar services and facilities, and hence are a local subsidisation in terms of local resources. This is important because it will then demonstrate to what extent 'national capital' is being augmented by this 'foreign investment', or to what extent it is being 'denationalised' and/or internationalised in its application and hence appropriation. This is a kind of 'cost/benefit analysis' that should form a quantitative aspect of the enquiry but by no means the basis, as is sometimes done one-sidedly.

Centralisation of 'national capital' will also take a number of forms. This will happen in its ideal form where a wholly owned subsidiary of a transnational corporation utilises local bank and other capital for its productive activities. Where the transnational monopoly accepts joint-ventureship it is in an even better position, even with a minority interest, to tap these locally-centralised resources, since it can now claim to be a 'national company'. Even in 'worst' situations, as when its sole interest is sales of technology and it is paid a percentage on net earnings of the company before tax, it will still be utilising the whole 100 per cent 'national share' capital and other productive resources to extract that surplus-value for its technology. Centralisation of national capital may also take the form of a *consortium* forming a finance corporation in which monopolies hold shares. An example of this would be the TDFC in Tanzania or ICFC in Kenya. Here foreign finance capital with local capital is lent out, and finance capital reaps surplus-value. All these and other forms of centralisation and control of 'national capital' should be investigated in any research on the transnational corporation.

The enquiry should also investigate the forms and diverse means by which the transnational corporation repatriates its vast earnings. This may be important to show the extent exchange-control restrictions are avoided by the corporations, or to show the rate of the flow of resources out of the country. Thus, although in management, marketing, consultancy and/or technical agreement remuneration is on the basis of a percentage of profits after tax, plus a technical fee or a fixed fee per year for management, plus a percentage of the purchase price for the services of a purchasing agent, plus, again, royalties for technical services as a percentage of sales, such remunerative heads may become a basis for cumulative repatriation of surplus-value. In addition to any of the above arrangements, there will be a percentage of the capital expenditure, and a fixed sum per year plus a percentage of net profits before taxes as payments for managerial and other services. There may be a mixture of the above arrangements and percentages may be subjected to a minimum (and sometimes to a maximum) fee. The above fees, which in many cases are cumulative, are *in addition to* dividends earned on its equity share in the enterprise if the foreign monopoly is in addition a shareholder.

The transnational has at its disposal transfer accounting and/or pricing techniques which would enable it to beat the foreign exchange restrictions. The ILO Report on Kenya had this to say:

> It is, however, widely accepted that repatriation of profits is often an
> inadequate measure of the total resources transferred by the foreign enter-

prises, particularly in the manufacturing sector. Generally speaking foreign-
owned enterprises are in a position to use a number of accounting procedures
falling under the heading of transfer accounting that enable them to maximise
profits (by minimising their tax commitments) over the whole of their international operations, by moving resources from one country to another.[10]

Thus the foreign corporation will through *transfer-pricing, over-
invoicing* or *under-invoicing,* to be in a position to siphon off its funds
to the metropole. In Kenya the ILO Report noted that a number of
these firms that had made losses consistently over periods of four or
five years were suspected of transfer-pricing intermediate goods and
accumulating outside Kenya. The overpricing sometimes was as high as
20 to 30 per cent of the prices on the open market. The report
concluded:

> If it becomes prevalent, this type of transfer pricing can have a particularly
> marked effect on an economy like that of Kenya, where imported inter-
> mediates comprise a very large part of gross output in the manufacturing
> economy. It requires only *a very small overpricing ratio to bring about
> transfers of resources* which can, since they are untaxed, constitute a very
> large proportionate addition to the resources transferred through the
> repatriation of profits.

In Latin America, Vaitsos cited overpricing of imports of up to
400 per cent in Colombia.[11]

In addition to transfer-pricing, a foreign corporation may remit its
funds out of the country under the exchange control regulations themselves, by duplicating heads of entitlement. The ILO Report on Kenya
quotes the result of a sample of ten foreign-owned enterprises which
were found to have made the following remittances abroad: £310,000
for dividends; £136,000 for management fees; £34,000 for technical
services and consultations; £36,000 for royalties. Non-dividend payments amounted to 67 per cent of dividend remittances and 40 per
cent of total remittances.[12] It was also noted that the other common
practice was the earning of dividends on the basis of capitalised know-
how, and at the same time a charge of royalties on the sale for
technology was made.

Finally, the enquiry should investigate the quantity and quality of
labour-power that the capital exports were aimed at exploiting. This
will involve of course mainly peasant labour but, with increasing
enclave-type of import-substitution, proletarianised or semi-
proletarianised labour will be involved. With sufficient scientific skill it
should be possible to work out the organic composition of the capital
and then establish on some average level the rate of exploitation of the
labour force. This would necessitate establishing the surplus-labour and
necessary labour involved. The degree of exploitation would then be
the ratio of the two ($\frac{s}{v}$). Only when this is done would the profitability

be established.

On this basis a more meaningful research would then be possible. Any economistic approach would reveal a one-sided phenomenon. Indeed, in our view a recent study of the Kenya soap industry by Steven Langdon shows how this economism produces results that are self-satisfying only to 'neo-Marxist' dogmatism. In his study Langdon starts off with a long list of 'should' dogmas based on neo-classical vulgar economy that only exist in the imagination but not in reality. And since they do not exist in *historical* reality, at the end of the study the 'shoulds' acquire a self-cancelling effect on the whole aim of the research. For instance, Langdon sets his research strategy thus:

> The article considers that genuine industrial development in poorer African countries should have relatively large employment effects, in terms of jobs provided per unit of capital invested; should generate considerable local linkage effects, particularly backward linkages to indigenous resources; should minimize wastage of resources through capacity underutilisation, changeover costs, advertising expenditure, etc; should have a relatively positive balance-of-payments impact, considering import intensity, exports, repatriations by foreigners, *et al;* and should contribute more to egalitarian social and regional distribution effects than most industrialisation has so far done in Africa.[13]

Why most industrialisation has not so far succeeded in Africa is not explained in the hypothesis that is the beginning of the study. On the contrary, it is assumed to exist on the basis of the 'shoulds', themselves *a priori* categories that exist only in the imagination. The reality of colonialism and neocolonialism is brushed aside in favour of the *a priori* non-reality. Langdon then 'assesses' the performance of the transnational corporation against these 'standards'. At the end of the research we are consoled by the 'discovery' that transnational investment

> has resulted in increasing unemployment and regional inequality, has made very little and possibly negative contribution to the balance of payments, and has failed to make linkages with the local economy and especially its resources.[14]

In our view most of these self-satisfying conclusions could have been assumed as a tendency based on imperialist exploitation. The research effort could then have been focused on those areas that reveal the real exploitative nature of exports of finance capital, rather than starting from a historically disproved hypothesis that the transnational is 'the agency through which advanced technology is transferred to underdeveloped countries', as Langdon does, only to end up in morally bemoaning the fact that this is not so after all. To quote Langdon:

> A final conclusion is evident. This study points out the serious shortcomings for the developing countries, of the mnc as an institution of technology

transfer from the developed countries. *The implication is that an important contribution to greater world equity could be the emergence of much less restrictive means of such transfer.* This suggests a priority for activity in the richer nations: *the development of alternative, non-profit institutions of technology transfer;* and the related *challenging of mnc control over much technology and most technological innovation.*[15] *[Emphasis added]*

Just as he started, he winds up the 'research' by moral demands for the establishment of 'non-profit' institutions for the transfer of technology in order to bring about 'equity'. Langdon and vulgar economy must understand that there can be a 'non-profitable' transfer of technology only on the grave of monopoly capitalism itself and not before!

We must reject these unscientific moral persuasions that ignore the real causes, and get on with real scientific research which shows us the way out of imperialist exploitation of the transnational monopolies based on exports of finance capital. This necessitates a scientific methodology based on the historical movement of capitalist production, which reveals to us the fact that the transnational corporation is a form of how monopoly capitalism operates under multilateral imperialism. This scientific methodology then raises only those questions that are based on what exists and what is the reality, rather than questions that are *a priori* formulations of a non-existent, ideal situation. Such scientific methodology should take into account the questions that we have proposed as a fundamental basis of the research. In our view a detailed questionnaire based on this fundamental methodology would bring us nearer to more useful knowledge than the one based on idealist *a priori* formulations. This is what constitutes scientific enquiry, to which social science must adhere if reality is to be fathomed and change brought about.

Until then, *forward!* Backward *never!*

NOTES

1. Vernon, Raymond: *Restrictive Business Practices. The operations of multinational US enterprises in developing countries,* pp. 1-3; UN (NY), 1972.
2. Main, Jeremy, in *Fortune* Magazine, December 1967, p. 143.
3. Jalée, P.: *op. cit.,* p. 129.
4. Economic Commission for Africa, *The Multinational Corporations in Africa,* p. 5; London, 1972.
5. *Ibid.,* p. 10.
6. *Multinational Corporations in World Development,* p. 49, UN (NY), 1973.
7. Beckford, G.L.: *Persistent Poverty,* pp. 114-8; London, 1972.
8. Tschannerl, G.: *Tanzania and the World Bank;* Dar es Salaam (mimeo), 1976.
9. *Ibid.*
10. I.L.O.: *Employment, Incomes and Equality in Kenya,* pp. 453-6; Geneva, 1972.

11. Vaitsos, C., in Bernstein, M.D., *Foreign Investments in Latin America,* New York, 1969.

12. I.L.O.: *op. cit.,* pp. 455-6.

13. Langdon, S.: 'Multinational Corporations, Taste Transfer and Under-development: a case study from Kenya' in *Review of African Political Economy* No. 2, 1975, p. 13.

14. *Ibid.,* p. 12.

15. *Ibid.,* p. 32.

CHAPTER 3

IMPERIALISM IN THE CONTEMPORARY WORLD

I

In this chapter we try to deal with the problems that imperialism poses in the contemporary world and the manner of resolving them. The methodology is a materialist interpretation of imperialism, and hence presents, to the best of the author's knowledge, a Marxist-Leninist viewpoint and working-class solution to the problem of imperialism.

In Section I an effort is made to grapple with the presentation of the problem of imperialism by the bourgeoisie. Schumpeter is presented as the theoretician on this question because of his serious approach and his rigorous analyses of aspects of old imperialisms. He is put forward as giving a general bourgeois position also because of his attempt to refute the materialist interpretation of modern imperialism, although adopting an ambivalent position towards the end. His strong argument that modern imperialism is not a stage of capitalism, but comes from the 'dim past', represents general bourgeois thinking on the question. This leads us in Section II to deal with the problem of false consciousness and its relation to the social sciences, in which it is demonstrated how bourgeois social science cannot penetrate the problem of imperialism nor provide any answer. This is done after analysing the neo-Kantian approach of the sociology of Durkheim and Max Weber, showing how it ends up in scientistic limbo unable to explain society. In the sphere of political science we present the arguments of Frankel and Morgenthau, and demonstrate Frankel's own conclusion that international relations theory has found itself in 'intellectual jail'.

In Section III we deal with science, education and culture under the grip of imperialism, and attempt to show how education inevitably reflects the false consciousness of the bourgoisie, how scientific research has been gripped by monopoly and how the question of culture is bound up with the national question and the class struggle. We end with Section IV in which the national question is raised, and in which the liberation struggle in general and in Southern Africa in particular is examined. Here we present what we regard as a working-class solution to the problem of imperialism. We demonstrate that the right of nations to self-determination only belongs to the political sphere in which the dual transformation of the acceptance of the principle of equality of all nations and territorial demarcation of national borders is necessary in advancing the democratic struggle against economic domination, which in the present epoch must lead to socialism.

Today's bourgeois political science or economics cannot unravel the power that is represented by imperialism in the contemporary world. Indeed, the bourgeoisie could not do so, since their class interest under

existing conditions, and the fetishism that capitalist relations under
imperialism imply, make it increasingly necessary for them to obscure
reality and to uphold an idealist world outlook which compels them to
analyse things from their appearances rather than from their content.
This is not a moral weakness of bourgeois scholars, nor does it have to
be seen as a wickedness on their part for mystifying the reality of
contemporary imperialism. Indeed, it is the fetishism that commodities
take on, reinforced by juridical relations in the market, that make such
ephemeral analysis real to the bourgeois. Yet it does not hold that their
analysis is correct because of it. Indeed, it is the demand that
phenomena be analysed *scientifically* and not *'scientistically'* that
makes the Marxist-Leninist theory of imperialism hard to brush aside.
The understanding of imperialism in the contemporary world and its
impact on all sectors of social life requires a materialist approach,
which analyses modern imperialism in its historical movement and
specificity, based on the laws of motion of society in general (historical
materialism) and on the laws of motion of capitalism in particular,
avoiding the banalities and generalities about imperialism as a general
natural phenomenon which bourgeois social science adopts.

In his effort to analyse the problem of imperialism, which he saw as
a problem of 'aggressive attitudes on the part of states', and which he
defined as 'the objectless disposition on the part of a state to unlimited
expansion', Schumpeter thought the way of understanding it lay partly
in analysing 'the real and concrete interests of the people', which were
not necessarily 'economic in character'. Such interests also did not
have to 'extend to the *entire* population of the state'. He discarded
what he called 'the economic interpretation of history', which derived
imperialist tendencies from the 'economic-structural influences that
shape life in general and from the relations of production'. He continued:

> I should like to emphasize that I do not doubt in the least that this powerful
> instrument of analysis will stand up here in the same sense that it has with
> other, similar phenomena—if only it is kept in mind that customary modes of
> political thought and feeling in a given age can never be mere 'reflexes' or
> counterparts to, the production situation of that age. . . Again, the attempt
> may be made to reduce imperialist phenomena to economic class *interests* of
> the age in question. This is precisely what neo-Marxist theory does. Briefly it
> views imperialism simply as the reflex of the interests of the capitalist upper
> stratum, at a given stage of capitalist development. Beyond doubt this is by
> far the most serious contribution toward a solution of our problem.
> Certainly there is much truth in it. We shall deal with this theory later. But
> let us emphasize even here that it does not follow from the economic
> interpretation of history.[1]

The quotation above may sound contradictory. In fact in many
places of his essay Schumpeter accepts the validity of Hilferding's
analysis in his book, *Finance Capital,* which had then come out. But
his purpose was to demonstrate that imperialism could be equally

explained otherwise. His method?

> We propose to analyse the birth and life of imperialism by means of historical
> examples which we regard as typical. A common basic tract emerges in every
> case, making a single sociological problem of imperialism in all ages, though
> there are substantial differences among the individual cases.

Schumpeter then went on to analyse these 'historical examples' of
'imperialisms', from the 'typical imperialism' (of Egypt), 'people's
imperialism' (of Persia), 'naked imperialism' (of Syria as compared to
that of Louis XIV), 'Arab popular imperialism', 'German imperialism',
the 'anti-imperialist warrior aristocracy' (of Morevingian imperialism),
and 'Roman imperialism', to the 'imperialism of the Absolute
Monarchy' (of France, Russia etc.). In his summary of the factors
contributing to these imperialisms, he points *first* to the 'objectless'
tendencies towards 'forcible expansion, without definite, utilitarian
limits, non-rational and irrational, 'purely instinctual inclinations
toward war and conquest'. This was because the majority of wars were
waged 'without adequate "reason" '. *Secondly,* there were the 'vital
needs of the situation that moulded peoples and classes into warriors—
if they wanted to avoid extinction', and here the psychological
dispositions and social structures, acquired in the 'dim past', once
firmly established tended to maintain themselves and to continue
'long after they have lost their meaning and their life-preserving
function'. *Thirdly,* there were 'subsidiary factors' that facilitate the
survival of such dispositions and structures—namely the orientation
towards war 'mainly fostered by the domestic interests of ruling
classes' and *also* by the influence 'of all those who stand to gain
individually from a war policy, whether economically or socially'.
He concludes:

> Imperialisms differ greatly in detail, but they all have at least these traits in
> common turning them into a single phenomenon in the field of sociology. . .
> [it] is atavistic in character. It falls into that large group of surviving
> features from earlier ages that play such an important part in every concrete
> social situation. In other words it is an element that stems from the living
> conditions, not of the present, but of the past—or, put in terms of the
> economic interpretation of history, from past rather than present relations
> of production.

Thus, for Schumpeter imperialism could be reduced to one common
element—atavism, i.e. having its roots in the 'dim past'. But he reminds
us in the footnote to the above that these atavistic 'sentiments',
although not explained in the present, 'became comprehensible only by
reference to their capacity and wishes' because this mentality was not
something that existed outside the economic sphere. To Schumpeter a
'purely capitalist world' offered no fertile soil to imperialist 'impulses'.
This did not mean that it could not maintain an interest in imperialist

expansion. Capitalism was essentially anti-war, and 'war tendencies are alien elements, carried into the world of capitalism from outside, supported by non-capitalist factors in life'. Schumpeter maintains his position although he admits that it is 'in the nature of a capitalist economy—and of an exchange economy generally—that many people stand to gain economically in war', since this means increased demand and panic prices, 'hence high profits and also high wages in many parts of the national economy'. The national economy however is impoverished by the tremendous excess in consumption brought on by war. Having said this, he nevertheless sticks to the 'free trade' dogma that 'where free trade prevails no class has an interest in forcible expansion'. Foreign raw materials and foodstuffs are accessible to each nation 'as though they were within its own territory', so that it does not matter who colonises the backward areas.

Schumpeter here was caught in the illusion of free trade so that in spite of Hilferding's analysis he maintained that it was only under free trade that *international* cartels would be possible. Any tariff barriers erected   benefited large landowners and were in any case

> fruit of political action—a type of action that by no means reflects the objective interests of those concerned. It follows that it is a basic fallacy to describe imperialism as a necessary phase of capitalism, or even to speak of the development of capitalism into imperialism. We have seen before that the mode of life of the capitalist world does not favour imperialist attitudes. We have seen that the alignment of interests in a capitalist economy—even the interests of its upper strate—by no means points unequivocally in the direction of imperialism.

II

What has been brought out above from Schumpeter in our view exemplifies what Marx called 'the illusion of the epoch', or false consciousness of the hitherto ruling classes. This illusion of the epoch constitutes the ideology of the ruling classes in a particular epoch and constitutes the substance of what has to be passed on as education and culture. Reality under such ideology is inverted to defend the existing as 'natural' and unchangeable. Reality is metaphysically mystified. Ideology and false consciousness remove from beings and things that reality that belongs to them and relegate them to abstractions. Then in platonic fashion they set out from the abstractions to reconstruct the world as it is, producing concrete being and reality from these abstractions.

To be sure, such conversion of reality, the falsification of consciousness, is not new nor characteristic of the era of modern imperialism alone. In primitive, communal society, the rudimentary conception of nature was expressed in magic and myth. The first served as the illusory technique of production and the second as the oral accompaniment to the first, and with the development of the productive forces came to represent an elemental theory of reality. This was because under this system of production, society produced only *use-values,* since the means of production were commonly owned, and both production and consumption were collective. The division of labour was elemental and social relations simple and direct, based on kinship. Thus primitive consciousness was under these circumstances bound to be uniformly subjective, concrete and practical. This was inevitable in situations where man was imperfectly aware of the objectivity of the external world, and of his power to change that objective world. His only knowledge of it was obtained through production and limited heritage. Moreover, the categories of his knowledge in this collectivity were of necessity social categories determined by the level of the productive forces and the relations into which he entered for such production. For this reason his thinking about the external world as something separate was thought of as a *social order.* Nature and society were one, because his relations were subject to collective control by the community, and in the same way the world of nature could only be controlled by collective action. This communality of being and nature was reinforced by totemic kinship groups which were tied together by common descent. Thus myths and the magical act represented this rudimentary stage of society and sufficiently explained it.

With the division of society into antagonistic classes the situation changed. This change was brought about by the developments in production arising from the discovery of the iron plough, which gave tremendous boost to the productive forces, enabling a surplus product much above the former consumption needs of producers. The surplus product increasingly went to the consumption needs of a class of non-producers, which slowly consolidated itself into a ruling class. These developments gave rise also to a division between mental and manual labour, with the implication that the thinkers no longer thought for a collectivity but for a divided society. As society divided itself in the actuality of production and consumption, manual and mental producers, so too the consciousness of the two diverged and only converged in hostility to each other. With a leisured class it now became possible for abstract science and philosophy to develop—a phenomenon we notice in ancient Greece, where the historical circumstances for its flowering converge for the first time around 500BC.

But for our purpose here we see the beginnings of *theory* being separated from *practice.* What arose from the thinkers were metaphysical mystifications, which reflected reality but in an inverted way. They reflected the class structure and interests of the various classes. The ruling classes now explained their existence and interest not as a product of history but as a product of nature in the abstract. This inversion of reality was reinforced with the appearance of commodity production—production of *exchange-values.* As *use-value* production is replaced, men emerge as individual owners of commodities which they exchange in the market. Thus emerges a relation beyond their control, based on laws of exchange. These laws appear as the reality, and the actual relationships which produce these market exchange-values are obscured by the overwhelming operations of the laws.

It is thus that the 'illusion of the epoch', the ideology of the existing ruling classes, emerges. It is not for nothing that Plato and Aristotle justified the existing relations based on slavery in Greece. When Plato coined his 'noble lie', it was contrived in the interest of his class. When he divided society in his Republic-to-be into Rulers, Auxiliaries and Producers as an old natural wisdom of the Phoenicians, he was coining the illusion of the epoch. So too Cicero in Rome, when he stated:

> Antiquity no doubt was deceived in many things, and has had to be corrected by time, by experience, or the spread of knowledge. And yet the reverence for augury and the college augurs and the practice of augury must be kept on account of the beliefs of the common people and for its great service to the state.[2]

So too with the feudalists; in the words of John of Salisbury: 'According to the law of the universe all things are not reduced to order equally and immediately, but the lowest through the intermediate and the intermediate through the higher.'[3] In the same way the bourgeoisie, struggling to stand on its feet, saw the *social contract* through Rousseau as the thing that made 'individuals come in contact and have mutual intercourse'.

Thus we see that the slave-owning class utilised the 'divine first mover' as the basis for its ideology which mystified and upheld the real relations in production based on slavery. The feudalists did so under *natural law* where the serf, having won for himself limited freedom, was regarded as a member of the community under the influence of the German mark. With the bourgeoisie the reality is even more inverted. Since capitalism advances commodity production to its fullest, the relations between men are veiled fully as market and hence juridical relations. Under the bourgeoisie history and nature receive the sharpest rupture. As George Thomson observes:

> Nature is regarded as the realm of necessity, standing outside of man—a realm which man can operate according to his will, provided that he understands its laws; but man himself is somehow 'free', his freedom being seen 'as a product, not of history, but of nature'.[4]

This dualism in bourgeois society is supported by Kantian philosophy in which the will has autonomy through pure *reason,* and reality exists but is fashioned by this inner human reason, namely the false consciousness of the bourgeoisie. Labour and its product (mental and

material) are counterposed by highly developed commodity production.
Says Marx:

> A commodity is therefore a mysterious thing, simply because in it the social
> character of men's labour appears to them as an objective character stamped
> upon the product of that labour; because the relation of the producers to the
> sum total of their own labour is presented to them as a social relation,
> existing *not between themselves, but between the products of their labour.* [5]
> *[Emphasis added]*

Marx, through his dialectical method, puts an end to that dualism,
re-establishing the unity between nature and history.

But it is false consciousness that characterises bourgeois social
science. Among the youthful revolutionary bourgeoisie it manifested
itself in the theory or *principle of utilitarianism,* under which they
fought the privileges and restrictions of the old class and enhanced
the demands of the new class rising under the new relations. The idea
that utilitarianism was that principle by which an act was judged
according to whether it augumented man's pleasure or increased his
pain, was attributed to revelation by man's 'inner reason' of the
unrevealed law of God. Bentham rubbed in this false consciousness
thus: 'Nature has placed man under the empire of pleasure and pain.
We owe to them all our ideas, we refer to them all judgments and all
determination of our life.'[6]

But what the bourgeoisie meant by pleasure and pain was not the
ordinary hedonism that some bourgeois scholars attributed to them.
Pleasure stood for the accumulation of capital, and pain for thefts or
the destruction of capital. John Austin, the jurist *par excellence* of the
bourgeois legal ideology, who drew heavily from Bentham, put it
squarely: God designs the happiness of all his creatures. Some actions
enhance that purpose and are therefore mischievous or pernicious. God
has enjoined and approved the useful tendencies and forbidden the
pernicious. God has given us the faculties of observation and reasoning
and hence we are able to know these tendencies in our actions. The
purpose of law is to assure *subsistence,* by creating opportunities which
lead individuals to provide for themselves; *abundance,* by creating
conditions for making new acquisitions; *equality* of opportunity and
not condition; and *security,* as the paramount goal of law and state to
assure individual property, life, honour and status, and protect
'established order':

> Without security of property, there is no inducement to save. Without
> habitual saving—there is no accumulation of capital. Without accumulation of
> capital, there is no fund for the payment of wages, no division of labour, no
> elaborate and costly machines [which help] augment [labour's] productive
> power, and therefore multiply the enjoyments of every individual in the
> community. Frequent invasions of property [thefts] would bring the rich to

poverty; and, what were a greater evil, would aggravate the poverty of the poor.[7]

Here through Kantian 'pure reason' we are brought circuitously to the realisation that the advancement of capitalist production is not a historically determined phenomenon but the realisation of the idea of pleasure, and the idea of combating thefts which, with the rise of bourgeois rule, due to wholesale impoverishment of the peasantry and due to the expropriation of their means of subsistence and production, were rampant at this time.

The other leg on which Kant's philosophy stood—*practical reason*—pushed bourgeois social science into greater obscurantism. While conceding to Hume's inner reason, he also recognised Newton's 'outer reason' of empirical observation through natural sciences. These were concerned with the physical world but the results of those sciences were to be fashioned by the knowledge of the inner mind conceived *a priori.* It is for this reason that Austin's 'positive law', made by men for men, had as its index the utilitarian principle derived from the faculty of reason. What *'is'* was therefore conditioned by *'ought'* through morality, which was knowledge *a priori.* The reality of man's historically accumulated heritage was turned into an idea, not historically determined but naturally determined, thus allowing the bourgeoisie to claim their rule as 'natural'.

This Kantian 'transubstantiation'—to borrow from Plato—was even more hideous under the sociology of the 1830s onwards. Neo-Kantianism, put forward by Rickert, Windelband and Dilthey, held that there could not be any complete scientific description of reality, since reality consisted of a complex divisible profusion of phenomena. Even if we were to focus on one particular element of reality, it too was infinite. According to them, social science therefore must select from the multitude of infinite phenomena aspects of study and investigation. This was a reaction against the influence of Auguste Comte, who in some quarters is regarded as the father of positivism and who held that all sciences are ordered in the form of empirical and logical hierarchy, in which each science is treated as involving the methods and pre-suppositions of natural science in the study of social phenomena. Comte's positivism of applying the laws of natural science to society soon led to irretrievable rigidity.

Durkheim tried to integrate socio-cultural systems in the study of society—in which the primitive society was to be seen as a 'growing concern'. Each culture was a distinctive living organism made up of interrelated parts of sub-groups and individuals which had to be seen in action, pursuing corporate goals through purposeful operations. According to him, the anthropologist must investigate, first, causal sequences or habitual behaviours of such societies, then the ends they serve and the part they play in these interlocking institutions. Other sociologists emphasised particular phenomena, e.g. Malinowski saw the central theme as survival, Parsons saw the determining principle of society as being the maintenance of 'a steady state' based on a consensual acceptance of mutually coherent and balancing roles and expectations.

Max Weber took off from these sociologists and went a point further. He started with Rickert's emphasis on the need to study the unique characteristics of each society and its special nature, to be grasped by intuitive knowledge. According to Rickert, we must study the purpose and motivation for which the society came into existence. Durkheim's 'group mind' was seen as unhelpful—because it was devoid of content. It was a mere abstraction. There could be no general formal system, for everything depended on the particular motivation and purpose. Weber held that in selecting what to study it would be naive to suppose 'neutrality' or a value-free position, but when one had shown the value-position one should be ruthlessly objective in showing exactly how it worked. Weber took western capitalism as the particular system to study and explained it on the basis of its motivation and purpose. He did this by a model system he called 'ideal type'.

The 'ideal type' was not derived directly from reality, since this involved the intrusion of value-presumptions. Since social phenomena could not be studied by methods of natural science, the 'ideal type' in this case was an abstract construct which interpreted and explained the objectives of capitalist society, without necessarily reflecting universally 'essential' properties of reality. The 'ideal type' was constructed by the abstraction and combination of an indefinite number of elements which, although found in reality, were rarely or never discovered in this specific form. It was not a hypothesis, either. Its only purpose was to facilitate the analysis of empirical questions. The construct was a delineation through empirical examination of specific forms of capitalism, the most important respects in which rational capitalism was distinctive.[8]

The 'ideal type' of rational capitalism which Weber examines in his writings is the outcome of men acting under common motivation and finding the appropriate means of attaining their chosen ends. This is the value orientation of all reasonable men from his class standpoint, and is the meaning of capitalist society based on his model. As to the methods of attaining these ends, Weber provides a theory of 'adequate causation'. This is the 'scientific method' of social science, which is necessary for obtaining the system of objective possibilities which constitute dependable regularities of society. In order to explain why a certain sequence of events happens in society, according to Weber it is enough if we can locate a factor which may be accepted as adequate to explain events. The cause is adequate if the end desired would not be achieved or the event we want to explain would not happen, without it. Thus the 'ideal type' explains on the basis of 'adequate causes' of the existing, functioning, on-going society, in terms of its 'frame of action', its total meaning, its intentions and its actions.

Weber's model seen from the characteristics of early capitalism provided adequate explanation of the system. But it was a system abstracted from historical movement as a whole. For this reason it could not explain the system of capitalist production in its motion. Seen from the standpoint of its contradictory development, it was an idealised version, a false consciousness, for Weber did not seek to understand reality in its ever-changing, historical movement, in which the old is negated and is always in the process of becoming. The crisis brought about by monopoly capitalism could not be comprehended by Weber's method of studying social phenomena. This period, unlike the earlier one of young capitalism, was characterised by *scientistic* methods increasingly detached from reality. The new philosophies that were developing also demonstrated the loss of vision of the bourgeoisie as a whole, as segmentation among them increased; the monopoly bourgeoisie was increasingly dispossessing the others, thereby turning them into a petty bourgeoisie.

An example is a philosophy called pragmatism which was articulated in the United States by one William James. According to James the world consisted of some neutral substance which was neither ideal nor material. According to him therefore the development of the world was neither law-governed nor knowable. John Dewey also denied the materiality of the world and laid the concept of experiment at the base of everything existing. It was impossible to know the world, he said. Scientific concepts, laws and hypotheses were merely instruments of man in his struggle for existence. Their usefulness was the only criterion of our knowledge. There was no objective truth. All instruments of science must help us to resolve situations. Only what was useful in this context was true. He advocated pluralism according to which all factors of social life are of equal significance for social progress.

All social science has adopted this scientistic, 'thing-in-itself' abstractionalism. A proliferation of 'schools' has increased with each rise in the intellectual division of labour. There is no meeting place for knowledge. The illusion of the epoch finds itself increasingly in confusion and crisis, as each individual actor sees his individual 'particular' knowledge as real knowledge, but which is increasingly abstracted away from reality. Engels was to the point when he stated:

> Still higher ideologies, that is, such as are still removed from the material economic basis, take the form of philosophy and religion. Here the inter-connection between conceptions and their material conditions of existence becomes more and more complicated, more and more obscured by intermediate links.[9]

Thus bourgeois sociology under imperialism has found itself increasingly in limbo, unable to explain reality. The tradition of the Comtes and Spencers has ended in narrower and narrower outlooks.

Weber's protestant ethic and his 'ideal type' showed no way out. Durkheim's socio-cultural systems avoided the category of social class in their analysis and equally gave no way out. Schumpeter's sociology of imperialism brought us no nearer to its understanding. His emphasis on psychological factors, and his 'typical' and 'objectless' causes did not help. J.D. Bernal correctly observed:

> The. . . insistence on accumulating simple and disconnected facts and on the comparative method, together with the rejection of historic and economic interpretation, doom from its very birth the nineteenth-century science of sociology.[10]

The introduction of sociometry (Moreno), socio-dramatic techniques, micro-sociology, social psychology, hyper-empiricism and sur-relativism (Garvitch) in the later period only went towards mis-interpreting human reality.[11]

Nor is bourgeois sociology alone in this limbo. Modern political science under imperialism is another example of how imperialism further enlarges the gap between reality and false consciousness. This is more glaring in the field of international relations, which should have enabled us to comprehend imperialism. Contemporary international relations theory has concentrated mainly on 'behaviour of states', and 'balance of power'. In this emphasis the political scientist is concerned with systems analysis, integrationist and functionalist approaches, actions of states analysis, or states in interaction approach. Thus, according to Frankel, although 'intellectual use of theory' enables us to 'play with material from various angles' in a scientific manner, as well as helping identify more clearly relevant factors at issue, it need not be bad if this tendency to abstract theory from social reality does not prevent the development of an applied social science which combines 'a fairly rigorous theory with consideration of actual reality'. This enables us to obtain John Stuart Mill's 'mid-term theories' which are 'reasonably adequate explanations for a given point of time and place although the explanatory power of these theories rapidly diminishes when they are applied to different periods and systems'. That is why according to him the 'balance of power' theory as well as Marx's theory was applicable to nineteenth-century international relations and earlier stages of the industrial revolution. Thus although international theory is unable to establish valid causal relationships it has 'begun' to establish well-documented and 'plausible correlations', and as the nation states increasingly integrate and increase to resemble one another, it is possible to learn from others

> through the use of analogies by specifying as precisely as possible the nature of the characteristic in respect of which the analogy is being drawn, or paradigms as a yardstick for comparison and evaluation when evaluation is difficult.[12]

Frankel correctly draws attention to the limitations of this type of theory. Unable to find causal explanation, the political scientists resort to 'scientific methods'. Here again they are confronted with lack of 'scientific precision' and so they are led to a search for a redefinition of political concepts leading to

> accumulation of conflicting and confusing definitions. . . resulting in a jargon which is sometimes scarcely understandable to those not versed in the theory, however much they may be interested in the field of international relations.

Moreover, he points out, analysis tends to become ahistorical, manipulating a few selected variables and thus ending in simplifications which are even 'more remote from real life and hence theory tends to become even more esoteric'. The resulting fragmentation of models and schools ('traditionalists' and 'scientists') linked to an 'unruly flock of activities' operates in 'intellectual jails' thus leaving 'large and crucial areas of social life unexplored'. Frankel continues:

> A striking example is provided by our ignorance of the working of international economics: both the economists and the political scientists work on the 'unseen colleague' assumption. Thus, even when they are willing to resort to some form of rational decision-making through relying upon (expert) advice, the politicians are left free to follow their hunches and prejudices and always find some theory available as rationalization.

Thus, Frankel concludes, international theory, like other social sciences, is preoccupied with methodology and devotes much more effort to improving methods than to reaching substantive results. The contributors themselves and their critics judge results by methodological prowess even when the substantive results are 'insignificant or banal'. He attributes this to nature!

> In a way, this preoccupation is natural in view of the two related facts that, in principle, human beings appear to have freedom of choice and also that they are activated by their own system of interpretation and sets of beliefs about the social world.

Here Frankel resorts to some 'hunch and prejudice' like the politicians he describes and has found some 'theory' to rationalise the failings of political science. But his rationalisation is no other than the one expressed by Kant's dualist philosophy which still, through neo-Kantianism, neo-Thomism and a hotchpotch of other philosophies, continues to haunt the bourgeois intellect. And since it does, should we be surprised by Frankel's conclusion? 'There is thus a dual division, not only between theory and methodology in general but also between individual theories and methodologies.'

Thus, reality is thrown overboard. Intuition of the individual 'scientist' has free rein depending on his 'model', 'type', 'paradigm', or what have you. Social science of the bourgeoisie truly finds itself in 'intellectual jails', with reality and the movement of history locking them up in tight corners. The ideology of the bourgeoisie can no longer explain anything. It has become decadent, reflecting the parasitic, moribund character of monopoly capitalism and modern imperialism.

All this social science is in defence of imperialism. Just as Frankel thinks the 'balance of power' concept is outdated, so the contemporary author of it thinks it is valid. Morgenthau uses it to defend imperialism. According to Morgenthau, balance of power is a 'device' for self-defence of nations 'whose independence and existence is threatened by a disproportionate increase in the power of other nations', so long as it is used genuinely for 'self-protection'.[13] The point is, however, argues Morgenthau, 'power drives of nations' utilise 'ideal principles' and transform them into ideologies in order to disguise, rationalise and justify themselves. 'They have done this with the balance of power.' Thus according to Morgenthau it is the conception of balance of power which determines whether a particular action be anti-imperialist or imperialistic. 'A nation seeking only to maintain the *status quo* has often tried to give a change in the *status quo* the appearance of an attack upon the balance of power.'

So for Morgenthau imperialist domination can be justified under 'self-protection'. Any struggle against it disrupts the balance of power and creates conditions for 'instability'. In this way all imperialist aggressions are justified. Morgenthau even questions the whole concept of imperialism.

> To enemies and critics of the US everywhere American imperialism is a standard form. To add to the confusion, certain economic and political systems and economic groups, such as bankers and industrialists, are indiscriminately *[sic!]* identified with imperialist foreign politics. The task of theoretical analysis is to break with this popular usage in order to redefine imperialism and give it an ethically neutral, objective and definable meaning that at the same time is useful for theory and practice of international politics.
> 1. Not every foreign policy aiming at an increase in the power of a nation is necessarily a manifestation of imperialism (e.g. US acquisition of the Virgin Islands). *We define imperialism as a policy that aims at the overthrow of the status quo, at a reversal of the power relations between two or more nations.*
> 2. Not every foreign policy aimed at preservation of an empire that already exists is imperialism. [To say so is to identify imperialism] with the maintenance, defence, and stabilization of an empire already in existence rather than with the dynamic process of acquiring one.

Morgenthau's rationalisation is directly from the monopolists' horse's mouth. It no longer veils over its intention. It sees imperialism as a rational system and national liberation as irrational. Unlike petty-bourgeois mystification, which also beautifies imperialism, Morgenthau puts across the illusion of the epoch of imperialism in an open way.

Like Schumpeter, his capitalist imperialism is peaceful. But unlike
Schumpeter he attributes imperialist attributes to the dominated.

Whether in sociology, political science or law, bourgeois social
science has a considerable gap between it and reality, signifying that
the relations of production no longer correspond to the level attained
by the developments in the productive forces. The gap can only be
removed when this contradiction between the two forces is corrected
by socialist revolution.

III

The impact of imperialism on science is as devastating to the forces of
production as it is on the entire store of human knowledge, but with a
difference. Scientific and technological acquisitions are an important
aspect of the development of capital and become fully integrated with
it as capital gears into monopoly. In its early history science was
connected with magic and generally therefore with non-producing
classes. The long spell in economic stagnation that characterised
Western Europe until the industrial revolution was itself evidence of the
imprisonment of science at the hands of mythology, religion and
theology. Scientific enquiry was anathema to the medieval social order.
When the first breakthrough was made in Italy in the fifteenth century,
it was as a result of the generally revolutionary trends which were
emerging in society with the rise of the towns and the long-distance
commerce that characterised the period of the Rennaissance. The
development of the towns with trade, the growing demand for money
to circulate the increasing commodities, all these led to a scramble in
mining, seafaring to look for gold, and piracy on the high seas for
riches of the East, Africa and the Americas. Thus wars and foreign trade
became inseparable. It is for this reason that the first scientific discoveries were connected with navigation.

But even then science was clouded with metaphysical abstraction,
with little freedom to develop the productive forces, themselves
backward and not calling for such change. Francis Bacon correctly
observed:

> The roads to human power and human knowledge lie close together and are
> nearly the same; nevertheless, on account of the pernicious and inveterate
> habit of dwelling on abstractions, it is safer to begin and raise the sciences
> from those foundations which have relation to practice and let the active part
> be as the seal which prints and determines the contemplative part.[14]

But it took three hundred years before this became a reality. It was
not until the basic accumulation of capital had been undertaken,
enabling organised manufacturing to take place, that science was
increasingly brought into the service of society. The manner and speed
with which this process took place was admirably analysed by Marx in
relation to the laws of capitalist development in Chapters 13-14 of his

Capital Volume 1. The discovery of the steam engine revolutionised not only production but also, because of it, social relations. Thus science became the handmaiden of capitalist production. The steam engine, by turning all manual tools into automatons, also turned man into a tool of the machine. A tool was a simple machine but the new machine became a complex tool. Whereas with a tool man was the motive power the machine changed all this, the motive power became something else, water, wind and later electricity. Man's expertise as a craftsman was lost in the process, as all labour was reduced to average abstract labour, now activated by machinery.

But most of the early machinery connected with the textile industry was simple, and all early scientific innovation was rapid and cheap. Technical change was therefore faster, also because the wear and tear was determined by the length of the working day, which at this stage was relatively longer. Machinery also underwent what Marx called 'moral depreciation', due to its loss of exchange-values as a result of better machinery of the same sort being produced or being produced cheaper. It followed that:

> The shorter the period taken to reproduce its total value, the less danger [there is] of moral depreciation; and the longer the working day, the shorter is that period. When machinery is first introduced into an industry, new methods of reproducing it more cheaply follow blow upon blow, and so do improvements, that not only affect individual parts and details of the machine, but its entire build. It is therefore in the early days of the life of machinery that this special incentive to the prolongation of the working day makes itself felt most accutely.[15]

This quick advance in technical change implied a rapid passing of scientific results to production needs. Thus although scientists claimed no part in the direction of industry, their work was easily acquired and paid for. Bernal observes:[16]

> Scientists claimed no part in direction of state and industry. They were concerned with pure knowledge. It was a satisfactory arrangement to both parties. The industrialists made use of the work of the scientists, and generally paid them for it, though not much; the scientists had the satisfaction of knowing that they were living in an age of indefinite progress to which their labours, in a manner which it was unnecessary to examine, were contributing the largest share.

He continues that although scientists should have been connected with the development of the machine age, they got bogged down into the idea of 'pure science' and left the results to an 'ideal economic system, ideal because natural and open to the free play of economic forces'. Such was the place of science and technology under free competition.

Imperialism changed all this. The intra-imperialist struggles and rivalries for colonies leading to wars, and the entry of the US and

Germany into the world market, challenging British hegemony, were partly responsible for all this. Adds Bernal:

> An incidental result was the further development of science. To cope with new problems of imperial expansion, the Imperial College and the Imperial Institute were founded, and a general overhaul of scientific teaching and research was made. . . The turning point in the history of science occurred with the War. The War differed from previous wars in that it involved whole nations and not only armies drawn from them. Agriculture and industry were pressed into direct war service.

A report of the Department of Scientific and Industrial Research emphasised the need for a closer match between British industry and science. This was because it was 'unfortunately' found that Britain was to a large extent 'dependent on foreign sources for some of the supplies necessary for war-like operations'.

> Our greatest enemy of those days had secured, by application of science, a hold upon certain manufactured products which was found to be of an extent and nature to threaten our national well-being.[17]

Thus science and monopoly industry which had arisen in the period under consideration merged under the cover of 'national interest'. They have never separated since.

With the rise of monopolies, the monopoly enterprise acquired a power to fix prices above cost, as we have seen. This development had real significance for scientific and technical change. Whilst monopoly made it possible either through process-sharing agreements or by sheer size of the enterprise to undertake large-scale scientific research which a small enterprise could not undertaken, at the same time there was no incentive for such research. It became merely one among a number of means for increasing profitability of the monopoly. A number of factors also went to hinder any scientific improvements. Because of the large capital outlay in such monopoly enterprise the danger of heavy capital losses through obsolescence and moral depreciation was greater. Under free competition, as we have seen, the enterprise which changed to a better machine was able to cheapen its products and therefore sell more of them cheaply. Under monopoly there was no such situation. When prices could be fixed above cost it was possible to delay change of the plant until it had fully worked itself out. Here monopoly appears as more 'rational' than free competition, which becomes 'wasteful'. But by control of obsolescence, monopoly tends to retard technical and hence scientific advance. This stifles invention by restricting research, secondly it holds up the application of scientific discoveries. 'This is especially so in connection with research which is liable to interfere with productive methods in which a large amount of capital has been sunk.'[18]

This holding up of applied science is assisted by the legal superstructure through the *patent system.* Whilst this system was intended to protect the inventor, by the 1880s it was increasingly being turned into its opposite. It was no longer the small inventor who was protected but monopolies, which increasingly bought new discoveries, put them under seal and patented them in the registry of patents against copying. Patenting was also intended to make this knowledge scarce so it could be sold and under monopoly conditions only at monopoly prices. As Professor Penrose has pointed out:

> Clearly the patent system is our attempt to include the production of other things, and to do this by creating scarcity—by limiting the use of the invention. . . So far as inventions are concerned a price is put on them not *because* they are scarce but *in order* to make them scarce to those who want to use them.[19]

It is for this reason that monopoly capitalism, which is intricately tied up with modern imperialism, becomes a fetter on the all-round development of science for the good of mankind. Today's grumbling and demands for a more 'equitable' transfer of technology are a reflection of this negative impact of imperialism on scientific and technical progress. Science and technology have become a monopolistic tool in which the bourgeois state works hand in hand with huge monopolies in sharing out scientific secrets for war and destruction in order to advance monopolistic profits.

Under such circumstances it can be seen that imperialism cannot advance either the arts, social sciences or scientific research. In advancing their cause the bourgeoisie can only pass on as education their illusions of the epoch. This is self-evident in the nature of the social sciences we have examined. Avoiding a scientific world outlook, the bourgeoisie are only able to deal with the problems in a one-sided, ahistorical manner.

Indeed, when the bourgeoisie began to agitate for popular education while still in the womb of feudalism, they fought against the type of education that tended to bolster up the feudal order. The revolt was against theology, and in days of persecution the ideological representatives of the bourgeoisie in embryo had to camouflage teachings in science under the label 'natural philosophy'. When materialist philosophy emerged the new class was feeling its strength. Once the bourgeoisie were in control, however, they themselves soon instituted their class control over the system. The earlier demands for universal education were no longer pursued. Although some amount of reading and writing was necessary to the new system of production, this was conceded only very reluctantly. Examples can be found in the factory legislation in England of the 1830s. Under these laws factory owners were required to put aside part of the working time for education of child labour. This was made necessary as Marx explained by the intellectual desolation artificially produced by converting immature human beings into mere machines for the fabrication of surplus-value, a state of mind that is clearly distinguishable from the natural ignorance which keeps the mind fallow without destroying its capacity for development, its natural fertility.[20]

While Parliament was compelled to pass the laws, no machinery however was provided to enforce them.

When it was possible to enforce these provisions for instruction in elementary education, Marx continued, it merely proved for the first time the possibility of 'combining education and gymnastics with manual labour and, consequently, of combining manual labour with education and gymnastics'. Thus the education system under the Factory Acts was aiming at increasing production for the capitalists and not towards producing a fully developed human being. The system could not do that without destroying itself and so it continued to operate in the service of capital. Education was made available only to the hereditary educated classes and the bourgeoisie. But the working class continued to agitate for education. 'Educate, agitate, and organise' became their slogan. By the end of the nineteenth century universal elementary education had generally been conceded. But the demand for higher education for the working class grew and was introduced with the growing need for skills and science for the new industries. Universal and higher education became possible, but again only within limits set by the bourgeoisie. Education was required to adapt itself to the needs of capitalism and imperialism, and educational theory was advanced to this end. Bernal correctly points out:

> The science of education, which had existed as an academic backwater for centuries, was now having to meet the requirement of educating the whole population. It must be admitted that it was not well constituted to do so. In part educational theory was a genuine attempt to find principles, largely psychological, behind the actual techniques of transferring information, and as such was no more and no less scientific than the rest of psychology. Even more, however, it was traditionally an attempt at a philosophy of education aiming at laying down its true purposes. As such it suffered from all the defects of the social sciences in an exaggerated form. Because it could not or would not recognize the changing character of society, or its class structure, educational theory, unconsciously as much as consciously, accepted that society as permanent, and aimed at finding ways of adapting the pupils to it. This inevitably made it conformist and apologetic.[21]

To ensure this class nature of education, discrimination was carried out in such devices as 'intelligence tests', which originally were applied to criminals. These now were used so that the doors to education were open to the rich and closed to the children of the working class as much as possible. To the bourgeoisie intelligence was a universal idea which should be present in every individual, and not itself a social product of the material conditions of society. In these circumstances it became almost impossible for working-class children to ever gain admission to the 'public school': too bad for them, because of their 'low intelligence'.

The crisis that imperialism implied gave rise to demands from the young to have knowledge about the system of oppression. In the 1950s this revolt was generally in the social sciences—sociology in particular— where for the first time Marx's writings became popular. The student uprisings of the 1960s coupled with the Vietnam War atrocities of the US imperialists represented this general revolt by the young for a scientific explanation of society and the need to change it. The 1968 French student uprising has left its permanent imprint on the working-class movement, and the recent revolts in France against the reduction in the teaching of social sciences and increase in the teaching of technical subjects was a revolt against the demands of monopoly enterprise. Those measures were intended to arrest the revolutionary potential of the students and to turn students' education to the needs of the monopoly industry, by providing technicians and not class-conscious workers and politicians. Monopoly firms are increasingly throwing in large sums of money to institutions of higher learning for their research in fields connected with imperialist policy. Education under imperialism in the centres of capitalism is therefore increasingly narrowing down and this is manifested in deepening crisis.

Imperialism in the colonies passed on the diseases of the class bias to the colonial state. Whereas as we have argued, the rising bourgeoisie opposed the hold theology had on education, in the colonies they used the churches as their ideological spearhead. It is not surprising there-fore that in East Africa almost all the education was undertaken by the churches. As late as 1955, the *Royal Commission Report* observed:

> The pioneers of education work in East Africa have been missionaries, and until the last thirty years they have had a practical monopoly. Missions of various kinds and denominations, sometimes disguised in official publications under the name [voluntary agencies] , still control about three-quarters of the schools.[22]

Thus missionary education was acceptable and encouraged by the colonial administration. Their role had been so effective that the Royal Commission observed that they were 'regarded almost as indigenous African institutions'. On the other hand 'independent schools' run by Africans were hunted down by the colonialists on flimsy grounds of 'high fees', 'untrained teachers', etc. However, the real threat they posed to colonialism was the fact that they provided some amount of political education to the student. In Kenya and Uganda the struggle against them was intensified with the rising anti-colonial struggle. Having been through one of these schools in Uganda, I recall vividly the type of harassments that was meted out to them. The *Royal Commission Report* did not disguise its feelings towards these schools in Kenya:

> The Emergency in Kenya has shown only too clearly the moral and political
> virus with which these schools which have been subject to little government
> inspection and control, may infect their pupils. . .
> We think it essential that all independent schools should be registered by the
> Government or by local authorities in accordance with the rules formed by
> Government and that no new schools should be opened without the consent
> of such authority. It is also necessary that the Director of Education should
> be empowered to close any such school which, in the opinion of the local
> education authority, is redundant [sic!] , or (in the words used in the African
> Education Ordinance of Northern Rhodesia) 'is being conducted in a manner
> detrimental of peace and good government or the physical, mental and moral
> welfare of the pupils'. We note that as a result of the present Emergency,
> legislation on these lines has been passed in Kenya to come into effect in the
> current year, and we think that similar action be taken in the other
> territories.[23]

Action was taken on similar lines in the other territories and the
churches with a handful of government schools had their sway. With
political independence these church schools have in some countries
been taken over, but religious influence continues unabated in
institutions of learning run by the state.

The neocolonial educational system has not brought about fundamental change in the educational system nor could it be expected to.
But some of the changes that have been made are significant and require
concrete study, although without the elimination of imperialist
exploitation and domination such changes can have only marginal
effect on education and society as a whole. The concentration and
exchange on a world scale that imperialism brings about under
monopolies imply an international system of education. In this way
education in our countries only supplements the reproduction of
monopoly capitalism. This is irrefutably proved by the so-called
'brain-drain'. Two observers writing on this phenomenon have pointed
out:

> In the Philippines, for instance, it was reported that a whole year's output of
> doctors from one medical school had together charted a plane to fly them to
> the States—a total clean-out. . . In British hospitals at the moment more than
> half the doctors are foreign-born; mainly from low-income countries, and
> although at a lesser level of skill, nurses are equally highly recruited from
> abroad. Indeed many of the National Health Service hospitals would not be
> able to function without the medical staff from the health services of
> countries much less able than ourselves to pay for their training.[24]

The same can be said for other spheres of learning, and is proof of the
domination by international finance capital of our countries. In a real
sense, therefore, there can be no real education for our countries unless

the yoke of finance capital is eliminated, just as without socialism there can be no education for the working class which develops their potentiality to the full as fully developed human beings and not as debased beings at the hands of machinery controlled by the exploiters. Let us remind ourselves of Marx's scientific observation in the 1860s:

> Though the Factory Act, that first and meagre concession wrung from capital, is limited to combining elementary education with work in the factory, there can be no doubt that when the working class comes into power, as inevitably it must, technical instruction, both theoretical and practical, will take its place in the working-class schools.[25]

With such a record all round, imperialism cannot advance the culture of the toiling people. Culture is a class product. There is no such thing as human culture devoid of class bias. The struggle for cultural freedom is indeed a struggle for political and economic freedom. The working class therefore sees the struggle for cultural freedom as part of this broad struggle against finance capital. As Lenin pointed out, the question of 'national culture' is an important slogan to Marxists,

> not only because it determines the ideological content of all propaganda and agitation on the national question, as distinct from bourgeois propaganda, but also because the entire programme of the much discussed cultural autonomy is based on it.[26]

Lenin's remarks were directed at those who put the question of 'cultural autonomy' in juxtaposition to the whole national question and who, like Proudhon, saw the question merely as an idea and not as a concrete question. There was no such thing as a 'cultural idea', but real cultures of real classes, he argued. The rise of the bourgeoisie represented an epoch in which the culture of the bourgeoisie became dominant. Just as its ideas became ruling ideas, so its culture became a ruling culture. To the extent that the advances the bourgeoisie carried out against the old class represented a progressive step for mankind, its culture enabled advances to be made in the field of art, the novel, the theatre etc. Such culture was enhanced with advances in education.

But with capitalism becoming moribund and parasitic with the rise of modern imperialism, bourgeois culture too became decadent. A bourgeoisie that had lost its vision through the contradictory development of capitalism, offered nothing new to humanity. It offered only decadence in culture. Its high ideals it fought for when it put forward slogans—liberty, fraternity and brotherhood—had disappeared in the smokescreen of the factory products, which increasingly isolated it from society. Its interest as a class became the interest of all society. But society was not one. It was divided into classes that did not exist before. The bourgeoisie was left in the illusion that it stood for freedom, but a freedom that was never available to all. Equality of *opportunity* was never the same thing as equality of *condition.* Each class found itself in different conditions and no amount of equal opportunity could remove this gap. As the gap widened with the concentration of capital and with imperialism, so also the gap between condition and opportunity widened increasingly into crisis, not only between classes, but also between peoples, countries and nations.

This crisis was reflected in all sectors of life. War was merely a violent expression of it. Crisis in ideology, science and culture reflected crisis in production due to the anarchy of monopolistic competition that imperialism implied. This crisis reverberated in all circles and continues to this day, and will continue to do so until the end of imperialism. A prominent bourgeois scholar in the 1930s expressed it in the following terms:

> We are living in a very singular moment of history. It is a moment of crisis in the literal sense of that word. In every branch of our spiritual and material civilisation we seem to have arrived at a critical turning point. This spirit shows itself not only in the actual state of public affairs but also in the general attitude towards fundamental values in personal and social life. . . Formerly it was only religion, especially in its doctrinal and moral systems, that was the object of sceptical attack. Then the iconoclast began to shatter the ideals and principles that had hitherto been accepted in the province of art. Now he has invaded the temple of science. There is scarcely a scientific axiom that is not nowadays denied by somebody. And at the same time almost any nonsensical theory that may be put forward in the name of science would be almost sure to find believers and disciples somewhere or other.[27]

A Marxist theoretician and activist writing in the same period,[28] an activist who found himself deep in the Spanish Civil War, also wrote a series of pamphlets outlining the illusions of the bourgeoisie in art, ethics, values, psychology, religion and science. His writings were truly an ontology of a dying culture of a dying class, whose development of the productive forces had increasingly left it in the cold, in stark contradiction with reality.

Culture of the colonised in these circumstances represented cultural domination and backwardness. To the extent that imperialism could not allow the colonial people to develop the productive forces to the full, it also hindered the advance of the cultural life of the oppressed people. Neocolonial culture as expressed in the writings of the neo-colonial intellectual reflected this depressed culture. Appeal to the past instead of to the future dominated so-called 'Black culture', 'Arab culture' or 'Asian culture'. This reflected generally backward conditions in the neocolony. Among the 'sophisticated' novelist, playwright etc., imperialism was represented by sexuality, violence and vulgar humour that these writings eulogised. A truly national culture could not emerge in a country still dominated and oppressed; and can never do so until such domination is eliminated. To the Marxist-Leninist such 'national culture' would have been the dominant culture of the bourgeoisie. But to the extent that such culture represented capitalist development of a non-oppressed nation, it would have implied its antithesis in proletarian culture. A truly progressive culture of the future is a culture of a socialist society without imperialism and would include the democratic and socialist culture of all nations. The future culture within grasp in the present epoch is therefore the international proletarian culture. As Lenin pointed out in a draft resolution to the Protetcult Congress of October 1920:

> Marxism has won its historic significance as the ideology of the revolutionary proletariat because, far from rejecting the most valuable achievements of the bourgeois epoch, it has on the contrary assimilated and refashioned everything of value in the more than two thousand years of the development of human thought and culture. Only further work on this basis and in this direction, inspired by the practical experience of the proletarian dictatorship as the final stage in the struggle against every form of exploitation, can be recognised as the development of a genuine proletarian culture.[29]

The struggle against imperialism for national liberation from all forms of exploitation, oppression and domination is a prerequisite of such future culture. The national question is therefore at the centre of such struggle for an international proletarian culture which will unite all mankind in the totality of all human history and endeavour.

IV

The national question is an important question in Marxist-Leninist theory and in relation to the struggle of the working class and other exploited and oppressed peoples for the broadening of democracy and for socialism. The question is not a general one. The national question has to be examined historically. In this manner we note that national states arise and achieve their full maturity with the rise of capitalism and the decay of feudalism. Engels pointed out that language groups constituted the basis for the bordering off of most national states in Europe in the Middle Ages:

> Once the language groups were bordered off. . . it was natural that they should serve as the basis for the formation of states and that nationalities began to develop into nations.[30]

True, he continued, by no means all language borders coincided with state borders, yet every nationality, excluding Italy perhaps, was represented in a specific major European state and the tendency to create national states, which came to the fore ever more clearly and consciously, constituted one of the most essential levers of progress in the Middle Ages. Engels stated that the motive power behind the rise of these nation-states was the rise of the town and the merchant, the introduction of money and the generally growing bourgeois property at the expense of feudal relations. All these went to consolidate the power of the monarch against the nobility, assuring that the new bourgeois classes could develop and consolidate their power economically.

Stalin, in a text which represents a clear Marxist-Leninist treatment of the national question, emphasises these arguments and formulates a theory on the question. Having pointed out the main characteristics of a nation, he summarises it in a definitional form as *'a historically constituted, stable community of people, formed on the basis of a common language, territory, economic life and psychological make-up manifested in a common culture'.* He concludes:

> A nation is not merely a historical category but a historical category belonging to a definite epoch, the epoch of rising capitalism. The process of elimination of feudalism and development of capitalism is at the same time a process of the constitution of people into nations.[31]

This process occurred in Western Europe. In Eastern Europe, on the other hand, the process was somewhat different. Here, Stalin pointed out, instead of nation-states emerging multinational-states were formed—states consisting of several nationalities. In these multi-national-states the national groups which proved to be 'politically the most developed' took it upon themselves to unite other nationalities into a state. This was because feudalism had not yet been eliminated and capitalism was feebly developed. Nationalities which had been forced into the background had not yet been able to consolidate themselves economically into integral nations. As capitalism developed 'nation-sentiments' strengthened, but it was 'too late'. These national-ities could no longer form themselves into independent national states. They encountered on their path the very powerful resistance of the ruling stratum of the dominant nationality which had long assumed control of the state. Such was the case with the Germans in Austria-Hungary and the Great-Russians in Russia. Thus the national movement arose in those countries, as part of the awakening that capitalism introduced. Lenin adds that where these multinational-states existed they represented backwardness and not progress.

These historical facts are important to recount, for they help us comprehend today's complex national question. Stalin's treatment of this question is attacked by Trotskyists and other petty-bourgeois elements on the grounds that a nation need not have a common language. One such attack which has bearing on the national question in a neocolony is by Banaji who, in the review of Horace Davis's book *Nationalism and Socialism* (itself petty-bourgeois), attacks this part of Stalin's definition as 'unscientific and vulgarised Marxism'. He states: 'A nation, to begin with, is not a community of any sort *[sic!]*, much less one which possesses a common language and a common culture.'[32]

As proof of his thesis he gives India as evidence of his 'refutation' of

Stalin. Apart from the vulgarisation and misrepresentations which Banaji engages in, it is clear that his understanding of the national question is petty-bourgeois and is no more than an idea. Nowhere does Stalin regard a nation as a 'community of any sort'. We have seen Stalin's treatment of the question wherein he emphasises that 'a nation is not merely a historical category *but a historical category belonging to a definite epoch, the epoch of rising capitalism'.* On the basis of Stalin's definition India is not a nation. We shall shortly see that Lenin substantiates Stalin on this question in his thesis on the right of nations to self-determination, wherein it can be understood that India and all colonial, semi-colonial and neocolonial countries are 'oppressed countries' and not nations. It can be seen that it is not Stalin but the petty-bourgeois opportunist Banaji who regards a nation as 'a community of any sort', for he identifies India—a dominated and oppressed country—as a 'nation'. Hence it is Banaji and his Trotskyist friends who vulgarise Marxism on the national question in the neo-colonies. Here the national question has never been solved and therefore constitutes today's fundamental contradiction between these countries and imperialism. Indeed, in other works of his Stalin pointed out that, whereas formerly the national question was regarded from a reformist view, in the era of the proletarian revolution it incorporated the necessity of overthrowing imperialism. The colonial peoples in their struggle against imperialism for national liberation joined the proletariat in this struggle. Henceforth, Mao Tse-tung added, the *new democratic revolutions* of the colonial, semi-colonial and other oppressed peoples led not to the building of capitalism but to the building of socialism. The national question took on a new characteristic which belonged neither to the revolutions leading to nation-states in Western Europe nor to those leading to the right to self-determination and secession from the multinational-states of Eastern Europe. All those went to the consolidation of capitalism, although in parts of Eastern Europe some of the movements were overtaken by events and found themselves amidst the socialist revolution, as in Russia. Thus the separation of former colonies into independent states did not lead to the elimination of national exploitation and oppression.

This question is important and we shall now turn to it. Why is it that India and for that matter Tanzania, although politically independent as separate states, are yet not nations? Lenin pointed out approvingly Hilferding's observation about the connection between imperialism and colonial and national oppression. Hilferding had correctly stated:

In the newly opened-up countries, the capital imported into these intensifies antagonisms and excites against intruders the constantly growing resistance of peoples who are awakening to national consciousness; this resistance can easily develop into dangerous measures against foreign capital. . . Capitalism itself gradually provides the subjugated with the means and resources to their emancipation and they set out to achieve the goal which once seemed highest to the European nations: the creation of a united national state as a means to economic and cultural freedom. This movement for national independence threatens European capital in its valuable and most promising fields of exploitation, and European capital can maintain its domination only by continually increasing its military forces.[33]

Lenin adds that this national oppression also increasingly applies to the old countries. Hilferding's observations have been born out by today's neocolonialism and national liberation struggles wherein imperialism increasingly intervenes to protect puppet regimes and its capital. Lenin, in his 'Discussion on the national question, summed up', pointed out that since the colonies have *no capital* of *their own* they have to submit to political domination in order to obtain it.

The situation in the neocolony inasmuch as reliance on foreign finance capital is concerned has never fundamentally changed. These former colonies now wielding national state status still continue to submit to political domination by the financially powerful states. In a speech at Ibadan University President Nyerere exposed this domination in very clear terms, and we quote *in extenso:*

The reality of neocolonialism quickly becomes obvious to a new African government which tries to act on economic matters in the interests of national development, and for the betterment of its own masses. For such a government immediately discovers that it inherited the power to make laws, to treat with foreign governments, and so on, but that it did not inherit effective power over economic developments in its own country. Indeed, it often discovers that there is no such thing as a national economy at all! Instead, there exist in its land various economic activities which are owned by people outside its jurisdiction, which are directed at external needs, and which are run in the interests of external economic powers. Further, the Government's ability to secure positive action in these fields does not stem from its legal supremacy; it depends entirely upon its ability to convince the effective decision-makers that their own interests will be served by what the Government wishes to have done.

This is a very serious matter. For it means that if deliberate countervailing action is not taken, external economic forces determine the nature of the economy a country shall have, what investment shall be undertaken and where, and what kind of development—if any—will take place within our national borders.

Neocolonialism is a very real, and very severe limitation on national sovereignty. The total amount of credit and its distribution to different sectors of the economy, for example, is determined by the banking system. The persons or groups who control the Banks therefore have a very fundamental—almost a deciding—effect at two points. The first is on the level of current economic activity in a money economy; the second is on the comparative expansion of, say, peasant agriculture as against estate agriculture, or agriculture in general as against the development of local industry or trade. The local agents of foreign banks may well be willing to co-operate with the national government's priorities; but in the last resort their loyalty is, and must be, to their overseas employers. In case of dispute at the top policy level, the government will not be able to enforce its decisions. It may be able to stop things; it will not be able to start things. Matters of vital interest to our development are thus determined externally, without any consideration being given to our interests.

In economic matters, therefore, our countries are effectively being governed by people who have only the most marginal interest in our affairs—if any—and even that only in so far as it affects their own well-being. That, in fact, is the meaning and the practice of neocolonialism. It operates under the cover of political colonialism while that continues. Its existence and meaning become more obvious after independence.[34]

But did this mean that political struggles for democracy were unnecessary or impossible under such conditions? Lenin emphasised in refutation of the Luxemburgists and Trotskyists that the right to self-determination of nations belonged to the *political sphere* of state independence and formation of nation-states. In the demand for self-determination and the struggle for liberation of oppressed nations a dual transformation in the *political sphere* was implied. *Firstly,* the principle of full political equality of nations, and *secondly,* the freedom of political separation, which refers to the demarcation of state frontiers, were accepted. All these transformations broadened the political democratic rights of the people, as far as colonial liberation was concerned. But this did not imply *economic self-determination.* On the contrary:

> The domination of finance capital and capital in general is not to be abolished by any reforms in the sphere of political democracy; self-determination belongs wholly and exclusively to this sphere. The domination of finance capital, however, does not in the least nullify the significance of political democracy as a freer, wider and clearer *form* of class oppression and class struggle. Therefore all arguments about the 'impracticability', in the economic sense, of one of the demands of political democracy under capitalism are reduced to a theoretically incorrect definition of the general and basic relationships of capitalism and of political democracy as a whole.[35]

Lenin added that all demands for self-determination are only partially practicable under imperialism. It did not follow that the proletariat would reject such demands. On the contrary, such a rejection would play into the hands of the bourgeoisie and reaction. But in order to bring about fundamental change such demands must be formulated in a revolutionary and not a reformist manner. The demands must go beyond bourgeois legality, beyond parliamentary speeches and verbal protests. The demands must draw the masses into decisive action, to extend and intensify the struggle for the fundamental democratic rights, 'up to a direct proletarian onslaught on the bourgeoisie i.e., up to the socialist revolution that expropriates the bourgeoisie'.

These scientific theses of Stalin and Lenin have been confirmed by *concrete experience* in the Soviet Union, in China[36] and in Indochina.[37]

They have shown that in order for the national liberation struggle to succeed it must be led by a proletarian programme which aims at involving the masses in decisive action, which leads to the bourgeoisie being expropriated and to the socialist transformation being introduced. Any programme aimed at safeguarding bourgeois property, whether in the form of state capitalism or private monopolies, also aims at safeguarding bourgeois dictatorship under imperialism. National liberation therefore implies a dual transformation from the political democratic rights in the political sphere to the economic expropriation of the exploiters in the economic sphere, and this is impracticable without socialism. Therefore national liberation in the final analysis is transformation to socialism.

Such transformation will not be impossible because of the lack of a large proletariat in the colony, semi-colony or neocolony. The same Luxemburgists and Trotskyists who argued about the 'impracticability' of self-determination of colonies under imperialism also argue the 'impossibility' of socialism under a large peasantry in our countries. Their assertions are as one-sided as those they made before. For whereas it is true that finance capital is exported to backward areas in order to take advantage of the cheap labour of the small working class and large peasantry, it remains true that the introduction of capitalism in the colony introduces there the awakening to nationhood, and a 'national-state', although possible at the political level, is historically impossible economically under capitalism. It follows that the proletarian elements, small as they are, are able on the basis of alliances with the peasantry to overthrow imperialism, expropriate the bourgeoisie and embark on the long road of socialist transformation. Lenin pointed out:

> The socialist revolution is not a single act, it is not one battle on one front, but a whole epoch of acute class struggles, a long series of battles on all fronts, i.e. on all questions of economics and politics, battles that can only end in the expropriation of the bourgeoisie.[38]

What is said above is of equal relevance to the national liberation struggles in neocolonial Africa against imperialism in general and Southern Africa in particular. It used to be said in the early days of Africa's political independence that there were no classes in Africa. Those days when all sorts of theories were advanced about African socialism are gone. The concrete experience of the last fifteen years has dispelled such beliefs. The sharp class struggles that are waged today in Africa have thrown sand in the eyes of those who wanted to obscure reality.

But there still linger on strong voices holding that Africans must work out 'their own solutions', and not follow 'foreign and alien ideologies'. This persistent line of argument is supported by imperialism, for was it not Kissinger who, in his recent preoccupation with African affairs, put forward the thesis: 'African problems must be solved by

Africans.'[39] He was saying this while a US imperialist solution in
Southern Africa was being worked out! What is clear is that this
argument is directed against Marxism-Leninism, against the working-class
—the most resolute opponent to finance capital in its effort to
rally the peasantry against imperialism. For it is only on the basis of the
working-class leadership and such alliance that foreign capital can be
fully expropriated and not merely juridically 'nationalised'. Without
such expropriation of the financial oligarchies and the elimination of
imperialist domination can there be a basis for socialist transformation in
our countries?

There is nothing uniquely African in an era where finance capital has
united all the peoples of the world under its rule. An African proletariat
is no less international than an Asian one or a European one. They are
all exploited by the same monopolies, the same class, the same capital,
only in different measure. There can therefore be no different general
solution to the problem of imperialist exploitation. Each situation has
to be concretely studied and each revolutionary struggle concretely
worked out, but this is quite different from maintaining that Africans
should solve 'their own problems in their own way'. This slogan is
reactionary. The national question, which will mean the total defeat of
imperialism, will be possible on the basis of an internationalist world
outlook and not on the outlook of a narrow nationalistic one, which
incidentally imperialism itself rules out, and which history has put away.

The truth of this is proved by the struggles against imperialism in
Southern Africa. Here the struggle against Portuguese fascists and
US-led imperialism was waged by African fighters, with the assistance
of the socialist world and a few African progressive states which were
themselves receiving considerable military assistance from the socialist
countries. This struggle was waged against the total imperialist support
for the fascist forces provided through NATO and other channels. It
continues to be so today. The machinations of US imperialism over
Zimbabwe, Namibia and South Africa are again proof of the inter-
nationality of the struggle in Africa. First it must be remembered that
the US 'awakening' on African liberation came after its total defeat in
Indochina. Its latest manoeuvres are intended to save what can be
salvaged from the socialist-oriented forces which are rampant throughout the world. About this there can be no doubt. The US excuse that it
is fighting to keep out the Soviet Union is itself a hegemonic imperialist
argument in its struggle against the Soviet Union. There are no 'natural
traditional spheres of influence' of the US imperialists in Africa which
give it a right in this rivalry to impose itself in Southern Africa. That is
why its dictated solutions in the area are utterly unacceptable to the
people of the world. The US is counting on puppet neocolonial regimes
to support its domination. In a report by Bruce Oudes in the US news-
paper *The Sun,* of April 25, 1976, headed *Kissinger in Africa wooing
seven dwarfs,* it was explained that the new US policy was nothing but
the policy which had been worked out in the Lusaka Manifesto. It drew

attention to the fact of US economic interests in South Africa; in 1975, 56 per cent of her investments in sub-Saharan Africa were in South Africa—'an 18 per cent increase in 2 years'. Many other European monopolies have their investments in this area. There should therefore be no doubt as to who is the real enemy here, and that this enemy is internationally united although enmeshed in contradictions. The defeat of this enemy also depends on internationally united action. This is what is scaring the US imperialists.

In their struggle to resolve the national question in South Africa, the people must correctly comprehend this fact. The struggle against apartheid is a struggle against cultural autonomy and racial autonomy backed by imperialism. This ideology is harmful because its aim is to isolate the black worker culturally from the white worker, and in this way exploit both by keeping the black worker backward and isolated from the white worker. In this process some of the white workers are turned into white-collar 'labour aristocrats'. All this is not in the name of racial or cultural 'purity', although some people may believe so and be motivated by it. What is of significance however is who gains from it in the end. Can there be any doubt that it is finance capital which gains, by exploiting the racial and cultural issue for its ends.

It follows that the working-class programme, which must advance the cause of all the exploited and oppressed, must formulate the strategy of struggle in such a manner that the basis of imperialist exploitation is undermined. Such formulation must aim at bringing the masses of the exploited and oppressed peoples into decisive action to struggle against imperialism, which enhances apartheid; and it must lead ultimately to the expropriation of the financial oligarchy, and to the transformation of the society towards socialism. Only then can we speak of liberation and solution of the national question. It seems to us that whether we call the problem in South Africa a colonial or racial one, we are still faced with the national question, and to solve it we have to address ourselves to the task of advancing the democratic rights for all within the nation-state borders. There must not be special privileges for particular social groups—which privileges go to obscure the real exploitative relationships under imperialism. It is also pointless to argue that South Africa is a sub-imperialist power. Today the US imperialists are running all over telling Vorster and Smith what to do. Talk of 'Boer national-capital' also goes to obscure the centralising and concentrating power of imperialist finance capital over South Africa, and hence obscures the enemy. The Boer petty-bourgeois ideology of 'separate development' is an ideology in the arsenal of imperialism and must be fought as such.

Thus, whatever the US imperialists do in Zimbabwe, in Namibia and South Africa, given correct proletarian strategies the struggle will continue until imperialism is defeated. This struggle will be assisted greatly by the solidarity and support of the proletariat in the liberated sector of the world and in the imperialist countries. To try to isolate or counterpose one against the other is to assist the enemy. Today's 'neo-Marxism', and other petty-bourgeois ideologies which try to demonstrate by theories of 'unequal exchange' etc. that the workers in the 'centre' exploit those in the 'periphery', serve the imperialists in creating confusion in the ranks of the working people, confusion which must be avoided if contemporary imperialism is to be removed from the face of the earth to give way to the triumph of socialism.

NOTES

1. This and the following quotes are from Schumpeter, J.A.: 'The Sociology of Imperialism, in a booklet entitled: *Imperialism and Classes: Two Essays,* pp. 1-7; New York, 1972.

2. Quoted in George Novack: *The Origins of Materialism.* pp. 264-5; New York, 1971.

3. Quoted in George Thomson: *The First Philosophers,* p. 342; London, 1972.

4. *Ibid.,* pp. 343-4.

5. Marx, K.: *Capital* Vol. I, p. 77.

6. Bentham, J.: *An Introduction to the Principles of Morals and Legislation,* p. 1.

7. Austin, J.: *The Province of Jurisprudence Determined. Lecture II,* London, 1954.

8. Lewis, J.: *Marx, Weber & Value-free Sociology;* London, 1975. See also Giddens, Anthony: *Capitalism and Modern Social Theory;* Cambridge, 1972.

9. Engels, F.: 'Feuerbach and the End of Classical German Philosophy' in Marx and Engels: *Selected Works,* Vol. 3, p. 371.

10. Bernal, J.D.: *Science in History: The social sciences* Vol. 4, p. 1083; Harmondsworth, 1969.

11. Engels, F.: *Anti-Dühring,* pp. 177-8; Moscow, 1969.

12. The quotes in this, and the following paragraph are from Frankel, J.: *Contemporary International Theory,* pp. 8-14, Oxford, 1973.

13. This and the quotes following are from Morgenthau, H.J.: *Politics Among Nations.*

14. Quoted in Bernal, J.D.: *The Social Function of Science,* p. 6; Cambridge, Mass., 1973.

15. Marx, K.: *Capital* Vol. I, pp. 380-2.

16. Bernal, J.D.: *op. cit.,* pp. 29-30.

17. Quoted in *ibid.,* pp. 30-31.

18. *Ibid.,* pp. 139-63.

19. Penrose, E.: *The International Patent System,* London, 1951.

20. Marx, K.: *Capital* Vol. I, p. 377.

21. Bernal, J.D.: *Science in History, op. cit.*

22. *East African Royal Commission 1953-1955.* Report Cmd 9475, 1955, p. 174.

23. *Ibid.,* p. 185.

24. Rose, H. & Rose, S.: *Science and Society,* pp. 205-6, Harmondsworth, 1961.

25. Marx, K.: *Capital* Vol. I, p. 458.

26. Lenin, V.I.: *Critical Remarks on the National Question and the Right of Nations to Self-Determination,* p. 21; Moscow, 1974.

27. Planck, M.: *Where is Science Going,* London, 1933.
28. Caudwell, C.: *Studies and Further Studies in a Dying Culture;* New York, 1971.
29. Lenin, V.I.: *On Literature and Art,* p. 155; Moscow, 1970.
30. Engels, F.: 'Decay of Feudalism and Rise of National States', Appendix IV in Engels: *Peasant War in Germany,* pp. 181-2; Moscow, 1974.
31. Stalin, J.V.: 'Marxism and the National Question' in Bruce Franklin: *The Essential Stalin,* pp. 60 & 65; New York, 1972.
32. Banaji, J.: 'Nationalism and Socialism', *Monthly Review* 1973. A Review in *Economic and Political Weekly* Vol. IX No. 36, Sept. 7, 1974; p. 1539.
33. Quoted in Lenin: *Imperialism, op. cit.,* p. 116.
34. Nyerere, J.K.: 'Process of Liberation'. Speech delivered to the convocation of Ibadan University, Nigeria, 17th Nov. 1976. *Daily News,* Tanzania, 18th Nov. 1976.
35. Lenin, V.I.: *Critical Remarks and Right of Nations, op. cit.,* pp. 99-100.
36. Mao Tse-Tung: New Democracy, *op. cit.*
37. See, for instance, Le Duan: *The Vietnamese Revolution: Fundamental Problems, Essential Tasks,* pp. 11-85; Hanoi, 1973.
38. Lenin, V.I.: *Critical Remarks, op. cit..* p. 99.
39. USIS News Release, Dar es Salaam report of address given by Dr. Kissinger in Lusaka, 27th April, 1976.

CHAPTER 4

GENERALISED SCHEMES OF PREFERENCES IN WORLD TRADE[1]

I

Generalised Schemes of Preferences (GSP) have been hailed as a significant 'breakthrough' for UNCTAD in its ten-year efforts to get the advanced capitalist powers to accept them.[2] Seen from this formal standpoint such acceptance and part implementation of some of the schemes is indeed a point of departure, for it amounts to an acknowledgement and admission by the monopoly capitalist groups that 'free trade' does not bring about development in the underdeveloped peripheries. It also amounts to an admission that the hitherto blind faith in the so-called principle of comparative advantage as propounded particularly by David Ricardo in the early nineteenth century, and as later brushed up by his neo-classical followers, has no validity in the modern international trade scene. It further goes to remove the veil over the official 'most-favoured-nation' principle which seeks to treat all trading nations as equals.[3] Of course this does not mean that the exploiters' ideologists will have no theory on the matter. They will on the contrary find a way of explaining this apparent contradiction in the form of a 'new' theory; but the point being made here is that the facts behind GSP have stood in challenge to the principle, in particular as it is spelt out in Article I of GATT. Some people will therefore be jubilant.

However, seen from the standpoint of the real world such jubilation must be short-lived. The imperialist system in its trade practices exists precisely because it is inherently based on exploitation, not only within its borders, but more importantly in all its dealings in all parts of the world where it sets its feet. This has been its record to date and unless we would wish to delude ourselves in thinking at this rather late stage that imperialism has changed its nature and no longer relies on exploitation for survival, it is well for us to regard the GSP as a new method of make-believe dished out by imperialism to the third world in an effort to earn it more time to scheme out new tactics. As we will show this is a necessity for imperialism to extend its life, which is in crisis.

To be sure, schemes of preferences are not new in the third world. These existed, albeit in different forms, as Commonwealth Imperial Preferences, French Union Preferences, the Benelux Union of Preferences, US Preferences with the Philippines, etc. They were used by the imperialist powers to spread their tentacles the world over; so that when the second world war ended and efforts were made to create a multilateral trade arrangement to replace the pre-war bilateral trade system, these preferences were seen as a stumbling block in the way of the new trading system. Whereas the US—the champion of the post-war efforts towards multilateralism—opposed these hitherto existing preferences, the former colonial powers were firm in their determination to retain them under the new system. What emerged was a statement of the 'non-conditional' general most-favoured-nation [mfn] principle in para. 1 of Article I of the General Agreement on Tariffs and Trade (GATT), followed by a saving provision in para. 2 of the same Article retaining the pre-existing preferences subject to diminishing preference-margins. Whereas the US was prepared to demand their abolition in its document,[4] it too finally insisted on retaining its preference with the Philippines when its proposal was rejected by the UK and France! Some of the preferences under GATT continue to exist and are now being phased out with the implementation of the GSP.

Another form of preferences saved under Article I of GATT, are the preferences maintained by the European Economic Community (EEC) under the guise of free trade areas. This is another of those phenomena that mark the checkered history of GATT. Whereas preferences were generally condemned, customs union and free trade areas were accepted, since they were supposed to promote trade.[5] The experience under GATT to date however has proved beyond doubt that what was supposed to be free trade areas, claiming exemption from the mfn principle under Article XXIV of GATT, are in actual fact preferential arrangements. Thus Association Agreements between the EEC and Turkey, Greece, the Yaoundé Group and the Arusha Group and the EFTA, as well as the New Zealand/Australian arrangement, are all such preferences which have been tacitly approved by GATT, in spite of this organisation's loud claims of unhindered 'free trade'.

The important logic to observe all the time is that preferences which perpetuate the exploitation of the third world by one or other of the imperialist monopoly groups, or which rationalise trade amongst the developed countries, are given a blind eye, whereas customs arrange-ments or free trade areas intended to establish horizontal contacts between the third world have always been thwarted, unless such arrangements directly or indirectly serve the interests of the imperialist countries. Moreover, in the rather weak bargaining position in which the third world countries find themselves in international bodies, they normally give in to arrangements which clearly are disadvantageous to them. This however is not surprising since the petty bourgeoisie in the third world cannot do otherwise. They are incapable of fundamentally changing the inequalities that imperialism set in motion. Seen in this perspective, the very 'independence' which imperialism was able to extend to the petty bourgeoisie was part of the global scheme of multi-lateral imperialism, in which the petty bourgeoisie as a stratum of the grand bourgeoisie fulfilled a role. Thus the 'equality' that the third world under the leadership of the petty bourgeoisie has fought for in international gatherings can be seen as efforts at reform. International conferences then become for the petty bourgeoisie great 'equalisers' for themselves: equality for *governmental* delegations rather than equality for nations.[6] A brief background to the GSP in their present form will reveal how inconsequential have been the demands of the third world petty bourgeoisie in GATT and other international conferences.

II

It has been said several times that when the General Agreement was concluded in 1947 the interests of the third world were not taken care of in the arrangement. This is not surprising, since most of the third world was still under colonial rule. To the extent that their presence would have meant some attention in the Articles of the General Agreement to the problems attaching to their trade with the developed countries (DCs), this was soon rectified in that by 1963 Part IV was added to the Articles dealing specifically with 'Trade and Development'. But such specific attention did not mean a solution to the problems. On the contrary, as this analysis will show, such a solution was only marginally possible within the framework of multilateral imperialism.

Be that as it may, the GATT's initial concern with the third world was, it should be underlined, in regard to *'the protection of infant industry'*. This was the so-called 'development clause' in Article XVIII. We underline this provision because it was so stringent that the only countries which tried to invoke it, and burnt their fingers in the process, were Sri Lanka and Cuba. Any protective measures proposed under the clause had to be reported and investigated by the contracting parties before implementation. It is not surprising in these circumstances that many third world countries resorted to the use of quantitative restrictions in Article XII, which was meant to apply to the DCs for balance-of-payments problems and was less stringent. Revision of Article XVIII in 1955 did not effectively alter the position, and the development clause remained a dead letter for most of the period. This is because the revised Article envisaged its application for prospective measures required to establish a particular industry. It was also to apply in cases of balance-of-payments problems only to the extent that the situation required 'equilibrium at a satisfactory reserve level'. This more or less brought Article XVIII in line with Article XII.

When third world countries wished to develop their infant industries the imperialist countries were disturbed, but they quickly grasped the fact that the aid, loans, investment, etc., which the third world would require to engage in such import substitution were good business for the monopolies since they would invariably be tied to the goods of the donor country. The global strategy of the transnational corporations was still in its infancy, being tried out in its new phase by the US in Europe. The opening up of the markets to the products of these industries was, however, a different matter, at least at that stage. So the immediate problem that faced the new industries in Latin America and Asia in 1954 was lack of markets for their export products, a fact which should have been foreseen. It was at this time that the Trade Intelligence Division of GATT, in the Annual Report, *International*

Trade, 1954, stumbled on a new discovery.

> Relative growth of trade within and among industrial areas, almost entirely
> accounted for by the rapid growth of trade in Western Europe, and the
> relative decline in trade between the non-industrial and industrial areas,
> accounted for by the failure of the value of exports from the non-industrial
> areas to expand. [7]

This discovery immediately led to great concern over the matter by the
Contracting Parties, and in a study churned out for the purpose it was
reported that

> if the gap between the need for development finance and available financial
> resources is to be reduced, a substantial expansion of the LDCs' export
> earnings is essential. [8]

The above is quoted to illustrate the almost unbelievable
obscuranticism. As early as 1949 a United Nations study of international trade had reported a deterioration in the terms of trade and a
drop in value of the exports of the third world. [9] The above quotation
from the GATT programme had, however, come out of a study of a
panel of experts—the so-called Harbeler Committee—which had
examined 'the failure of the trade of the. . . LDCs to develop as
rapidly as that of industrialised countries'. The experts had come to
the conclusion in 1958 that the prospects for exports of LDCs were
very *sensitive to internal policies in the DCs* and that in balance 'their
development will probably fall short of the increase in world trade as a
whole'. [10] The Committee recommended that due to many technical
changes in agriculture necessitating large requirements of capital and
land,

> relatively poor countries with high population like India and Hong Kong
> should export cheap labour-intensive manufactures in order to import food-
> stuffs like wheat from the developed countries like Australia, Canada and the
> United States which are rich in land and capital.

Here clearly the comparative advantages were being reversed to suit a
new development. If these gentlemen had paused a moment to ponder,
India would have been the last country to be recommended for the
export of manufactures (cheap at that!) in order to pay for the importation of food! The Contracting Parties whereupon appointed a Special
Committee 3 to

> consider and report. . . measures for the expansion of trade with particular
> reference to the importance of the maintenance and expansion earnings of
> the LDCs to the development and diversification of their economies. [11]

The Committee got down to its work and its immediate concern was to find out what were the manufactured and/or primary products the LDCs had available for export and what were the obstacles to their exportation. The Committee sorted out eleven products which it examined in detail, and according to Curzon 'the examination brought out some interesting facts'.[12] The eleven products examined were: vegetable oils, tobacco, cotton textiles, tea, coffee, cocoa, jute products, cotton, timber, copper and lead. The 'interesting facts' found by the Committee were that for manufactured products like cotton and jute goods the industrialised countries used *high* tariffs as one of the means of protection, while for lead, oilseeds, copper or cocoa in their original form *low* tariff rates were used, while any transformation of these products was submitted to a very high protective tariff rate. Here it was observed that where a nominal tariff was imposed on, say, processed cocoa, the effective rate of protection was found to be much higher than what appeared on the surface. A duty-free rate on unprocessed cocoa compared to a 10 per cent duty on processed cocoa, where the value added by the transformation was 10 per cent, turned out to be 100 per cent effective protection for the processors in the DCs. This protection had the tendency to thwart the efforts of the LDCs to improve the quality of their products to earn more, and ensured their role as perpetual suppliers of raw materials to the DCs. To quote Curzon again:

> The effect of the collected knowledge of these trade obstacles on the underdeveloped countries was impressive. The studies showed them how pervasive and iniquitous obstacles to trade expansion really were for them. For the first time in GATT history, they met as a distinct group and agreed on a note to be submitted to the Contracting Parties.[13]

What the LDCs knew by actual experience was made to appear as a discovery by GATT. What is of more interest to us, however, is that the Note to the Contracting Parties reflected the dragging of feet, as was to be expected. It pointed out that the goods of the LDCs met with other barriers besides tariffs, and that their exports were few in number hence their capacity to negotiate on tariffs was limited; therefore, they demanded removal of the non-tariff barriers unilaterally since they had no concessions to offer. They needed to retain tariffs on imports for fiscal and developmental needs. They felt that the problem of increased export earnings should be considered as 'extremely urgent'.

Although some steps were taken in various countries, these had marginal effect. The UK and Japan for instance reduced the duty on jute from 30 per cent to 20 per cent; whilst Japan alone liberalised on imports of coffee beans from all sources. Although various other studies were made, there was no progress in the implementation of any of the proposals in any meaningful way. On the contrary, increased exports of products like textiles in those areas where there had been a relaxation of barriers resulted in a clamp-down there. The result of the influx of textiles was the short-term cotton textile agreement limiting their importation to the markets of DCs on the ground that such increased imports created 'market disruption' in the DCs, a fact which put one more nail in the coffin of the 'theory of comparative advantage'! As one author on the GATT has aptly commented: 'There was no suggestion that the exporting country was doing anything improper. Rather, the principle of comparative advantage was itself being called into question.'[14] That cotton textiles were singled out for this treatment is more than ironic, since the DCs themselves 'took off' in the nineteenth century in the early stages of their capitalism with this industry, and it happened to be the only product in which the LDCs had a clear comparative advantage because of its labour-intensive structure. This is a pointer to those who argue that industrialisation is possible under neocolonialism.

It is not surprising that in such circumstances India, for example, found it necessary in 1961 to carry along with them to the Ministers' Meeting of the six-nation consortium their Third Five-Year Development Plan in one hand, and a bowl in the other for a first instalment of the $2,225 million created by the 'trade gap'.

But what is interesting is that the Committee, after three years' investigation, came up again with ten 'specific recommendations'. These ranged over the usual spectrum of prayers and requests, which later came to be referred to as the Action Programme, calling for removal of quantitative restrictions on imports of LCDs and requesting that DCs 'should adopt a sympathetic attitude to the question of reciprocity of tariff concessions to meet the special needs of the LDCs', etc.

At this rate there was bound to be concern from other quarters. It came from ECOSOC, where for a long time the Soviet Union had been pressuring for a world trade organisation, since in its opinion—and justly so—the GATT with its Ricardonian rules was a capitalist businessman's club. The sympathetic response from the third world in spite of rejections from the Western capitalist states put the matter outside GATT's hands at least for a time. The GATT however manoeuvered to forestall what UNCTAD might do by drafting a three-part Article (XXXVI-XXXVIII) to be added to the GATT, dealing specifically with 'Trade and Development'. This was in November, 1965. It was but one of the usual tactics to give the impression that something was really being done. The addition turned out to be nothing more than a declaration of the facts already known, namely that the GATT stands for the raising of standards of living of all countries; that the export earnings of the LDCs are vital for their development; that there exists a trade gap, and that in the circumstances a 'joint' effort is essential 'to further develop the economies of the LDCs'. The Contracting Parties added nothing of substance but notably conceded that 'the DCs do not expect reciprocity for commitments made by them in trade negotiations to reduce or remove tariffs and other barriers to the trade of

LDCs'.[15] In their 'commitments' (which were to be given effect *'to the fullest extent possible,* that is *except* when compelling reasons, which may include legal reasons, make it impossible'), the DCs resolved to 'accord high priority to the reduction and elimination of barriers to products currently or potentially of export interest to LDCs'. etc.[16] Dam has correctly called this 'a great deal of verbiage and very few precise commitments'.[17]

No commitment on general preferences for all LDCs was made. But to keep the tradition of structuring and restructuring going, Committee 3 was replaced by a new Committee, to be known as the Trade and Development Committee. Marx and Engels had correctly observed that one thing which distinguishes the bourgeois epoch from all the other epochs so far is the capacity by the bourgeoisie to constantly disturb all social conditions, creating everlasting uncertainty and agitation; 'All fixed, fast, frozen relations are swept away, all new-formed ones become antiquated before they ossify.'[18] In their struggle to survive and to continue the exploitation under different guises and covers, it becomes a lifetime necessity.

The emergence of UNCTAD on the international trade scene in 1964 was heralded as the new hope for the third world, since GATT was 'unsuited' to their developmental needs and its rules were too stringently in favour of the stronger imperialist economies, denying them markets for their products. Tied up in this vicious cycle, it can readily be seen why they should feel compelled to press for access to markets of the DCs for both their agricultural products and rudimentary manufactures. We have already observed that after the era of open colonialism the imperialist powers, at the insistence of the US, found a collective interest in creating multilateral markets in the former colonies or semi-colonies to the greatest extent possible. Although associate preferences continued to exist, as pointed out, these preferences nevertheless existed over and above the multilateral markets. Thus when the third world embarked on import-substitution as a strategy of 'economic development', the imperialist monopolies saw no harm in financing them either by way of direct investment or by official loans. Such investments and loans, needless to say, helped the monopolies to expand their markets further in the neocolonies, and these channels were effectively used to extract ever-increasing surplus from the labour and resources of the third world. With the import-substitution factories on their feet the problem of markets for the products became more pressing, hence the pressure for non-reciprocal concessions by DCs to the entry of these products in their markets. Such pressures however ignore the fundamental law of capitalism, namely the law of the tendency of the rate of profit to fall, leading to ever-increasing accumulation of capital on a world scale and concentration, which is not possible without third world markets.

The first step taken by the UNCTAD I in Geneva in 1964 was to lay down General and Special Principles on the question of preferences for the products of the LDCs. The Secretary-General in his proposal to the Conference pointed out that the objective of the Conference should be to adapt those existing preferences to the new system of

> Special and General Preferences in such a way that there is no discrimination among the LDCs whilst ensuring that existing beneficiaries receive *equivalent* preferences under the new system.[19]

In a resolution the Conference, in conformity with this proposal, resolved that:

> Preferential arrangements between DCs and LDCs which involve discrimination against other LDCs, and which are essentially for the maintenance and growth of export earnings and for the development of the LDCs at present benefiting therefrom, should be abolished *pari passu* with the effective application of international measures providing at least equivalent advantages for the said countries.[20]

But this was to be within General Principle 8 which was henceforth to guide trade relations between DCs and LDCs. This principle laid down that 'DCs should grant concessions to all LDCs. . . and should not, in granting these or other concessions, require any concessions in return from LDCs'.

These resolutions and principles were not wholly accepted by the DCs. The US particularly objected to preferences. Their view was shared by Canada, Switzerland, Japan, and to some extent Sweden and Norway. Although France and Belgium advocated selective as opposed to general preferences based on the abortive Brasseur Plan, first put forward by Belgium in 1963 in GATT, this was seen as propaganda. The paper submitted by France based on the Plan was also rejected by the US.[21] However, between Geneva and New Delhi there emerged a certain consensus on the matter in the OECD block. Equally, although there were differences between the Latin American and African states, a certain unanimity prevailed amongst them. For the US this turned out to be a strategic problem, which had to be resolved if it were to maintain its leadership over its 'Allies' and put monopoly capital on a footing to meet the challenge. This the US was able to do in time, at Punta del Este on April 14, 1967, when the US President Johnson announced the strategy:

> We are ready to explore with other industrialised countries—and with our own people—the possibility of temporary preferential tariff advantages for all developing countries in the markets of all industrialised countries.[22]

Thus US monopoly capitalists ('our own people') and the other monopoly groups ('other industrialised countries') quickly worked out a general approach, although not without difficulties and contradictions. But US agreement on this issue was at a price: it demanded abolition by the EEC of 'reverse preferences' granted by the African associated states to the EEC. Branislav Gosovic in his recent book has tried to explore the reasons behind the US reversal of policy:

> Why did the American decision-makers change their strategy against the traditional policy, and in spite of fear of 'low-wage' products in the US market and the related opposition to such tariff liberalization. In its negative stance toward the GSP, the United States became increasingly isolated politically from the developing and developed countries, while its influence on the content of the scheme was diminished. The tendency towards proliferation and solidification of the Yaoundé Convention based EEC preferential arrangements on the African continent was viewed with alarm in Washington. At the same time, the Latin American countries were getting more restless. The GSP was not taking shape and the special preferences were becoming more extensive so their clamour for vertical preferences in the US—as 'defensive measures' against the 'Afro-European block'—began to intensify. Of course, any such move would have a negative impact on US relations with the developing countries of Asia and Africa, and would have added to the trend which divided the developing world into tighter spheres of influence.
>
> With the aid of a new strategy, the United States could alleviate some of the above mentioned challenges. For example Latin American countries could be mollified by showing that the US was, after all, doing something active to secure better access for them to the European market, and especially to the EEC. Also, Washington could state that it would extend preferential treatment to all developing countries, excepting those that discriminate against [US] products, and give reverse preferences to some industrialised nations. In this manner, a wrench of sorts could be thrown to the EEC's, mainly French-promoted, policy of consolidating the preferential links with a substantial part of Africa. Furthermore the GSP could have a dampening effect on the further proliferation of special arrangements, while the significance of the existing ones would be reduced. All of these elements called for a reassessment of the situation and played a role in convincing President Johnson of the need to change the policy stand of his country.[23]

This passage is quoted extensively because it shows more brazenly the back-room motivations of post-war imperialism based on multilateral neocolonialism. We shall later have opportunity to refer to the mechanics or tactics of implementing this policy which clearly underline the above strategy.

Thus the common positions arrived at by the LDCs in the Algiers Charter and the OECD group formed a basis for a compromise recorded at New Delhi in UNCTD II, in 1968. In a resolution, the Conference,

> *Establish[ed]* to this end, a Special Committee on Preferences, as a Subsidiary organ of the Trade and Development Board, to enable all countries concerned to participate in necessary consultations. . .
> *Request[ed]* that the aim shall be to settle details of the arrangements in the course of 1969 with a view to seeking legislative authority and required

waiver in GATT as soon as possible thereafter.

Not[ed] the hope expressed by countries that the arrangement should enter into effect in early 1970.[24]

But the crux of the problem was to agree on the content of the schemes and to take positions on existing preferences and the abolition of reverse preferences. Although the Special Committee was scheduled to meet in November 1968 and early 1969 to draw up their final report, no progress was made by the DCs. It was only around July 1969 that the OECD members submitted their illustrative lists, each putting forward a negative list specifying products from Chapters 25-99 of the Brussels Nomenclature (BTN) on which it was not prepared to grant preferential treatment. Each list was also accompanied by statements of assumptions, qualifications and conditions on which countries based policy. By November 1969 the co-ordinated list was submitted to UNCTAD and to the LDCs. In all, eighteen countries agreed to participate in the GSP. After lengthy consultations in 1969 and 1970 consensus was reached on mutually agreeable arrangements for Generalised Scheme of Preferences to be introduced in 1971. The Rules of Origin were also agreed in December 1970. In the meantime steps were taken by the eighteen to obtain waivers under Article XXV of the GATT to introduce the GSP. The ten-year waiver from Article I (mfn) obligations was granted in June 1971 on condition that the waiver would not be used to raise barriers to trade, the intention of the GSP being 'to facilitate trade'. The Contracting Parties of GATT were to review the waiver at the end of the period and to decide whether it was to be renewed. The Socialist countries—USSR, Poland, Hungary, Czechoslovakia and Bulgaria—announced their intention to contribute to the aims of the GSP and undertook *inter alia* to include their provisions in their respective plans and to grant technical assistance for the construction of 'industrial undertakings' in LDCs.

On 2nd June 1971 the EEC Council of Ministers approved their scheme to come in force on 1st July for six months. In 1972 a number of countries submitted their schemes. It is fitting at this stage to examine some of these schemes.[25]

III

Between 1st July 1971 and 1st July 1972 a number of DCs and Socialist countries implemented their schemes. They were Austria, the EEC (6), Ireland, Japan, New Zealand, the Nordic countries, Switzerland and the United Kingdom. The USA and Canada did not implement their schemes, due to the fact that the USA insisted on the elimination of special preferences and the accompanying reverse preferences, or at least guarantees that the preferences would be phased out in two or three years, before it could get its Congress to endorse the scheme. Moreover, the Japanese scheme stipulated that countries maintaining discrimination against Japanese goods in trade or tariffs would cease to benefit under the scheme after three years from the date of its coming into force (1st August 1971). The Socialist countries which introduced the schemes were Bulgaria, Czechoslovakia and Hungary. The USSR had been granting preferential treatment to the LDCs since 1965, and Poland, which does not have a customs tariff, introduced special preferential arrangements to expand its imports from the third world.

Since it is not possible to go into each and every GSP we can only make an attempt to examine the schemes in general. All the schemes indicate (i) product coverage, (ii) depth of tariff cuts, (iii) safeguard measures, and (iv) rules of origin. We will examine each of these, first dealing with GSP of the capitalist countries.

A. PREFERENTIAL ARRANGEMENTS BY THE CAPITALIST COUNTRIES

(i) *Product Coverage.* The schemes in general over only agricultural and fishery products in BTN Chapters 1-24. These products, moreover, account for a minor share of the imports of DCs from the LDC beneficiaries. The precise product coverage varies from scheme to scheme. The important thing to note is that *agricultural products of current export interest to many LDCs are excluded from the schemes!* This is the crux of the matter and is an indicator of the nature of the schemes.

Moreover, although the schemes cover manufactures and semi-manufactures in BTN Chapters 25-99, *the schemes exclude textiles, leather and petroleum products!* They also cover all primary commodities in these BTN chapters, except that the EEC (6) scheme excludes all primary commodities as well as base metals up to the stage of ingots. The exclusion by the EEC (6) of these products is intended to preserve the market for products from its Yaoundé countryside and to some degree the Arusha hinterland, to the extent those areas can enjoy the preserved markets, since they too are subject to quotas and other restrictions due to the EEC's common agricultural policy. New Zealand extends treatment only to selected primary products. The countries most affected by the exclusion of textiles and petroleum products include Egypt, Pakistan, Kuwait, Iraq, Saudi Arabia and Bahrain. The EEC (6) exclusion of the agricultural commodities extends of course to all the tropical products from LDCs except those with special preferences mentioned above, namely the Yaoundé and Arusha groups.

Although the number of manufactured products in BTN Chapters 25-99 in the various schemes which are entitled to preferential treatment is small, the trade involved is substantial, averaging 62 per cent of the 1970 preference-giving countries' imports of all dutiable products from the beneficiaries.[26] But at the same time they are products which are subject to high tariff and non-tariff barriers. For certain products considered 'sensitive' from the point of view of domestic production in the EEC, preferential imports are subject to predetermined community tariff quotas whereby each member of the EEC is allocated a quota in value or quantity, viz: Federal Republic of Germany 37.5 per cent,

France 27.1 per cent, Italy 20.3 per cent, Benelux 15.1 per cent.

(ii) *Depth of Tariff Cut.* The cuts differ from country to country and from product to product. As far as agricultural products in BTN Chapters 1-24 are concerned, the only schemes that have granted 'duty free' treatment are Finland, Norway and Sweden. The UK accords similar treatment with the exception of a few items. The other schemes of Austria, Denmark, EEC (6), Japan, New Zealand and Switzerland give various degrees of cuts, ranging between one and four points. The 'duty free' cut gives considerable advantage to the extent that these products are generally highly protected in these markets. The crucial point however is that the so-called 'duty free' treatment is subject to 'safeguard provisions' (see below).

With regard to products in BTN Chapters 25-99 covered by the various schemes, EEC (6), Denmark, Finland, Norway, Sweden and the UK apply 'duty free' treatment—with Japan applying 50 per cent reduction of the mfn rate on certain products of special interest to LDCs. Austria and Switzerland apply a linear cut of 30 per cent of the mfn rates; Ireland applies one-third reduction and New Zealand applies various rates of reduction, depending on the product. These apparently generous cuts have to be viewed with caution, since the margin of preference will diminish with the progressive increase in the mfn rate as the degree of processing of the products increases. This does not apply to 'duty free' products, where the margin of preference corresponds to the mfn rates of duty.

(iii) *Safeguard Measures.* All the schemes have safeguard measures which are intended to provide some degree of control by the preference-giving countries over the trade that might be generated by the tariff cuts. These can be classified into two broad categories: (a) *a priori limitations*—applied by EEC (6) and Japan in BTN Chapters 25-99, and (b) *escape clauses,* which are applied by all the other preference-giving countries with respect to all the trade, and by EEC (6) and Japan with respect to BTN, Chapters 1-24.

(a) *A priori limitations.* The purpose of this formula is to regulate preferential imports on the basis of past trade performance of beneficiaries ('basic quota'), plus a certain increment ('supplementary quota'). The effect of the formula is to limit imports at a ceiling which falls short (in many cases) of the current level of imports and potential expansion. To be sure, the actual mechanics of the *a priori* limitation in the case of the EEC quota is to take the c.i.f. values of imports from the beneficiaries in 1968 (basic quota) and add on it 5 per cent of the c.i.f. value of imports from other sources (supplementary quota), to be calculated on the latest information available. These quotas would be subject to the community quotas (quotas-within-quotas) referred to already. In the case of Japan, the supplementary quota is 10 per cent of imports from other sources, but many items of special interest to the beneficiaries as pointed out are subject to a 50 per cent reduction of mfn rate only.[27] The reasons for these *a priori* limitations are obvious: they are inbuilt safeguards against *market disruption* which would be created by increased importation of products from the LDCs taking advantage of the cuts. As usual, the old game of imperialism is clear: give with one hand and take back with the other! Its only net effect is to transfer the tariff revenue to the beneficiaries if the beneficiaries increase their prices to take advantage of the tariff cut, in which case it is aid and not trade that is generated. In whatever event the 'aid' is intended to finance the imports of the preference-giving country in the market of the 'beneficiary'; and the position is as it was before. It is all very smooth.

(b)*Escape clause.* The safeguard in this clause involves the withdrawal of the preference offered where the import of any product from the beneficiary country or countries is in such quantities, or under such conditions, as 'to cause or threaten to cause serious injury' to domestic producers of the like or directly competitive products in the preference-giving country. This is a cruder and more straightforward form of denial of the preference. The Nordic countries (Denmark, Finland, Norway and Sweden) provide for invoking the clause if the preferential imports 'cause or threaten to cause *market disruption*'. Other reasons include the need to assist the establishment of any new industry or development of an existing one (New Zealand), or the existence of *'critical circumstance'* (Sweden). The withdrawal is normally invoked on notice but some schemes provide for unilateral withdrawal (Ireland and New Zealand). Many countries have not spelt out the conditions attached to the clause. The UK, for instance, invoked the clause against four Latin American countries against the importation of certain leather products for 1973. The duration is not normally specified but some schemes state that the withdrawal will remain in force 'to the extent deemed necessary to correct the adverse situation' (EEC (6), Switzerland, Sweden). None of the schemes have, however, defined the criteria for application of the clause, and uncertainty surrounds it. Only Austria provides for certain statistical guidelines prior to invocation. The effect of the escape clause in practice is in the final analysis the same as the *a priori* limitation. Moreover, the product coverage is spelt out in such a way as to exclude those products in which trade could have been expanded where the third world has 'comparative advantage', namely, textiles, footwear (leather products) and petroleum products.

(iv) *Rules of Origin.* To ensure further 'tightening' of the trade the schemes provide for direct consignment and other origin criteria specified by each scheme.

(a)*Origin Criteria.* A product will be considered originating from the preference-giving country if the product has been produced *wholly* in the preference-giving country or when the product has undergone *substantial transformation* from materials and/or components imported of undetermined origin. All schemes (except New Zealand) base their origin requirement on the process criterion. The process criterion specifies a transformation that would lead to the exported product being classified under a BTN heading other than that under which the imported materials and/or components used in production were classified. The value-added criterion which New Zealand uses and which the USA and Canada are likely to adopt specifies a value-added of as high as 50 per cent of the ex-factory price of the exported product. The immediate result of these criteria is to exclude from the scheme traditional products of the beneficiaries of export interest to them. When you add together *the exclusion* of textiles, footwear, petroleum products (which are the products substantially transformed by most beneficiaries with 'comparative advantage' in those products) from most schemes; and *the exclusion* of other products in which the value-added is *below* 50 per cent of the ex-factory price, as well as the transformation process require-ment, what remains for the majority of the 'beneficiaries' is very little if not nothing. In such circumstances it is not surprising that the Tanzania Minister of Commerce and Industry, in his address to UNCTAD III at Santiago de Chile in 1972, should have found it necessary to state: 'Certainly the generalised schemes of preferences are of no practical significance or relevance to so many poorly developed countries.' To return to the process criterion, the follow-ing illustration given by the UNCTAD Secretariat reveals its intention:

> Under most schemes garments must be manufactured not from imported woven fabrics but from imported yarn, in order to qualify for preferential treatment. Also plastic goods qualify only if they are manufactured from imported basic chemicals and not from plastic raw materials. Radio sets qualify only if the transistors used in production originate in the develop-ing countries of exportation. It is estimated that during the first eight months of operation of the scheme of Japan, about one quarter of the preferential trade in that market [would have] failed to receive preferential treatment because of the substantial transformation requirement.[28]

(b) *Direct Consignment*. The other major requirement for satisfying origin criteria is direct consignment. Products eligible for preferential treatment must, in general, be consigned directly to the preference-giving country from the preference-receiving country. This means that transportation must be effected without passing through the territory of one or more countries with or without trans-shipment or temporary storage facilities. Where direct consignment is not possible the goods must remain under customs transit control and not enter into trade or

consumption there. The UK and Japanese schemes further provide that
at the time the goods leave the beneficiary country it must be the
intention of the exporter to ship them to the UK or Japan, respectively,
provided that in the case of a land-locked country like Uganda, goods
may be consigned from a port in a neighbouring country like Kenya or
Tanzania. In any case this requirement and latter 'concession' to the
landlocked countries are intended to preclude the possibility of the
beneficiary country storing a product in a suitable port for a period
necessary to obtain the most favourable terms for its resale in whole or
in part. In the opinion of the Chambers of Commerce of North Sea
Ports: 'Such a rule is contrary to the most advantageous commercial
practices with regard to storage and distribution of imports from
developing countries.'[29] The UNCTAD Secretariat concludes:

> It seems, therefore, that the direct consignment rules as presently applied
> not only are disadvantageous to trading circles but also do not meet the
> interests of the developing countries.

(c) *Certificates of origin.* Some of the schemes specify that, even
after satisfying the above requirements, the products should be
accompanied by a 'certificate of origin'. The preference-receiving
countries must provide information on the relevant government
authorities empowered to endorse the certificates of origin and in
some cases they are required to furnish specimen impressions of
stamps used by these authorities and the specimen signatures of the
officers issuing the certificates. Those countries which have not
complied have had exports excluded from preferential treatment.

B. PREFERENTIAL ARRANGEMENTS OF THE SOCIALIST COUNTRIES
(i) *Product Coverage.* Bulgaria grants tariff preferences to all manufactured and agricultural products with the following exceptions: dead
poultry, manufactured tobacco, essential oil, articles of furskin,
knotted carpets, other carpets, footwear, wrought lead and wrought
zinc. Primary commodities are admitted 'duty free'.
   Czechoslovakia also grants tariff preferences to all agricultural
and industrial products, including primary commodities, with the
following exceptions: white sugar, cigarettes, poultry of all kinds, not
including feathered game, beer, meat sausages, carpets other than hand-
made, hats, ready-made articles of textiles.
   Hungary grants tariff preferences to 299 tariff headings or sub-
headings in BTN, Chapters 1-99. The USSR grants tariff preferences to
all products falling within BTN, Chapters 1-99.

(ii) *Depth of Tariff Cut.* Bulgaria and Czechoslovakia grant respectively
a 30 per cent and 50 per cent reduction in mfn rates. Hungary's cuts
range from 50 per cent to 90 per cent of mfn rates on most products
and duty-free treatment on a large number of products, the average

reduction being around 50 per cent of the mfn rates. The USSR grants duty-free treatment to all the products.

(iii) *Safeguard Measures.* The schemes of the socialist countries reserve rights to take protective measures in accordance with customs regulations in force in their countries in exceptional circumstances, and many schemes provide for reduction or increase of preferential rates for determined periods, or for suspending their application. Czechoslovakia subscribes generally to the above. It however accepts the GATT definition of the criteria for determining injury or threat of injury to domestic production. Czechoslovakia is prepared too to hold prior consultations on a bilateral or multilateral basis before escape action is taken. The USSR has made no provision for reintroduction of duties abolished or for adoption of any measures of a protective character.

(iv) *Rules of Origin.* The Bulgarian scheme insists on the criterion of goods wholly produced or mainly processed in the beneficiary country. A certificate must accompany the goods. Czechoslovakia applies the same criterion and alternatively requires that the goods should undergo a manufacturing process which increases the original value of the goods by 100 per cent. The government of Czechoslovakia however states that it has no experience in applying the process criterion, but that until it has gained experience from other countries it will rely on the judgment of its customs officers on whether the component percentage has been observed.

Hungary applies a 50 per cent value added criterion and like Czechoslovakia relies on the judgment of the customs officials. Documentary evidence is required for goods with customs value exceeding 50,000 forints. Where the value-added includes a Hungarian-made component the treatment accorded is duty-free. The USSR scheme gives no details but merely requires that the goods must have originated in the beneficiary country.

C. SPECIAL PREFERENCES AND SPECIAL MEASURES FOR THE LEAST
   DEVELOPED AMONG THE DEVELOPING COUNTRIES (LLDC)

As pointed out earlier, the introduction of GSP by many of the preference-giving countries was conditional on the elimination of special preferences. In this connection the UNCTAD Special Committee on preferences stated that the developing countries which shared their existing tariff advantages in some preference-giving countries as a result of the introduction of these schemes, would expect the new access in other preference-giving countries to provide export opportunities at least to compensate them. These were the two African groups (Yaoundé and Arusha), the association agreements with Tunisia and Morocco, and the LDCs which enjoyed Commonwealth preferences in the UK and New Zealand. Experience under the EEC scheme showed that as far as the African associated states were concerned their exports were unaffected by the scheme. Only 5 per cent of the Yaoundé exports, 6 per cent of the Arusha exports and 21 per cent of Tunisia and Morocco were affected by the EEC GSP. As far as the Commonwealth preference was concerned, the UK scheme safeguarded its beneficiaries either through the negative list or through duty margins and quota allocations. The UNCTAD Secretariat worked out an estimate of the extent to which the special preference beneficiaries shared their protected markets with other GSP beneficiaries. This showed that the imports from the African associated states with the EEC and those enjoying Commonwealth preferences of products included in the EEC and UK schemes altogether amounted to $72 million, which these states have to share with the other GSP beneficiaries. As against this figure the African associated states' exports to other markets in 1970 amounted to $43 million c.i.f. value, which would offset any 'loss' by other beneficiaries gaining entry to the EEC through the GSP. It must however be noted that special preference margins were greater than the GSP margins; and hence special preferences still played a role in spite of the GSP.

As regards industrial products, special preferences offered duty-free treatment to the associates for all products in BTN 25-99 (subject to rules of origin). In 1970 these accounted for $62 million of EEC imports from the associates, as opposed to agricultural products which amounted to $10 million in imports. The EEC GSP excluded industrial raw materials which the EEC obtained cheaply from the associates in Africa.

The Commonwealth preference beneficiaries exports in 1970 amounted to $525 million to the UK and New Zealand, but they had access under GSP from other DCs amounting to $800 million which these DCs imported from them. With the EEC enlargement these Commonwealth schemes became irrelevant and the Commonwealth beneficiaries were taken care of under Protocol No. 22 to the Accession Treaty under which the 'Three' joined the 'Six'.

As far as East Africa's exports to the UK were concerned, these enjoyed Commonwealth preferences which averaged around 10 per cent. The commodities included coffee (unroasted), cashewnuts and kernels, tobacco (manufactured), canned beef, meat extract, cloves, pineapples (fresh, tinned and juice), groundnuts, and cottonseed cake. All these items were imported into the UK duty-free except tobacco (unmanufactured), which was imported at a preferential rate.

UNCTAD Resolution 21(ii) called for special attention to exports and export earnings of the twenty-five LLDCs, among which Uganda and Tanzania feature prominently. A Special Committee was set up to 'further investigate and consult' in regard to special measures in favour of these countries. The Special Committee emerged with a report showing the measures that might be taken with regard to improvements in the product coverage and depth of tariff cut, as well as the application of safeguards and rules of origin. The conclusions which are drawn from the 1970 trade flows are pregnant with 'new discoveries', for instance: imports by preference-giving market economy countries from the LLDCs 'are at present very small and limited to a narrow range of mainly agricultural products and industrial raw materials'; most imports of non-agricultural products (BTN, Chapters 25-99) are already admitted duty-free under mfn treatment and thus fall outside the scope of the GSP; the remaining dutiable imports are largely covered by GSP; unless the product coverage under the GSP is extended to dutiable products currently imported from LLDCs and, as appropriate, deeper tariff cuts are provided for these products, 'the LLDCs are not likely to derive much benefit from GSP in the short run'.

The UNCTAD secretariat estimated that about *one-fifth* of imports subject to duty under mfn treatment (8 per cent of total imports) were covered by the various GSP. The estimate also showed that the LLDCs would have enjoyed generalised preferences on imports worth $51 million.

IV

In addition, the trade 'liberalisation' which took place with the enlargement of the EEC to nine and the on-going negotiations under the GATT (the so-called 'Nixon Round') were bound to have an impact on the GSPs.

The enlargement of the EEC on 1st January 1973 meant in effect the progressive removal of tariff and other barriers to trade, which ended by 1st July 1977, resulting in a full-fledged customs union for the EEC (9). The effect of this was that the preference-receiving countries were less favourably treated in the enlarged community than formerly, since the new members' products received more favourable treatment. In the case of East African exports, they continued to gain duty-free access into the UK market as well as the EEC at least during 1974. There was some reduction in East Africa's margin of preference, since the EEC CET tariff rates were somewhat lower than the UK tariff rates. Among the products affected were cashewnuts and kernels (UK 10 per cent, CET free). But East Africa gained some 'marginal advantage' in the UK market in the case of those products for which the EEC CET rates were higher than the current UK tariff rates. Such products included pyrethrum flowers (CET 3 per cent, UK free), pyrethrum extracts (CET 5 per cent, UK free), and fresh pineapples (CET 13 per cent, UK free).

The main impact on East African agricultural exports to the UK fell on those products which came under the Common Agricultural Policy of the EEC. Community preference for agricultural and farm products was introduced the moment Britain became a member, and this affected a number of East African products such as dairy products, meat products, sugar and horticultural products. The 'Six' had surpluses in the first three, while the UK was an importing country. Meat products were increasingly being exported and the bulk of it entered the UK market.

Moreover, by January 1974 the new members (including the UK) were required by the Accession treaty to align their GSP with that of the EEC (6). As a result, the enlarged community had a new scheme which came into force by that date. A proposal by the Commission to the Council for the new GSP for 1974, replacing the 1973 scheme, was put to the Council in late 1973 for products in BTN Chapters 1-24, without waiting for proposals for manufactured and semi-manufactured products. In the proposal the Commission proposed: (a) an increase in the margin of preferences in respect of products which were listed in the regulations then in force; (b) an extension of the number of products covered.

Thus under the proposal processed agricultural products subject to a single duty underwent an overall increase from 20 per cent to 40 per cent, except in the case of certain 'sensitive' products where the margin was widened from 10 per cent to 20 per cent; and in case of products subject to a two-tier duty (fixed component and variable component), the reduction in the fixed component was increased to 50 per cent wherever it was less than previously. The product coverage was widened to include: products with certain forms of pasta, Chinawood oil, certain other oils (coco) for technical uses, fish-meal, tea in packings of 3 kg or less, certain cereals, certain vegetables, cigarettes, cigars, and smoking and chewing tobacco. The improvements were supposed to add $160 million to imports in these new preferences.[30] The benefits from 'open-ended' UK and Danish schemes were 'lost' under the enlarged EEC GSP.

Moreover, free trade area agreements between the enlarged community and a number of EFTA members like Austria, Iceland, Portugal, Sweden, Switzerland and Norway conferred higher preferential treatment to the products of these countries than under the GSP. What was more, the EEC sought a 'global solution' to its relations with the Mediterranean countries. The coup in Portugal further opened up the possibility of free trade areas between the EEC and Portugal and possibly Spain. 'This global solution' was clearly intended to re-allocate markets to products of Western capitalist countries among themselves first, and then whatever remained to products of the third world. This meant, as the UNCTAD Secretariat pointed out:

> the developing countries dependent on the GSP for access to preferential markets of the enlarged Community will enjoy preferential margins in those markets only over competing exports from third countries mainly the USA, Japan, Canada, Australia, New Zealand, South Africa and socialist countries of Eastern Europe.
>
> The same also holds for all the developing countries as regards access to the markets of other preference-giving developed market economy countries in Europe: Austria, Sweden and Switzerland and eventually Norway and Finland also. . . Only the schemes of Japan and New Zealand (as also the USA and Canada when implemented) offer preferencial margins to beneficiary developing countries over all other countries.[31]

The multilateral trade talks got off the ground with the Tokyo Declaration. The declaration set off with two basic objectives, namely:

> to achieve expansion and 'ever-greater liberalisation' of world trade. . .
> through the progressive dismantling of obstacles to trade. . . and to secure
> additional benefits for the international trade of LDCs so as to achieve a
> substantial increase in their foreign exchange earnings, the diversification of
> their exports, through a substantial improvement in the conditions of access
> for the products of interest to the LDCs.[32]

These broad aims were bound to contradict each other, as indeed the results of the Tokyo Round revealed. This is because any multilateral reduction of the mfn rates will correspondingly reduce the margins of preference for the various GSP on the preferred products, the depth of tariff cuts and the period over which the preferences are to be realised. The achievement of zero liberalisation on mfn rates on preferred products would in effect wipe out any preferential effect of the GSP! In this case 'free trade' may mean 'no trade' for the LDCs in most products, bearing in mind that manufactured products over which they have 'comparative advantage' like textiles, leather goods and petroleum products are excluded from GSP. Moreover, they would still be under disability under 'free trade', since various non-tariff barriers exist which cannot be removed without causing 'market disruption'!

V

The UNCTAD Secretariat made some estimations of the probable benefits to the beneficiaries of the schemes already implemented, by taking the 1970 trade flows which would have been covered by the different schemes, and for which computer data was available in sufficient detail. This investigation excluded Ireland, since no such data was available. The estimations showed that $15 billion worth of trade, two-thirds of the imports valued at $24 billion from the beneficiaries, were admitted duty-free under mfn tariff treatment. This means that the flow was unaffected by the schemes but was subject to the usual non-tariff barriers. Of the remaining $9 billion imports, agricultural and fishery products accounted for 43 per cent ($3.9 billion). As is to be recalled these products are excluded from the schemes, with various small exceptions amounting to $200 million. This left $5.1 billion, or 21 per cent of total imports of dutiable industrial products including raw materials, which would have been eligible for preferential treatment under the existing schemes, even then with a number of exceptions. For instance, the EEC excludes *all* industrial raw materials from the beneficiaries. The excluded items account for one-third of the dutiable products in BTN Chapters 25-99 from the beneficiaries. Most other preference-giving countries (except Denmark) as pointed out already exclude textiles, leather goods and petroleum products. As far as Japan, the EEC and UK are concerned, these latter

exclusions accounted in 1970 for 78 per cent, 38 per cent and 11 per
cent respectively of their dutiable products (BTN Chapters 25-99)
imported from beneficiaries, with Sweden accounting for 70 per cent
of its imports.

The imports excluded from preferential treatment can be
summarised as follows:

All products	IMPORTS FROM BENEFICIARIES ($ billion)	SHARE OF TOTAL (%)
	24.00	100
less Duty-free under mfn	15.00	63
less Dutiable agricultural and fishery products not covered by the schemes	3.7	15
less Dutiable industrial products not covered by the schemes	3.2	13
equals Products covered by schemes	2.1	9

Thus in the final analysis only $2.1 billion of imports by preference-
giving countries, from the beneficiaries, or only one-fourth of their
total dutiable imports, would have qualified for the GSP had they been
in operation in 1970.[33]

It should also be borne in mind that this benefit would not have been
available to all the beneficiaries. The more developed of the LDCs
would have benefited more than the least developed. It is estimated that
the major beneficiaries accounted in 1970 for $829 million or 39 per
cent of the total trade which would have been covered by the schemes
(i.e. of $2.1 billion). But due to tariff-ceilings and tariff-quotas or
maximum amount limitations in the EEC and in Japan, only $600
million of this amount would have entered under their GSP. Of the
least developed, many of their products could have found no access to
the markets of the preference-givers.

The experience of the socialist countries with the schemes cannot be
assessed, but a number of countries (Hungary, Bulgaria) indicated that
the response so far had been unsatisfactory. The reason given was that
the export drive of the LDCs was directed mainly at countries with
convertible currencies. It was also observed by these countries that the
beneficiaries tended to raise their prices by an amount equal to the
preferential margin. As a result the tariff revenue foregone could not be
passed to the consumer through lower prices and sales, therefore
showed no tendency to increase. The USSR reported that

in practice no difficulties have been encountered in commercial transactions
between the Soviet Union and the developing countries since the introduction

of the preferential regime on 1st January 1965.[34]

Apart from the above UNCTAD estimate, there have been other academic estimates. One estimate done by Grant L. Reuber, based on the assumption that mfn rates were maintained at zero, concluded that the total effects at 1961 trade levels would have been an increase in LDCs' exports of the order of $600 million. He further estimated that if quantitative restrictions were removed from competing LDC goods, the additional exports would have come to about $1.1 billion. He concluded that these effects were negligible compared with the then current levels of trade and aid.[35] John Pincus makes similar estimates, and his conclusions are 'not significantly different'. His method assumed that the preferences would be on product-to-product basis rather than generalised (as they turned out to be), and made a further three assumptions of different rates, excluding all competing products of LDCs from the estimation. He concluded that the total increase in imports at 1963 levels would have been $2.5 billion based on a duty-free 5 per cent tariff quota or under, and $5.2 billion based on a duty-free 10 per cent tariff quota. He is also firm on an estimation of $1-2 billion, which in his opinion is negligible in terms of market access of the LDCs' products.

VI

The analysis to date has revealed that the export increases of the GSP are negligible. Hindley has argued that the schemes *per se* will do very little if nothing to attain the declared ends of the 'Group of 77' to increase exports through improved access to the markets of the DCs. This is because, as he correctly points out, 'the ability to restrict exports from developing countries remains securely with the advanced countries'.[36] It is submitted here that the little 'gain' made by the LDCs under the GSP will also be to the benefit of the DCs. As far as the aid element in the GSP is concerned it has been argued that this will ultimately end up in the DCs through increased exports to the LDCs. Hindley estimates the aid effect at $4-5 million, which is miserable compared to the OECD aid of $7 billion for 1967. Be that as it may, to the extent that the GSP will tend to strengthen import substitution strategy leading to increased manufacturing, this too in certain circumstances is no longer detested by the new *multinational corporate* strategy of the monopolies. It is clear that the leading capitalist powers are scheming out a new international division of labour in which field, because of their lead in science and technology (particularly the USA), they have a great advantage. This will of course enable them to control managements of joint ventures and sources of raw materials by their technological superiority. In this way certain aspects of manufacturing can be pushed to the third world. *Le Monde* correctly summed up the situation when it pointed out:

But why have they chosen preferences instead of an aid programme? The most obvious reason is that it will benefit firms established in the poor countries, which are equipped to take advantage of the opening up of the markets of the rich countries.

The system of special preferences will thus enable the international companies to profit from both the cheap labour of the poor countries, as a factor of production, and the high salaries of the rich countries, in terms of purchasing power.

To this redistribution of activity within the international firms must be added a redistribution of the economic activities on a world scale. The rich countries tend to specialise in the most advanced capital-intensive technological sectors. By 'abandoning' the other sectors to the poor countries this trend towards an ever-increasing specialisation will be intensified.[37]

Professor Johan Galtung in his study of the European Community (EC) comes to the same conclusion and adds three conditions under which the EEC can implement its GSP: (a) that the processed goods do not compete with EC industry because they are no longer produced inside EC. Hence they are bound to be goods like textiles and 'not-too-processed' iron and/or goods produced by highly polluting industries that EC would prefer produced outside; (b) that the processed goods are produced in the mncs with headquarters in EC countries. This would give the mncs sufficient room to maneouvre financially. 'Thus the mncs may fix prices so that profits show where taxes are lowest'; (c) that the EC will still be free to export goods at a higher level of processing than what they import from third world countries. This division of labour is maintained in all the fields of capital (from centre), labour (from periphery) and land (from periphery).[38]

VII

This analysis has tried to show that imperialism is still centrally concerned with markets of the third world. That whatever new structures are created these are intended to obscure this reality. Neocolonialism can therefore be seen as a stage in the evolution of imperialism. The post-war multilateral trade system was meant precisely to cater for this situation. The 'problems of under-development' that have attracted ever-increasing numbers of petty-bourgeois ideologists should not come to us as a surprise. The objective laws of capitalist development *do not* in the final analysis *obey* the juridical rules that may be constructed in their way. They operate quite independently of these rules and of the will of all those involved. Just as the workers and peasants have to produce for the system on penalty of death; so the system has to expand to its grave. But such death to the system does not come of its own but out of violent class struggles, which are the dialectical result of the evolution of the system. At a certain stage these existing productive forces will come in conflict with the production relations now existing on a world scale, resulting in a consciously organised social revolution, thus liberating the productive forces from the fetters of capital, and in turn creating conditions for man to liberate himself. There can be no short-cut to this dialectical law, as all history has hitherto shown.

Thus the existing unequal relationships between the imperialist centres and the exploited third world peripheries will only be finally resolved through such fundamental changes in property relations; a task which the revolutionary petty bourgeoisie working closely with an alliance of forces of the workers and the peasantry can bring about. In the meantime the GSP and any new rabbits coming out of the old hats of imperialism must be seen to be what they really are: CAMOUFLAGED CHANNELS FOR THE EXTRACTION OF THE SURPLUS FROM THE THIRD WORLD.

NOTES

1. This chapter was first published as an article in *East African Law Review* Vol. 7, No. 3, 1974.
2. Dell, S.: 'An Appraisal of UNCTAD III', *World Development,* Vol. I, No. 5, p. 11.
3. Pincus, J.: *Trade, Aid and Development,* New York, 1967.
4. *Suggested Charter for an International Trade Organization of the United Nations,* Department of State Publication 2598, Commercial Policy Series 93, 1946.
5. Wilcox, C.: *A Charter for World Trade,* pp. 70-71, New York, 1949.
6. Galtung, J.: *The European Community: A superpower in the making,* p. 44, London, 1973.
7. *International Trade, 1958,* GATT, p. 4, Geneva, 1965.
8. 'GATT Programme for Expansion of International Trade, Trade of LDCs', Special report of Committee III, GATT Geneva, 1962, p. 5. Gerald Curzon in reference to this notes that: 'It was clear that with the emphasis given to the monetary aspect *(sic!)* of development during the 1950's and the shortage of capital from private and public funds, export earnings were rightly to be given greater attention.' Curzon, G.: *Multilateral Commercial Diplomacy,* p. 225, London, 1965.
9. United Nations, *Relative Prices of Exports and Imports of Under-developed Countries;* quoted in Emmanuel, A.: *Unequal Exchange,* pp. xxiii; xl, London, 1972.
10. *Trends in International Trade: A Report of a Panel of Experts,* GATT, Geneva, October, 1958. The experts were Roberto de Oliveira Campos— Brazil; Gottfried Harbeler—Harvard, USA; James Meade—Cambridge, UK; Jan Tinbergen—Rotterdam, Netherlands.
11. Terms of reference Committee III, 2/939, 27/11/59.
12. Curzon, G., *op. cit.,* p. 227.
13. *Ibid.,* p. 231.
14. Dam, K.W.: *The GATT: Law and International Economic Organisation,* p. 299; Chicago, 1970. 'Market disruption' was defined by the contracting parties as occurring when the following elements combined:
    (i) a sharp and substantial increase of imports of particular products from particular sources;

(ii) these products are offered at prices which are substantially below those
prevailing for similar goods of comparable quality in the market of
the importing country;

(iii) there is serious damage to domestic producers or threat thereof;

(iv) the price differential interventions in the fixing or formation of prices
or from dumping practices.

This definition was not taken as exhaustive. [Basic Instruments, 8th
Supplement (1960) p. 26] Patterson in *Discrimination in International
Trade: The Policy Issues 1945-1965* lists woollen textiles, leather and
leather manufactures, cutlery, linoleum, rugs and carpets, footwear and
various electrical appliances as likely candidates for such arrangements as the
Long Term Textile Arrangements; pp. 321-2.

15.   These countries were: USA, UK, FRG, Japan, Canada, France and their
multilateral international organisations IBRD and IDA.

16.   Article XXXVI: 8. Many DCs have never ratified this Article.

17.   Dam, *op. cit.,* p. 237.

18.   *Communist Manifesto,* pp. 45-6.

19.   Prebisch, R.: 'Towards a New Trade Policy for Development', pp. 118;
U.N., 1964.

20.   UNCTAD I: Resolution Annex A. 11.1.

21.   'Memorandum concerning certain items on the Agenda of UNCTAD'
submitted by France at Geneva Conference. *Proceedings,* Vol. VI, pp. 23-5.

22.   *Department of State Bulletin* Vol. 56, No. 1454, (8th May 1967), p. 709.
See also Reston, J.: 'Punta de Este: Least-Favoured Nation Doctrine', *The
N.Y. Times Int. Ed.,* April 15-16, 1967.

23.   Gosovic, Branislav: *UNCTAD Conflict and Compromise,* pp. 70-1; Leiden,
1972. Gosovic acknowledges Denmark as first making this latter suggestion:
quoted by Weintraub in *Trade Preference for LDCs,* p. 136; New York,
1966.

24.   Resolution 21(11) Proceedings, New Delhi, Vol. I, p. 38.

25.   See *Journal of World Trade Law,* Vol. 5, 1971, p. 712.

26.   No effort is made here to deal with the 'pioneer' Australian Scheme of
Preferences introduced as early as 1965 which many observers have
described as meant to win friends but with very little effect.

27.   Although Egypt is the main supplier of textiles to Denmark it is excluded
from Sweden, etc.

28.   *Review of the GSP—General Report on implementation of the GSP.* Study
by UNCTAD Secretariat TD/B/C. 5/9—9th March 1973, p. 4. Most of the
data in this section is from this study.

29.   See Hindley, Brian: 'The UNCTAD Agreement on Preferences', *Journal of
World Trade Law,* Vol. 5, No. 6, p. 698.

30.   *Review, op. cit.,* p. 8, quoting TD/B/C. 5/6 para. 92.

31.   *Op. cit.,* p. 9; being direct communication to the UNCTAD Secretariat,
dated 24th October 1972.

32.   The Tokyo Declaration, GATT; Geneva, 1975.

33.   *Review, op. cit.,* p. 9.

34.   Commission of the European Community Proposal from the Commission
to the Council: Brussels, 13th July 1973.

35.   *Review, op. cit.,* p. 35.

36.   *Review, op. cit.,* p. 20.

37.   *Le Monde Weekly,* April 15-21, 1971, p. 5.
38.   Galtung, J., *op. cit.,* p. 76.
39.   *Review, op. cit.,* p. 28.

CHAPTER 5
THE LOME CONVENTION AND THE CONSOLIDATION OF NEOCOLONIALISM*

I

The ACP-EEC Lomé Convention (hereinafter referred to as the Lomé Convention or Convention unless otherwise indicated) was signed at Lomé, the Togolese capital, on 28th February 1975, almost twenty months from the date the negotiations began, 25th July 1973. The Convention was signed by the Plenipotentiaries of the Heads of States of the nine EEC Member States and the forty-six African, Caribbean and Pacific (ACP) States. The result of the twenty months' work was a voluminous documentation of 350 joint documents, all the effort of some 183 sessions of the two groups, and 493 meetings of the ACP States.

The Lomé Convention was a continuation on an enlarged scale of the earlier conventions and agreements between the EEC (6) and the Yaoundé Group, as well as the Arusha Group. The Yaoundé Group comprised the eighteen Associated African and Malagasy States (AASM) and the Arusha Group comprised the three East African States of Kenya, Uganda and Tanzania. The first Yaoundé Convention was put into effect by an Implementing Declaration incorporated within the Rome Treaty itself, whereas the second Yaoundé Convention was entered into after negotiation in 1969 under Article 238 of the Treaty. In 1963 a Declaration of Intent by the EEC enabled 'association status' to be granted to those countries which were not colonial territories of the six European imperialist powers, but which were at a similar level of development to the Yaoundé Group, namely those which were colonies of the other imperialist powers. This enabled countries like Nigeria, Kenya, Uganda and Tanzania to apply for association with the EEC on similar terms to those which were open to the AASM.[1]

The enlargement of the EEC from six states to the present nine enabled Britain, Denmark and Ireland to join it and created conditions for putting on a more permanent basis the relationships of the non-AASM States with the EEC. Under Protocol No. 22 to the Treaty of Accession, under which the three joined the EEC, it was stipulated that the EEC

> shall offer the independent Commonwealth countries listed in Annex V to the Act of Accession the possibility of ordering their relations with the Community in the spirit of the Declaration of Intent adopted by the Council at its meeting on 1/2 April 1963.[2]

---

*This chapter is drawn from an essay of the same title, combined with my paper 'Stabilisation of Export Earnings ('STABEX') in the Lomé Convention, *Ghana Law Journal*, 1977

The following formulae were offered to these countries as alternatives: participation in the Convention of Association, which upon the expiry of the Convention of Association signed on 29th July 1969 (i.e. the second Yaoundé Convention) would govern relations between the Community and the AASM which had signed; the conclusion of one or more special Conventions of Association on the basis of Article 238 of the EEC Treaty comprising reciprocal rights and obligations, particularly in the field of trade; the conclusion of trade agreements with a view to facilitating and developing trade between the Community and those countries.

Under the provisions of the Protocol, the independent Commonwealth countries listed in the Annex were to take up a position with respect to this offer as soon as possible after Britain's accession; and to this end the Community proposed that negotiations based on the above formulae should begin on 1st August 1973. Those countries which chose to do so were asked to participate side by side with the AASM in negotiating a new Convention to follow the Convention signed on 29th July 1969. In this case it was made clear that the Community was prepared to pursue its policy of association both with regard to the AASM and with the independent Commonwealth countries, which became parties to the same association.

For Botswana, Lesotho and Swaziland it was stipulated that, should they choose one of the first two formulae contained in the offer, then 'appropriate solutions must be found for the specific problems arising from [their] special circumstances' connected with their being in a customs union with a third country, i.e. South Africa. Secondly, the Protocol stipulated that in the territory of those States, the Community must enjoy tariff treatment not less favourable than that applied to South Africa. Thirdly, the provisions of the system applied, and particularly the rules of origin, must be such as to avoid any risk of 'trade deflection' to the detriment of the Community resulting from the participation of those States in a customs union with a third country, namely South Africa.

The Protocol further made it clear that the accession of the three new Member States to the EEC and the possible extension of the policy of association to the independent developing Commonwealth countries, 'should not be the source of any weakening in the Community's relations with the AASM' which were parties to the Convention signed on 29th May 1969. The Community's relations with the AASM, according to the Protocol

ensure for those States a range of advantages and are based on structures which give the Association its distinctive character in the fields of trade relations, financial and technical co-operation and joint institutions.

The Community's objective in its policy of association should therefore remain the 'safeguarding of what has been achieved and of fundamental principles referred to'.

The Protocol finally pointed out that the provisions of this association, which were to be defined during the negotiations, must similarly take account of the special economic conditions common to the independent developing Commonwealth countries and the AASM, the experience acquired within the framework of association, the wishes of the associated states, and the consequences for those states of the introduction of the generalised schemes of preferences.

The Community was to have as its firm purpose the safeguarding of the interests of all the countries referred to in the Protocol 'whose economies depend to a considerable extent on the export of primary products' and particularly sugar, which was to be settled within this framework, bearing in mind its importance for the economies of several of these countries and of the Commonwealth countries in particular.

The position of the AASM, the Arusha Group, and the countries not as yet associated with the EEC, was at this stage not very clear in relation to the new association. No clear strategic position in regard to the negotiations was emerging. This situation, which clearly reflected their inherent weakness, soon gave way to a number of steps taken to create a *modus operandi* for the group as a whole. The possibilities of a united front emerged during a number of meetings of the AASM, the Arusha Group, and other African countries. The earlier meetings culminated in the Nairobi ministerial conference, which spelt out the strategy. By the time of the Egemont Palace (Brussels) meeting which set in motion the negotiations on 25-26th July 1973, a 'united position' had emerged. This position, which was put across by Mr. Wenike Briggs, Commissioner of Trade of the Federal Military Government of Nigeria, as spokesman of the 'African Group', was later endorsed by Mr. Ratu Sir Kamisese Lara, Prime Minister of Fiji, speaking on behalf of the Pacific States, and Mr. S.S. Ramphal, Minister of Foreign Affairs of Guyana, on behalf of the Caribbean States. The positions were now converging into an 'ACP platform'.

The substance of the 'united front' position as outlined by Briggs was contained in a number of 'principles'. Firstly, it was emphasised that there would be no reciprocity in the trade deals to be arrived at, as such a principle was only suitable for countries at the same level of development. Ramphal said at this meeting, 'there can be no equality among unequals'. Secondly, it was pointed out that any rights of establishment accorded to the EEC by the ACP States would have to be extended to third countries non-discriminatorily. This took a position against the Yaoundé and Arusha agreements in which such rights were available only to the EEC.

Thirdly, the principles pointed out that the revision of the rules of origin must be formulated so as to 'facilitate the industrial integration' of ACP countries, and in particular the rules had to grant the status of 'originating products' to all goods which had been produced in one or several of the ACP countries, or which had been processed in accordance with mutually accepted criteria, irrespective of whether or not they enjoyed preferential relations with the EEC.

Fourthly, a revision of the provisions relating to the movement of payments and capital movements was to take into account the objectives of monetary independence of the ACP States, and the need for their monetary co-operation. Moreover, there was need to dissociate financial and technical aid from any particular form of relationship with the EEC.

Fifthly, 'free and assured access' to EEC markets for all products of ACP States including processed and semi-processed agricultural products, whether or not they were subject to the Common Agricultural Policy of the EEC, was demanded. Finally, the ACP insisted on 'guaranteed stable, equitable and remunerative prices' in the EEC markets for their main products, to enable them to increase their export earnings. They also requested the EEC to place special emphasis on the transfer of technology to them on 'easy and acceptable terms'. These principles set the ground for the prolonged negotiations that ensued in the next twenty months, beginning as we have observed with the Egemont Palace inaugural meeting.

II

When the Egemont Palace inaugural conference assembled, the position of the ACP countries was crystallising. The EEC however appeared to play it cool, for they had nothing to gain by being forthright at this stage. They were well-advised to do so, since putting firm positions from the start might have made the negotiations impossible. Moreover, in dealings with their former colonies they knew how best to handle particular situations with them. This paid them ultimately, and although the ACP States in the end emerged declaring 'victory', it was not so clear-cut a victory for them as they assumed.

The EEC general stand was enunciated by Mr. Ivar Norgaard, Foreign Minister of Denmark, at the Egemont Palace meeting on 25th July 1973. He merely spelt out the provisions of Protocol No. 22 already referred to. He also contented himself with an outline of the history of the AASM Conventions and the Arusha agreements, and stressed that in choosing the three alternative options the ACP States were 'absolutely free' in doing so. He outlined principles for future agreement but these were general and non-committal. Firstly, trade arrangements providing especially for free entry into the Community of most of the products of the associated states would be defined during the negotiations for similar and competitive agricultural products. Secondly, there would be the safeguarding of interests of the associated states whose economies depended to a large extent on the export of primary products. Thirdly, the financial aid provisions, securing for the ASM advantages which overall were equivalent to those they currently enjoyed, and the placing of the new associated states on an equal footing, would be assured. Finally, the implementation of the agreement by the parties would be through joint association institutions, which the Community suggested should consist of an association council assisted by an association committee; a parliamentary conference of association assisted by a joint committee on the basis of parity; and a court of arbitration of the association. He also suggested that the association should last for five years.

If nothing dramatic emerged in this first conference it was because it was left to the negotiators to go into detailed discussions between major conferences. For the ACP countries these were the ambassadors and representatives at Brussels, who were entrusted after Egemont Palace to prepare for the African Trade Ministers Conference to be held in Dar es Salaam 1st-3rd October 1973. At the end of the Dar es Salaam meeting it was agreed to maintain the agreed platform. Furthermore, the negotiating procedures drawn up by the ambassadors and representatives were adopted.

A roundtable conference was expected to be held in October between the ACP and the EEC, but by then not much progress had been achieved between the two sides. Indeed, the progress reported at the end of the third stage, at the beginning of June 1974 at Dakar, showed that no agreement had as yet been reached on a majority of the issues raised by the ACP, not even on general principles. Thus whereas the EEC had responded to the issue of free and unlimited access, all that they could assure was free entry for certain processed agricultural products subject to special arrangements. No agreement was recorded on the issue of the removal of all tariff and non-tariff barriers. Elimination of these barriers required action at EEC national level, for instance in health and sanitary regulations. The EEC took a position that these were to be left to individual EEC governments. The ACP demand that all quantitative restrictions applied to trade be removed only elicited a minor response from the EEC. It was prepared not to include restrictions which hitherto had been applied to a number of products. On products falling within the Common Agricultural Policy in the EEC, the ACP request for all their agricultural products subject to the policy to be admitted free with unlimited access was not accepted by the EEC, on the grounds that not all these products were of economic importance to the ACP States and they could not accept a blanket approach. They could instead be considered on a case-by-case basis.

With regard to the rules of origin, not much progress was recorded at this stage. While all agreed that the rules should be simple, flexible and liberal, the only agreement recorded was that the ACP and the EEC accepted to continue with the current rules defining a wholly-produced commodity. Whilst both parties considered it desirable to redefine the expression 'their vessels', there were still divergent views. Whereas the ACP would have preferred a definition based on a more than 25 per cent ownership of the vessel by the public authorities or nationals and companies, or vessels chartered or leased by these, the EEC preferred a distinction between fisheries taken from territorial waters and outside them in order to 'enable the development' of the ACP fishery fleet. Nevertheless, no agreement could be recorded.

As regards the transformation criterion, where the ACP regarded a 25 per cent processing and value-added which resulted in a change in the Brussels Nomenclature (BTN) heading,[3] the EEC rejected the 25 per cent stating that such a criterion could not 'stimulate any genuine industrialisation'. It would appear that the EEC still insisted on the 50 per cent criterion in the Yaoundé and Arusha agreements. Moreover, the EEC could not accept the non-cumulative treatment of origin which would have regarded all materials imported from developing countries used in the processing of commodities as originating from the ACP countries. Instead it was prepared to limit the cumulative treatment of origin to member countries of regional groups such as customs unions which were existing or about to be so. There remained outstanding issues on basic materials list and on direct consignment, on which agreement also could not be recorded.

On the 'rights of establishment' the ACP position had been that these rights should be open to all countries. At this stage the EEC could only say that they were prepared to replace the term with 'rules or arrangement of establishment' in order to eliminate 'ambiguities'. They agreed that the ACP should work out their respective policies on this as 'sovereign nations', and that they should be entirely free to decide what treatment they would give nationals and firms of the Community countries. But they insisted on two principles. First, there should be no discrimination as between nationals or companies, of the member states of the EEC. Second, if the ACP apply a favourable treatment to a third country, then the ACP must apply the most-favoured-nation treatment to the EEC countries, except that they would be prepared not to insist on this if the third country were a developing country. On this basis they were prepared on grounds of reciprocity to extend similar rights in the EEC to the ACP countries.

On the crucial question of current payments and movement of capital, the ACP position was similar to that advanced in relation to the rights of establishment. Whilst the EEC were ready to recognise the 'monetary independence' of the ACP, ruling out any monetary links between the EEC and the ACP, it however insisted on three main points. First, the parties should authorise payments connected either with trade or with arrangements relating financial and technical co-operation. Second, there should be no discrimination against nationals or companies of the different EEC member states in matters relating to investment or capital movements. Third, the most-favoured-nation principle ought to apply to all current payments and capital movements, save that this would not apply where the third country involved was a developing one.

No economic, financial or technical co-operation proposals were forthcoming at this stage. Whereas the ACP wanted provisions aimed at achieving the overall objectives through 'joint approach' in this field, with the aim of correcting the 'structural imbalances' in the various sectors of ACP economies, as well as to 'bring about economic development' of ACP States, the EEC on the other hand suggested dealing with this issue when all the patterns of co-operation on industry, commerce etc., had been definitely worked out. Similarly the scope of aid, the EEC pointed out, should be determined in the light of the objectives of the Association. Here several procedural agreements were recorded which paved the way for the drawing up of the final document, as we shall see. These procedural matters were basically concerned with the manner and purposes of giving aid, the type of projects, and the management and administration as well as the tendering and awarding of contracts. The ACP wanted the ceiling of the amounts of aid to be raised from the 500,000 units of account proposed by the EEC to 3 million units of account. The EEC could only go as far as one million units of account. This was before the panic over the 'oil crisis' impact on reserves was voiced. This demand for aid, as we shall see, was to be raised by the ACP to 8,000 million units. Certain percentages of preferential margins in the granting of tenders to ACP firms were also proposed.

Various other matters of co-operation were proposed by the ACP, including regional groupings of the ACP countries to 'promote and accelerate the diversification' of their economies, as well as the elimination of the 'dependence on imports' in order to maximise the production of those products for which the ACP States had 'production potential'. It was further proposed that markets of the ACP States should be opened up in order to promote trade, and to encourage the 'maximisation of resources and services' in those countries. To these issues the EEC added four points. First, that technical assistance for regional bodies be encouraged; second, that there should be a regional 'dimension' in the planning and use of aid; third, that there should be financial support for individual 'agreements to open up markets'; and fourth, there should be a reserve of EDF for regional co-operation measures.

As can be seen from the survey above, the EEC was not moving in a hurry. It played a game which persuaded the other side to put on the table all they proposed before responding. Since the ACP had exhausted themselves it fell on them to make the next move. This was forthcoming when the ACP ministers took the initiative of inviting the EEC to a conference at ministerial level in Kingston, Jamaica, at the end of July 1974. This conference opened with an impassioned speech by the Jamaican Prime Minister Michael Manley, in which he expressed despair at the 'insensitivity of our metropolitan friends' to the ACP positions. Very soon some dramatic 'breakthroughs' were announced, on 27th July 1974.

First, the EEC was now prepared to abandon any reciprocity requirement on the trade side. This was because 'the participants recognised that the keynote should be stability', and further that the developing countries 'were in an unequal position *vis-à-vis* their partners'. For this reason 'the main feature of these arrangements will be free access for the ACP States to the Community market, no corresponding commitments being required of the ACP States'.[4] Second, the parties recorded their definite agreement on the system of export receipts stabilisation as proposed by the EEC Commission. A list of products to which the envisaged provisions were to apply was to be drawn up by common agreement between the parties. The criteria to be taken into account were to be non-restrictive and these had to take into consideration factors such as employment, decreases in export earnings, fluctuations on world markets affecting exports to third countries, the deterioration of terms of trade, the level of development of the country concerned, and its geographical position (favouring landlocked and least-developed countries and islands). In the event of there being a decrease in export earning for one year, due to fluctuations in price or quantities, the country affected would be entitled to ask for a financial transfer.

Third, it was agreed that industrialisation should receive special attention and a chapter in the Convention should be devoted to it. The EEC 'took note' of the ACP memorandum on this issue, 'confirmed its agreement on the general aims of the memorandum', and agreed that the two parties should continue to examine the subjects in Brussels. This memorandum envisaged an 'international division of labour' which took into account 'our interests and priorities', which involved: (i) the transfer of technology; (ii) the transfer of techniques adapted to the specific needs and requirements of the ACP States; (iii) the conclusion of agreements between European private industry and the ACP States, with a view to strengthening control of the industrial sectors; and (iv) adjustment of the types of production in the Community. These proposals were basically incorporated into the Lomé Convention.

Fourth, as regards rules of origin it was agreed that the principle for determining origin was that of change in the BTN heading, but that exceptions had to be examined including the protective element thereof. Where however the required tariff heading did not take place, then there had to be a certain minimum percentage in the value-added of the product. It was 'noted' that the ACP proposed a twenty-five percentage minimum. As far as non-tariff barriers were concerned, the Community acknowledged the fact that the existence of health, plant-health, and administrative provisions represented a restriction on free access to its market. They however drew the attention of the ACP countries to the fact that these rules, by virtue of their basis, applied *erga omnes,* and that it would be very difficult to derogate from them. It was however agreed that the Convention should make provision for consultation procedure in any cases where practical difficulties arose, due either to existing regulations, or to the harmonisation of the regulations of the Member States of the Community, in order to minimise the adverse effect on free access.

No concrete agreements were reached on financial aid, but it became apparent in the corridors that the EEC were prepared to treble the EDF resources to 3,000 million units of accounts, while the ACP were now putting up the figure of 8,000 million units of account. But clearly the EEC was the only one that could decide this matter. Since the Yaoundé Convention and the Arusha Agreement were due to expire on 31st January 1975, and since it was becoming clear that no Convention would be ready by then, thoughts were entertained for transitional measures, but these did not materialise. Two further ministerial meetings were scheduled for 13th and 30th January 1975. The last meeting was a marathon one covering last-minute issues including rum, bananas, sugar and the amount of financial aid. One of the last problems, of sugar, was resolved with a sugar protocol which provided that the Community would buy 1.4 million tons of sugar from ACP countries. The Lomé Convention thus was ready for signature on 28th February 1975 in the Togolese capital.

III

The Convention has seven titles, seven protocols, a final act, an agreement on products within the province of the European coal and steel community, and twenty-four annexes containing joint declarations. The titles each contain chapters and articles dealing with specific areas of agreement, as follows:

Title I:	Trade co-operation
Title II:	Export earnings from commodities
Title III:	Industrial co-operation
Title IV:	Financial and technical co-operation
Title V:	Provisions relating to establishment, services, payments and capital movements
Title VI:	Institutions
Title VII:	General and final provisions

The protocols contain detailed treatment of concepts; administrative arrangements for financial and technical co-operation; particular commodities (sugar, bananas and rum); operating expenditure of the institutions, as well as the privileges and immunities of the personnel. The Convention is signed by the heads of states of the nine European States, both severally and jointly as Contracting Parties to the Treaty establishing the European Economic Community signed at Rome on 25th March 1957, on the one part and the forty-six ACP heads of states, severally only, on the other part, since they negotiated as a group formally but in actual fact as separate entities. This constituted the basic point of strength and weakness, since the nine were an imperialist economic group and the forty-six weak States were still under the monopoly control of post-war multilateral imperialism.

To be sure, this fundamental distinction is mystified in the preamble to the Convention wherein it is declared that the parties are 'anxious to establish, *on the basis of complete equality between partners,* close and continuing co-operation, in the spirit of international solidarity' [emphasis added]. It was emphasised throughout by the ACP States in their negotiations with the EEC that they were not equal with them. Indeed, as the Guyanese Minister of Foreign Affairs, Ramphal, stated in the inaugural meeting:

> Reciprocity between those who are unequal in economic strength is a contradiction in terms. In contemporary international economic relations, Aristotle's dictum that 'justice requires equality between equals but proportionality between unequals' must surely mean as between those who are unequal in economic strength. Equity itself demands non-reciprocity.

Unfortunately, the court of equity in which such nice principles of human ethics would be argued is nonexistent, and the brutal facts of life under multilateral imperialism do not need an agreement of 'equal partners' to assert themselves. Indeed, the provisions of the Convention attest themselves to the inequality of the parties, and inequality in the material conditions of existence of the forty-six and the nine necessarily implies the exploitation of the one by the other—reciprocity or no reciprocity. If agreements were able to remove these exploitative relationships, then the history of the last five hundred years, and of the last one hundred in particular, would be otherwise. Such is the story and essence of the provisions of the Convention.

A. TRADE CO-OPERATION

The provisions relating to trade co-operation in the Convention are contained in two chapters and 15 articles. It is stated that the object is to promote trade between the parties, 'taking account of their respective levels of development', and in particular of the need to secure 'additional benefits' for the trade of ACP States, in order to 'accelerate the rate of growth' of their trade and improve conditions of access of their products to the European market, so as to 'ensure a better balance' in the trade of the contracting parties [Art. 1].

To this end it is provided that products originating in the ACP States shall be imported into the Community 'free of customs duties and charges having equivalent effect', save that such treatment shall not be more favourable than that applied by the Member States among themselves [Art. 2:1]. This treatment however is subjected to qualification, as is to be expected. Products originating in the ACP States which are listed (in Annex II to the Rome Treaty), when they come under the 'common organisation of the markets' as stipulated under

Article 40 of the Rome Treaty, or those subject, on importation into the Community, to specific rules under the common agricultural policy of the Community, shall be imported into the Community duty-free if the provisions in the EEC for their importation do not provide, apart from customs duties, for the application of any other measures relating to their importation. For other products the Community is to take necessary measures to ensure, as a general rule, more favourable treatment than the general treatment applicable to the same products originating in third countries to which the most-favoured-nation clause applies [Art. 2:2].

The effect of this qualification is to exclude a wide range of products from automatic 'duty-free' treatment and to subject them to levies under the rules of the Community's common agricultural policy, or to the most-favoured-nation treatment, subject to the EEC according them a more favourable treatment. The products listed in Annex II to the Treaty are quite wide-ranging and are of 'particular interest' to the ACP States. They include products such as live animals, meat, fish, edible vegetables, fruit, coffee, tea and spices, cereals, fats and oils, beet sugar and cane sugar, molasses, syrups, cocoa, beans, and unmanufactured tobacco. Although there are provisions for consultations in the Council of Ministers which is established under the Convention, the decision as to which products will enjoy the most-favoured-nation treatment is entirely in the EEC hands.

It is further provided that the Community shall not apply to the imports originating in the ACP States any quantitative restrictions or measures having equivalent effect, other than those applied by members among themselves, save that products referred to and listed under Annex II to the Treaty which are subject to residual quantitative restrictions are to be unaffected by this provision, and save that products which come under international commodity agreements to which ACP States are parties are also to be unaffected by this provision [Art. 3]. This would exclude products like coffee, cocoa, and sugar.

The Community is granted the right to exclude products from importation into the Community on grounds of public morality, public policy or public security; the protection of health and life of humans, animals and plants; the protection of national treasures possessing artistic, historic, or archaeological value, or the protection of industrial and commercial property [Art. 4]. This is a normal umbrella provision which most states reserve, but which specifically in the case of the ACP States would exclude products produced under infringed patent rights for one, or products considered 'harmful' on security, health and moral grounds.

The 'victory' of the ACP States in their twenty-month-long negotiations on the question of reciprocity is recorded in Article 7 of the Convention. It is provided here that, in view of their present development needs, for the duration of the Convention the ACP States shall not be required to assume obligations, in respect of imports of products originating in the Community, corresponding to the commitments entered into by the Community in respect to the products originating in the ACP States, except that the ACP States shall not in their trade with the Community discriminate among Member States, and shall grant to the Community treatment no less favourable than that granted to the most-favoured-nation, save those as between developing countries. The effect of this provision is to discontinue the so-called reverse preferences that the Yaoundé and Arusha accords granted to the EEC, something the US and Japanese monopolies detested.

These apparent liberal 'concessions' by the EEC to the ACP States must not however obscure the fact that the products 'originating' from the ACP are subjected to a stringent definition in a Protocol which covers more space than the trade concessions themselves. We will look at this definition in a later section. Moreover, it is provided that the Community shall be entitled to take 'the necessary safeguard measures' if, as a result of the application of these provisions, 'serious disturbances occur in a sector of the economy of the Community' or of one or more Member States, or which 'jeopardise their external financial stability', or difficulties arise which may result in a deterioration in a sector of the economy of a region of the Community.

These safeguard measures are however to be taken in a way which gives 'priority' to such measures as would least disturb the trade relations, and shall not exceed the limits of what is strictly necessary to remedy the difficulties that have arisen. A number of provisions are made for consultations either within the Council of Ministers, or by each of the Contracting Parties informing the other in matters connected with these measures [Art. 11].

Finally, provision is made for trade promotion activities, with a view to attaining the objectives set as regards trade and industrial co-operation. The ACP States are to be assisted in these activities to 'derive maximum benefit' and to participate under 'most favourable conditions' in the Community, regional and international markets. These activities are to include the improvement of the structure and working methods of organisations, departments or firms contributing to the development of the foreign trade of the ACP States, or their setting up. It is also intended to provide training or advanced vocational training of staff in trade promotion, as well as to provide for the participation by ACP States in fairs, exhibitions, specialised international shows and the organisation of trade events. Other activities are to include carrying out and making use of market research and marketing studies; as well as producing and distributing trade information in various forms in the Community and ACP States. Applications for financing of these activities are to be lodged to the Community by the respective ACP States under conditions provided for financial and technical co-operation in Title IV.

B. EXPORT EARNINGS FROM COMMODITIES—'STABEX'

One of the 'most important' agreements recorded for which ACP States pressed the Community is in regard to the stabilisation of export earnings. A list of commodities is drawn up taking account of factors such as employment, deterioration of terms of trade, the level of development and the particular difficulties of the least developed, land-locked, or island ACP States listed in Article 24 [Art. 7].[5] These products include groundnuts, cocoa, coffee, cotton, coconut palm, palmnut and kernel products as well as raw hides, skins and leather, wood products, fresh bananas, tea, raw sisal, and iron ore.

The system of stabilisation is only to apply to the ACP export earnings if during the year preceding the year of application earnings from the export of products to all destinations represented at least 7.5 per cent of its total earnings from merchandise exports, but for sisal the percentage is fixed at 5 per cent. Exception is made for the least developed, landlocked or island ACP States and the percentage here is fixed at 2.5 per cent. Provision is made for adding to the list of products; and for special cases the system is to apply irrespective of destination of the product, but the ACP States must certify that these products originate in their territory [Art. 17]. A total of 375 million units of accounts is set aside by the Community for this stabilisation system for the duration of the Convention, covering 'all its commitments under the said system', which is to be managed by the Commission of the European Communities (the Commission). The amount is to be divided into five equal instalments, and for every year except the last, the Council of Ministers may authorise, where required, use in advance of a maximum of 20 per cent of the following year's instalment [Art. 18].

In order to implement the system a 'reference level' is to be calculated for each ACP State for each product, which shall correspond to the component of export earnings during the four years preceding each year of application. On this basis an ACP State shall be entitled to a financial transfer, if on the basis of the results of the calendar year its actual earnings, as defined in Article 17 referred to, from each of the products considered individually, are at least 7.5 per cent below the reference level, and 2.5 per cent for the least developed, landlocked and island states. The request for the transfer is to be addressed to the Commission, which is to examine it in the light of the resources available. The difference between the reference level and actual earnings shall constitute the basis of the transfer. No transfer however will be made if the fall in earnings is the result of 'a trade policy of the ACP State concerned adversely affecting exports to the Community'. The transfers are to be made rapidly, by means of advances, normally six-monthly [Art. 19].

Thus if we were to assume a reference value of 10,000 (which is obtained by multiplying a reference unit value of 100 by a reference quantity of 100), and country X is assumed to have received during the preceding year a transfer of 1000, if then for the current year:

Case 1:   Actual unit value is 120 and the actual quantities are 80,
so that actual earnings are 9,600; country X will receive a
transfer of 400, despite the fact that the unit value had risen.

Case 2:   Actual unit value is 105 and the actual quantities are 100
so that actual earnings are 10,500; country X would pay
back 500.

We will see that these computations are important for another reason.
The Convention requires that the countries that have received transfers
under Stabex are to reconstitute the transfers.

Provision is made to the effect that the ACP State is to decide how
to use the transferred resources but it has to inform the Commission
annually of the use to which it has put the resources [Art. 20]. There is
no interest chargeable on the transferred amounts, but the recipients
are required to contribute in the five years following the allocation of
each transfer, *towards the reconstitution of the resources made
available for the system by the Community,* if its earnings are found to
so permit. For this reason the Commission has to determine whether
the unit value of the exports is higher than the reference unit value;
and the quantity actually exported to the Community is at least equal
to the reference quantity. *If the two conditions are met at the same
time, the recipient shall pay back into the system, within the limits of
the transfers it has received, an amount equal to the reference quantity
multiplied by the difference between the reference unit value and the
actual unit value.*

Thus in the above example, Case 1 country X will not reconstitute.
In Case 2 country X will reconstitute by paying back 500. Two other
illustrations will help to clarify the point further:

Case 3:   The actual unit value is 120, the actual quantities are 100,
the actual earnings being 12,000. In this case because
country X would have received a transfer of only 1000, it
will have to pay back into the system 1000, though its
actual earnings are 12,000.

Case 4:   The actual unit value is 100, the actual quantities 110.
Although its actual earnings are 11,000, country X will not
be required to pay back, since the actual unit value does not
exceed the reference unit value.

If at the end of the five-year period the resources are not fully
reconstituted, the Council of Ministers may decide to take one of two
decisions. It may decide that the sums outstanding are to be reconstituted wholly or partially, in one or more instalments; or that
rights to repayment are to be waived. This the Council will do after
taking into consideration the situation of and prospects for the balance
of payments, exchange reserves and foreign indebtedness of the ACP
State concerned. It is however provided that the reconstitution provisions in this Article are not to apply to the ACP States listed in
Article 48 which are to be regarded as least developed, and to which
special measures established under that Article are made applicable

[Art. 21].[6]

It is further provided that each transfer is to be concluded in a 'transfer agreement' which is to be signed by the Commission and the ACP State concerned [Art. 22]. Provision is also made for the Council of Ministers by mutual agreement to make practical measures to facilitate exchange of information and the submission of requests for transfers by 'producing a form for requesting transfers'. Moreover it is stipulated that in order to ensure the smooth functioning of the stabilisation system, statistical and customs co-operation shall be instituted between the Community and the ACP States [Art. 23].

Specific provisions are made for guaranteeing prices and definite quantities of cane sugar. It is provided that, notwithstanding any other provision in the Convention, the Community undertakes for an indefinite period to purchase and import, at guaranteed prices, specific quantities of cane sugar, raw or white, which originate in the ACP States producing and exporting cane sugar and which those states undertake to deliver to it [Art. 25]. The conditions for the implementation of this provision are contained in a Protocol No. 3 annexed to the Convention. The Protocol stipulates that the safeguard measures in Article 10 are not to apply to this scheme, which is made fixed for a period of five years from the date the Convention comes into force. After that date, changes in the provisions may be made provided that the conditions for implementing the guarantee shall be re-examined before the end of the seventh year of their application. It is not indicated as to what effect this latter provision would have if the Convention were to irrenewably come to an end after the stipulated period of five years. But it is provided in Article 10 of the Protocol that the provisions of the Protocol shall remain in force for five years, i.e. up to 1st March 1980, and after that date the Protocol may be denounced by the Community with respect to each ACP State and by each ACP State with respect to the Community, subject to two years' notice.

The Protocol lists the quantities of cane sugar guaranteed against each country, with Mauritius taking the greater share of 487,000 metric tons of white sugar, and Kenya and Uganda taking the least share of 5,000 metric tons.[7] These quantities cannot be reduced without the consent of the individual states concerned. Nevertheless, for the period up to 30th June 1975 the agreed quantities are fixed in the Protocol.[8]

The white and raw sugar sold under the Convention is however to be marketed on the Community market at prices 'freely negotiated between buyers and sellers', and the Community is not to intervene if and when a Member State allows a selling price within its borders to exceed the Community's threshold price.[9] The Community however undertakes to purchase, at the guaranteed price, quantities of white or raw sugar, within agreed quantities, which cannot be marketed in the Community at a price equivalent to or in excess of the guaranteed price. The guaranteed price, expressed in units of account, is to be negotiated annually, *within the price range obtaining in the Community,* 'taking

into account all relevant economic factors'. Nevertheless, under an
Annex to the Protocol it is stipulated that for the period from 1st
February 1975 to 30th June 1976, and in respect of the quantities
specified, the guaranteed price shall be 25.53 units of account per 100
kilogrammes of raw sugar, and 31.72 units of account per 100 kilogrammes of white sugar standard quality as defined in Community
rules, unpacked, CIF European ports of the Community.

C. INDUSTRIAL, FINANCIAL AND TECHNICAL CO-OPERATION

With regard to industrial co-operation, the Convention seeks to achieve
the following objectives, among others:

(a) to promote the development and diversification of industry in
the ACP States and to help bring about a better distribution of
industry both within those states and between them;

(b) to promote new relations in the industrial field between the
Community, its Member States and the ACP States, in particular the
establishment of new industrial and trade links between the industries
of the Member States and those of the ACP States;

(c) to facilitate the transfer of technology to the ACP States and to
promote the adaptation of such technology to their specific needs and
conditions;

(d) to promote the marketing of industrial products of ACP States
in foreign markets in order to increase their share of international trade
in those products;

(e) to encourage participation of nationals of ACP States in small
and medium-sized industrial firms, in the industrial development of
those states;

(f) to encourage Community firms to participate in the industrial
development of the ACP States, where those states so desire and in
accordance with their economic and social objectives [Art. 26].

To those ends the Community is to help carry out, by all means
provided in the Convention, projects and schemes submitted to it on
behalf of or in agreement with the ACP States in the fields of industrial
infrastructures and ventures, training, technology, and research, small
and medium-sized firms, industrial information and promotion, and
trade co-operation [Art. 27]. The Community shall contribute to the
setting up of the infrastructure necessary for industrial development,
particularly in the fields of transport and communications, energy,
industrial research, and training [Art. 28]. It shall also contribute to
the setting up of industries processing raw materials and industries
manufacturing finished and semi-manufactured goods [Art. 29]. The
development of small and medium-sized firms shall, as far as possible,
be 'conducive to the complimentary relationship' between them and
'their links with large industrial firms' [Art. 32].

A Committee on Industrial Co-operation is to be set up, to be
supervised by the Committee of Ambassadors, to see to the implementation of the Title on industrial co-operation and to guide, supervise,

and control the activities of the Centre for Industrial Development, whose function is to gather and disseminate all relevant information on the conditions of and opportunities for industrial co-operation, as well as to carry out studies, organise and facilitate contacts and meetings between community and ACP 'industrial policy-makers, promoters, and firms and financial institutions' [Art. 36].

The financial and technical co-operation is intended to 'correct the structural imbalances in the various sectors' of the ACP States' economies. Hence the co-operation shall 'relate to the execution of projects and programmes which contribute essentially to the economic and social development of the said states' [Art. 40]. Protocol No. 2 to the Convention then stipulates that these programmes must ensure growth of the national income of each of the ACP States; and the improvement of the standard of living and the socio-cultural levels of populations and of the 'most unprivileged in particular'. It is also stipulated that more balanced economic relations with other countries should be established in order to bring about the improvement of the conditions of development, diversification and integration of the structure of the economy, as well as the encouragement of regional co-operation between ACP States.

The Council of Ministers is to define the policy and guidelines of financial and technical co-operation and it shall formulate resolutions on the measures to be taken by the Community and the ACP States. For the duration of the Convention the overall amount of the Community's aid is put at 3,390 million units of account, which will comprise 3,300 million units of account from the European Development Fund (EDF), and 390 million units of account from the European Investment Bank (EIB) in the form of loans at 3 per cent interest rate subsidy, which are to be charged against the aid from the EDF as stipulated above. The unit of account is defined by Annex XVII as equivalent to an IMF special drawing right (SDR), which is about a dollar. The duration of loans is up to 25 years according to the Protocol, and the interest rates subsidy may be adjusted so that the interest rate borne by the borrower is not less than 5 per cent or more than 8 per cent, where the loan is in the oil or mining sectors. Of these total funds, 2,100 million units of account will be in the form of grants; 430 million units of accounts in the form of special loans; and 95 million units of account in the form of risk capital. A total of 150 million units of account are to be spent in the French Overseas Territories and Countries (OTC) [Art. 42]. The tabulation below summarises this situation.

	ACP	OTC	TOTAL
Non-repayable grants	2,100	120	
Loans on special terms	430		2,650
Risk capital	95	5	100
Stabex*	375	25	400
Total from EDF	3,000	150	3,150
EIB loans on normal terms	390	10	400
	3,390	160	3,550

*stabilisation of export earnings

It is provided that, with the agreement of the ACP States concerned, financial aid from the Community may take the form of co-financing with participation by, in particular, credit and development agencies and institutions, firms, Member States, ACP States, third countries and international finance organisations [Art. 44]. The projects and programmes are to be in the field of agriculture; technical co-operation particularly in the fields of training and technological adaptation and innovations, industrial and sales promotion, as well as microprojects and 'grassroots development'. The aid may also cover import costs and local expenditure required for execution of projects and programmes [Art. 46]. It is stipulated that 10 per cent of the total financial aid is to be spent on the economic and social development of ACP States in the area of regional co-operation. These regional projects are intended to create 'sufficiently wide markets' within the ACP States and neighbouring states by 'removing the obstacles which hinder the development and integration of those markets' in order to promote trade between ACP States [Art. 47]. Furthermore, special attention is to be paid to the needs of the twenty-four least-developed ACP States listed in the Article, on most favourable terms of financing [Art. 48].

It is emphasised that the financial aid shall be 'complimentary' to the ACP States' own effort, and shall be integrated in their economic and social development plans and programmes, so that projects undertaken with the financial support of the Community dovetail with their objectives and priorities. For this reason at the beginning of the period covered by the Convention the Community aid shall be programmed on the basis of proposals made by each ACP State in which it has fixed its objectives and priorities [Art. 51]. The Community may provide technical assistance for drawing up the dossiers of projects and programmes. The Community is given a right to appraise these projects and programmes in close collaboration with ACP States and 'any other beneficiaries' [Art. 53].

The financing proposals, which summarise the conclusions of the appraisals, are to be submitted to the Community's decision-making body, which shall in turn submit the final version simultaneously to the Community and the ACP State concerned. Provision is made for exceptional aid, which initially shall be fixed at 50 million units of account, but may not exceed 150 million units of account. This aid shall be non-reimbursable and is to be granted on a case-by-case basis, to help finance the most serious difficulties resulting from natural disasters or comparable extraordinary circumstances, but not from the harmful effects from the instability of export earnings [Art. 59]. Elaborate provisions are made in Protocol No. 2 for implementing these provisions, which it is not possible to summarise here, but which are all intended for the smooth execution of the aid.

D. ESTABLISHMENT, SERVICES, PAYMENTS AND CAPITAL MOVEMENTS.
   INSTITUTIONS; AND GENERAL AND FINAL PROVISIONS
Consistent with the post-war strategy of imperialist predivision of markets on the basis of the open door policy, the Convention requires the ACP States to 'treat the nationals and companies or firms of Member States and firms of the ACP States respectively on a non-discriminatory basis' on matters connected with establishment and provision of services, unless for a given activity the ACP States and Member States wish to withhold such treatment [Art. 62]. With regard to capital movements linked with investments and to current payments, the Contracting Parties are expected to refrain from taking action in the field of foreign exchange transactions which would 'be incompatible with their obligations under this Convention resulting from the provisions relating to trade in goods, to services, establishment and industrial co-operation'. Although this is apparently addressed to all the Contracting Parties, it has effect only on ACP States in actual fact. The ACP States are however allowed to adopt 'necessary protective measures should this be justified by reasons relating to serious economic difficulties or severe balance of payments problems' [Art. 65]. The ACP States and Member States are expected not to take discriminatory measures against each other, or accord more favourable treatment to third countries. The parties must take into full account the evolving nature of the international monetary system, the existence of specific monetary arrangements, and balance of payments problems, as well as the international monetary rules [Art. 66]. Specific provision is made for foreign exchange to cover payments of interest on loans and risk capital [Art. 67].

The Convention sets up a number of institutions for the association. A Council of Ministers is established, as well as a Consultative Assembly. A Committee of Ambassadors is also set up to assist the Council of Ministers [Art. 69]. The Council is to be composed of, on the one hand, members of the Council and Commission of European Communities, and on the other, a member of the Government of each of the ACP States. The proceedings are only valid if half the members of the Council of Europe and one member of the Commission, as well as two-thirds of the ACP-accredited members, are present [Art. 70]. The Council is to be held once a year at least [Art. 71]; and the Presidency is to be held alternately between EEC and ACP States

[Art. 71]. An 'internal Protocol' is to lay down the procedure for arriving at respective positions, and the Ministers are to act by 'mutual agreement' [Art. 73]. The duties of the Council are spelt out in detail in Articles 74-75. A Committee of Ambassadors is to be composed of one representative of each of the parties as well as a representative from the Commission [Art. 76]. The Consultative Assembly is to be composed *on the basis of parity* of members of the Assembly on the side of the Community and of representatives designated by the ACP States on the other. It is to meet once a year and the Council is to report on its activities to this Assembly [Art. 80]. Any dispute about the interpretation of the Convention is to be settled by the Council, but should they fail to do so arbitrators may be appointed by the Council [Art. 81].

The General Provisions stipulate that Title I of the Convention is to apply to relations between the French Overseas Departments and the ACP States [Art. 85]. The Convention is to enter into force on the first day of the second month following the date of deposit of at least two-thirds of instruments of ratification of the Member States and the ACP States, and of the act of notification of the conclusion of the Convention by the Community. Any ACP member which would have not done so would be allowed to complete these formalities within twelve months, unless notice is given that these will be completed in six months after this date, in which case the Convention will become applicable to those countries on the first day of the second month after such completion [Art. 87]. The Convention is to expire after a period of five years from the date of its signature, namely 1st March 1980. Eighteen months before the end of this period, the Contracting Parties are to enter into negotiations in order to examine what provisions shall subsequently govern relations between the Community and the ACP States. In the meantime the Council of Ministers may adopt transitional measures until the new Convention comes into force [Art. 91]. The Convention may however be denounced by the Community or the ACP States upon six months' notice [Art. 92]. Finally, it is provided that all the Protocols to the Convention are to form an integral part of it [Art. 93].

One such Protocol which requires our attention is Protocol No. 1, which is concerned with the definition of the concept of 'originating products'. It is stipulated in the various articles of the Protocol which products qualify as originating from the ACP States. It is provided that for the purpose of implementing the Convention the following products shall be considered as products originating in the ACP States, provided they are transported directly within the meaning of Article 5 of the Protocol: (a) products wholly obtained in one or more of the ACP States; (b) products obtained in one or more ACP States in the manufacturing of which products other than those in (a) above are used, and provided that they have undergone sufficient working or processing within the meaning of Article 3 of the Protocol.

It is further provided that, for the purposes of the provisions above, the ACP States shall be considered as being one territory, to the extent that the products 'wholly obtained', or 'worked and processed', within the meaning of Article 3 to the Protocol will be considered 'wholly obtained', or 'worked and processed' in the ACP States where the last working took place, on condition that the products were transported directly within the meaning of Article 5 of the Protocol [Art. 1].

The following products are considered 'wholly produced' in the ACP States: mineral products, vegetable products, live animals and products therefrom, products of sea-fishing and other products taken from the sea by 'their vessels', products made aboard their factory ships, as well as waste and scrap resulting from manufacturing operations [Art. 2].

Article 3 stipulates the manner in which a product may be worked and processed in order to qualify as 'originating product'. Two criteria are spelt out: (a) the working and processing must result in a classification under a tariff heading other than that covering each of the products worked or processed, with the exception of certain products listed in List A in Annex II to the Protocol, where the special provisions of that list apply; (b) working or processing in List B in Annex III. The lists spell out the percentage of the value of products to be added before the products qualify, which in most cases require a 50 per cent value-added of the value of total product [Art. 3].

Article 5 lays down conditions for 'direct transportation', and provides that originating products whose transport is effected without entering into the territory other than that of the parties concerned are considered as transported directly from the ACP States to the Community or vice versa. Originating goods constituting a single consignment may be transported through the territory otherwise than provided above, if the crossing of the latter territory is justified for geographical reasons or needs of transport and provided that the products have not entered into commerce or been delivered for home use and have not undergone operations other than unloading, reloading or any operation designed to preserve them in good condition. Evidence that these conditions have been fulfilled are to be supplied to the responsible customs authorities in the Community by the production of certificate or any substantial document [Art. 5]. Detailed provisions including approved forms are made for the proper administration of the Protocol.

The term 'their vessel' is specifically defined. This as we observed was one of the crucial areas of negotiation. It is provided that the term shall only apply to vessels which are registered or recorded in Member States or ACP States; which fly under the flag of the Member States or ACP States; which are owned to the extent of at least 50 per cent of nationals of the parties, and whose manager, chairman of the board and the majority of the members of such board are nationals of the parties; and of which at least 50 per cent of the crew, captain and officers are nationals of States party to the Convention.

These in brief constitute the summary of the provisions of the Convention.

IV

The trade provisions of the Convention have to be looked at closely with the other provisions, particularly those relating to financial and technical co-operation as well as payments and capital movements. They constitute the central logic of the 'deal'.

To be sure, the provision relating to non-reciprocity, under which the ACP States have 'free of duty' access to the markets of the EEC for certain types of 'their' products, is not a 'victory' for the ACP States but more correctly a victory for multilateral imperialism. The US and Japanese monopolies have insisted all the time that the ACP States must not grant 'reverse preferences' to the EEC if they expect the US and Japan to grant them 'preferences' in their own markets. It is for this reason that the two countries withheld the application of their generalised schemes of preferences to these ACP States in 1971. Indeed, the then President Nixon instructed his trade representative, William Erble, to demand at Brussels on 5th October 1973 that the EEC drop the idea of reverse preferences in the Lomé Convention and instead abide by 'international regulations', under the GATT rules.[10] This demand was indeed in line with the post-war policy of dissolving colonial markets and substituting open door neocolonial ones, under US hegemony. Indeed, US exports to the AASM alone had risen by 61 per cent between 1961 and 1971, and her insistence was clearly rooted in her interest to 'open up' ACP markets for this trade.

Thus the continuing efforts by the former European colonial powers to continue to 'associate' with their erstwhile colonial territories are part of this post-war struggle by the monopolies of the European countries against US and Japanese monopolies. This struggle (which is at the same time present within the EEC itself, as we have seen) is manifested in the various tariff and non-tariff barriers erected by each of the monopoly groups to protect its products produced by its capital in the ACP States and other third world countries. It is here that the 'paradox' of the imposition of barriers by the imperialist countries against cheap agricultural products from third world countries is explained. There is also the fact that the neocolonial strategy was not at the voluntary behest of the imperialist countries. The emergence of countries with a limited amount of independence, in an international environment where the socialist states existed, created a security problem for imperialism.

For this reason imperialism adjusted its policy of reliance on the colonies and neocolonies for the supply of certain vital food and other agricultural products, by encouraging through subsidy their production in the imperialist countries themselves.[11] This fact also meant that the imperialist countries would endeavour to export their products either to dispose of 'surpluses' or as a way of cutting costs. This is why today it is ironically possible for imperialist countries to export food products to the third world countries.

It is because of these combined circumstances that the so-called 'duty free' treatment is severely limited by the provisos enumerated in Article 1 (a) and (b), as well as the provision relating to the 'concept of originating products', the 'safeguard measures' and the non-tariff barriers. These provisions considerably limit the 'duty free' provisions and are compounded by inbuilt constraints, for instance in the stabilisation of export earnings which are restricted to particular products in particular quantities as well as the extension of aid and technical assistance to particular types of production in particular quantities.

The trade carried on under the Arusha Agreement clearly illustrates some of the above contradictions. Since we have already analysed this agreement before, it is not intended to go into it here again. But it is sufficient to note that the main peasant-produced crops like coffee, cotton, cashewnuts, etc., have continued, with slight diversification overall, to play the central role in these countries' export-oriented economies. There is no visible effort to develop an internal market in these products since their values must be realised in order to service the finance capital inputs in these and other sectors. Indeed, coffee alone accounted for about 50 per cent of all exports to the EEC (6) under Arusha. Then other crops followed like cotton, plantation sisal fibre and tow. The plantation crops apart from coffee and sisal, like pineapples, tea, and pyrethrum, exported as East African products, were products of monopolies like Del Monte (pineapples, passion fruits), and Brooke Bond (tea), which competed in the EEC with other monopoly exports of similar products from the USA etc. Del Monte is an interesting case because it is an American monopoly, and the keenest competitors in pineapple exports in the EEC were American monopolies. The tinned pineapple, passion fruit, meat, and pyrethrum extracts were 'processed and semi-processed' products subject to monopoly patent and trademark controls, and hence were subject to restrictive marketing provisions under the Paris Union Conventions.

The provisions regarding export stabilisation are not new in international trade, and more so in products from the ACP States and other 'Third World' countries. Indeed the price control schemes go back to the period before the First World War, and these were connected with and formed part of the 'general movement towards industrial combination, which ha[d] long been proceeding in all industrialised countries'.[12] These schemes themselves were 'fundamentally forms of monopolistic combination of the cartel type adapted to the rather different problems of and conditions of primary industries'. In the 1930s crisis these schemes included products like tin (Feb. 1931), sugar (May 1931), tea (April 1933), wheat (Aug. 1933), rubber (June 1934), and copper (Jan. 1936). After the second world war direct government control became a factor. The Havana Charter which was to be the basis of the International Trade Organisation had chapters devoted to commodity control schemes. The principles under the Charter have been applied with the approval of GATT, and under these principles a number of Commodity Agreements have been concluded, all with the purpose of stabilising prices among other things. These agreements have so far covered coffee, tin, sugar, wheat, and cocoa. They have however failed in stabilising the prices of these commodities, and some have ended up in collapse (e.g. coffee) in spite of efforts to reactivate them.

Under the first Yaoundé Convention the EEC provided 'aid' amounting to $33 million to maintain prices and ensure a minimum income to producers of certain products which were particularly exposed to fluctuations on the world market. The second Yaoundé Convention 'dropped' this type of 'rigid institutionalised price support system' and substituted a 'new more flexible form of aid', amounting to $80 million from the EDF. This was intended to 'meet exceptional circumstances' such as a 'drastic drop' in world market prices affecting 'a vital product' of the country concerned. In spite of this 'flexible form of aid' the EEC itself reported continuing fluctuations in the prices of these 'vital products', and the fluctuations were now blamed on the 'lack of provisions' in the Conventions to solve 'this problem in its general and long-term aspects'.[13]

The instability, which was due not only to price fluctuations but to quantities exported, was recorded between 1965 and 1969 in the AASM to a fall in average volume of groundnuts by 28 per cent 'under conditions where price instability at no time exceeded 10 per cent'. In the case of cotton the corresponding figure was 15 per cent volume fall and 3 per cent price instability. On these grounds the EEC concluded that the problem of the instability 'cannot be resolved simply by stabilising prices, on the one hand, or simply by concentrating on quantities, on the other'.[14]

The Lomé Convention comes no nearer to finding that 'long-term' solution. Indeed, the provisions are clear on its aim: to 'remedy the harmful effects' of the instability but on a limited number of products, 'taking account' of factors like terms of trade, employment etc. The amount of 375 million units of account (equivalent to $375 million) is part of the financial and technical 'aid'. There is no machinery for removing the tendencies to deterioration in terms of trade, since this is an inherent feature of monopoly capitalism. Moreover, the ACP States benefiting under the scheme are required to 'reconstitute' the amount unless the repayment is waived. This means that the so-called stabilisation transfer is in actual fact a short-term loan to tidy up the ACP State concerned while the prices are low, and to be repaid when they rise. The fact that thirty-four states are excluded from the requirement to reconstitute is not due to the 'magnanimity of mind' of the EEC to these countries, but is evidence of the brutal exploitation of these countries by imperialism. The amount if transferred would be 'aid', but an 'aid' that is intended to continue to tie them up in the same exploitative relationships which gave rise to their being 'least developed' in the first place. There is moreover no attempt to tie the drop in prices of these commodities to the increase in prices of manufactured products. This would be some solution to instability, but it is crying in the wilderness since it would rob monopoly of its essential attributes and such surrender never occurs over Conventions. The Tanzanian Minister of Commerce and Industries was perhaps expressing the feelings of his colleagues in the ACP when he made reservations on this scheme. He said, 'we do not regard this as a very significant step without price indexing for the essential items'.[15]

The list of products covered—12 products if treated by family and 29 if treated individually—gives a small proportion of the total number of products subject to instability. Most products which fall under the EEC CAP were excluded, as well as minerals. The only exception in this respect was iron ore, which was inserted for purposes of reaching agreement. Products of export interest vital to a number of countries, like beef products, fruits, manganese and bauxite, were excluded. Moreover, the amount of $375 million is rather meagre. If we take the earnings for 1973 from the 'Stabex' products, these amounted to 1,984.7 million units of account. [See Annex B.] This means that if these earnings fell by 7.5 per cent, $149 million units of account would be needed for a single year to stabilise prices. At present only a maximum of 90 million units of account can be made available under Stabex. This shows the restrictiveness of the scheme at best.

Again, the fixing of the reference level is arbitrary and excludes the possibility of transfers, except in very exceptional circumstances. If we look, for instance, at the prices of cocoa over the last four years we get the following picture:

YEAR	PRICE PER TON
1971-2	£250
1972-3	£400
1973-4	£700
1974-5	£650

Thus the price on the average was £500 per ton. On the present Lomé calculation, cocoa prices would have to fall below this reference level by 7.5 per cent before transfer. That is, the price must fall from £650 per ton to 7.5 per cent below £500 before Stabex can come into operation.

Finally, the requirement to reconstitute the transfers turns Stabex into no more than an AID scheme—which tides over the ACP States in rainy season only, and as soon as the day is brighter the EEC insists on settling accounts, with the dialectical effect of creating another rainy season. The fact that 'the least developed' need not reconstitute should not blind us, for this is evidence of imperialist exploitation of these countries.

This new craze of price stabilisation is likely to be a trump card in imperialist hands for a number of years. Indeed, UNCTAD has picked up the idea, and a proposal for the international stabilisation of eighteen major commodities as part of an 'integrated programme' has been drummed up from the UN General Assembly Special Session on Raw Materials. A total amount of $10 billion has been proposed to provide the stability to these eighteen basic commodities. This 'multi-dimensional' approach is supposed to work out an indexation of prices system to assist the bridging of the gap between commodity prices and the prices of manufactures. A programme for international commodity stocks is also proposed.[16] More, we are quite sure, will be heard about this 'new solution', but feelings of dissension have already been expressed. A Nigerian delegate, Akporode Clark, speaking at one of the UNCTAD meetings 'for the developing states', called the new pro-gramme 'an insurance scheme which benefits only when one is on one's deathbed'.[17]

The industrial co-operation provisions are closely linked to the financial and technical provisions. It would not be otherwise, for the amount of 'aid' and 'technical assistance' that can be extended are made possible through exploitation of labour in the EEC and in the ACP States, and through the monopoly control of technology. It is there-fore unrealistic to expect monopolies to grant meaningful aid and technical assistance to the ACP States, for them to use to interfere with the exploitation of that labour. Moreover, the use of such techni-cal assistance would enable these states under given conditions to develop their own industry and in the process their own technology, thus depriving the monopolies of their sole property which enables them to exercise the present world economic control.

As we have seen, monopoly capitalism and hence imperialism become a reality when a few large firms begin to concentrate technological know-how and protect it as a property against the whole world. In many cases a monopoly acquires new inventions and patents them to keep them away from competitors. The whole international patent system, based on national legislation and a convention on industrial properties of which the majority of ACP States are members, is intended to protect this basic 'right' of the monopolies, to the extent that no ACP State would dare to touch a patent of a monopoly registered in its own country without becoming a leper in the 'international community'.

In any case, a country would never sell products based on such infringed patent outside its own borders without being subjected to lengthy legal litigations by those monopolies which had 'lost' their patent right. But even more important, such patent cannot be exploited without the detailed processes contained in the manuals, which a mono-poly maintains at its headquarters. It is this knowledge that a monopoly sells and 'transfers'. For the same reason a monopoly becomes the only vehicle for such transfer across national boundaries.

These facts were noted by the Group of Eminent Persons which carried out a study of the impact of transnational corporations on development and international relations, under the UN aegis.[18] The group however missed the point when they made recommendations which are clearly unimplementable, for they border on moral persuasions to monopolies that are motivated not by sentiment but by profit.

It is for this reason that the Lomé Convention simply engages in a lot of phrase-mongering. The several 'objectives' spelt out in Article 26 are the very things that the European monopolies have been avoiding doing in one way or another, and this for very objectively understandable reasons. No monopoly can entertain programmes, projects, and schemes in the field of industrial 'infrastructure and ventures' unless these assist it to reap a higher rate of profit in the ACP States than it is able to do at home. Neither can the monopolies engage in training, research, promotion, trade co-operation and furnishing industrial information, if these would in the long run work against their monopolistic control of the techniques which alone assure their control of markets as well as raw material bases in the ACP States. For the same reasons they will not contribute to setting up industries and semi-finished goods. The types of ventures they would encourage to service the monopolies are small and medium-sized firms, since these are not competitors, and since in any case these, according to the Convention, are 'as far as possible, [to] be *conducive to the strengthening of the complementary relationship between [these] small and medium-sized industrial firms of their links with large industrial firms'.* [Art. 32] [Emphasis added.]

The financial provisions are clearly bound up with the above provisions. Article 46 clearly shows this link, as well as the provisions of Protocol No. 2 to the Convention. In short they provide, as we have seen, that the financial and technical assistance is to be provided to further the execution of projects, in the production of raw materials such as energy and mining, among others, in which fields the technological control of the monopolies is assured. The aid is also to assist in schemes to improve agriculture and 'microprojects for grass-root development'. All these activities would require the importation of finance capital and technology, which are the very essence of neo-colonial exploitation, and so long as the exploitation continues there can be no real 'transfer of capital and technology', the very resources that would assure our development. In such circumstances it is pointless in our view to talk about amounts of 'aid' available, since this volume would be a function of the rate of exploitation of the 'beneficiary'.

It might be asked why the monopolies would be opposed to the implementation of measures that bring about development, if in fact they have agreed to their inclusion in the Convention. Surely the point here is that it is part of the political and legal ideology of imperialism to mystify the relationship, and to the extent that we would be 'duped' by such 'concessions', there is nothing to be lost by such maneouvres. On the contrary, such maneouvres and mystifications become the very basis of neocolonial control and exploitation. If one wanted to know what the monopolies think about the provisions of the Convention on industrial co-operation, the following view of the German publication which reviews weekly the German press is perhaps representative: 'A number of terms [in the Convention], such as the article on industrial co-operation, will no doubt prove very much an empty shell.'[19] Such is our view too.

The other provisions of the Convention need not detain us long. They are straightforward in their wider implications. The generalisation of the 'rights of establishment' as we have shown is in conformity with the open door multilateral imperialist policy, upon which the US and Japanese monopolies have insisted. All that this provision in the Convention means is that, instead of allowing EEC monopolies the sole right to establish themselves in the ACP States, the monopolies of the US and Japan can do so too. This cannot be regarded as 'victory' for the ACP States, on the contrary it is a victory for those two monopoly groups. Moreover, as we have shown this open door policy is insisted on by the EEC monopolies themselves *inter se,* hence the insistence on 'non-discrimination' between nationals and firms of 'Member States' [Art. 62].

The provisions on current payments and capital movements are the cornerstone of the Convention. Insistence on making available to the monopolies convertible currencies ('foreign exchange') for their loot ('current payments') and capitalised surplus-value ('capital') is the very meat of the transactions. This insistence is matched by the constant pressure on the peasantry to 'work hard' to earn the foreign exchange, and the frantic efforts made to 'conserve' it.

The institutional provisions in our view ensure the proper integration at a political level of the ACP States into the imperialist political system. Under the Convention we have a kind of Euro-ACP government, under which the Council of Ministers decides on measures to execute the neocolonial 'development plan' (the Convention). In its day-to-day activities the Council relies on both the Commission of European Communities and the Committee of Ambassadors. These two constitute the civil service of the Euro-ACP government. The activities of the government are then reported to the Euro-ACP Consultative Assembly, which 'democratically' debates them and 'adopts resolutions' on matters concerning and covered by the Convention [Art. 80:6]. In such circumstances pronouncements about disengagement from capitalism/imperialism become mere populist claptrap of the highest obscurantism, intended to dupe the masses into slumber.

V

Firstly, it is in our view quite misleading to examine the Lomé Convention in isolation from the historical experience of the earlier conventions, agreements and other deals with the imperialist world. Indeed, it is unscientific to do so in isolation of a clear analysis of imperialism as a system. It comes as no surprise that after sixteen years of the Yaoundé Conventions with the EEC, and after all the BDE/CIB 'aid' and technical assistance, the *per capita* incomes of the AASM went up by only $3 over the entire period. If we are to be surprised at this phenomenon then we have not grasped the full significance and implication of imperialism for our countries.

Secondly, the question of 'development' is not to be viewed as a process which takes place through 'assistance'. It is too often claimed that the real road to development in the ACP States is self-reliance, but too infrequently is the significance of this statement realised. Historically capitalist development took place through internal development of the productive forces coupled with reception of capital goods from the more developed areas through trade. In the earlier stages the 'primitive accumulation' from outside was vital to the development of the productive and class forces that later consolidated capitalism. In our case trade with the EEC is not between 'national' capitalist groups, but is 'trade' in products which are in one way or another financed by the same monopoly capitalist groups; the development of a 'national capitalism' in our countries having been arrested by monopoly capitalism itself. To talk of 'economic and social development', as the Convention does, under these conditions is to overlook these historical facts.

Finally, the real issues that we need to seriously address ourselves to are how and in what manner self-reliance and disengagement from the imperialist yoke can take place. Once we realise that this is essentially a political question and not an economic one, then it becomes necessary to clarify the politics that are a prerequisite for the struggle to ensure us victory. Mere repetition of statements like 'we are building socialism', or 'we are disengaging from imperialism', will not in itself bring about the desired transformation. On the contrary, such slogans just help to mystify the exploitative relationships caused by the imperialist domination of our countries.

It is clear that imperialism has denied us the development of nations. The national question is therefore still on the agenda. But this national question arises in historical conditions which cannot allow us to develop capitalist economies. It follows that the socialist path of development is not just the only rational choice but the *only alternative* open to us. But then the struggle for socialism is a struggle of the working class and other exploited people against the international monopoly bourgeoisie and hence imperialism. It is a class struggle. And such a class struggle is impossible without a scientific ideology of the working class. It follows therefore that as long as the national question remains unsolved—the question that cannot be resolved within the armpit of imperialism—and so long as the class struggle is suppressed, any talk of disengagement or of building socialism becomes empty phrase-mongering. These are the politics we need to address ourselves to.

NOTES

1. For a fuller discussion of the Arusha Agreement see my paper: 'The Arusha Agreement between the EEC and East Africa', in *East African Law Review,* Vol. 6, No. 2, December 1973; Dharam Ghai: 'The Association Agreement between the EEC and the Partner States of the EAC', discussion paper No. 14, I.D.S., University of Nairobi.

2. Protocol No. 22 to the Accession Treaty relations between the EEC and the Associated African and Malagasy States (AASM) and also the independent developing Commonwealth countries situated in Africa, the Indian Ocean, the Pacific Ocean and the Caribbean, p. 1144 of The Treaties establishing the European Communities 1973.

3. BTN stands for Brussels Nomenclature for Classification of Goods in Customs Tariff. This tariff contains, in 'sections', 'chapters' and 'tariff headings', all merchandise traded in the world.

4. Press release dated Kingston, Jamaica, 27th July 1974.

5. These countries are: The Bahamas, Malawi, Niger, Rwanda, Barbados, Mali, Somalia, Burundi, Botswana, Mauritania, Chad, Central African Republic, Sudan, Dahomey, Ethiopia, Equatorial Guinea, Swaziland, Tanzania, Togo, The Gambia, Fiji, Grenada, Guinea, Guinea-Bissau, Jamaica, Lesotho, Tonga, Trinidad and Tobago, Madagascar, Uganda, Zambia, Western Samoa, Upper Volta.

6. These countries are: Botswana, Mauritania, Burundi, Niger, Central African Republic, Rwanda, Chad, Dahomey, Ethiopia, Somalia, Sudan, Swaziland, The Gambia, Guinea, Tanzania, Togo, Tonga, Uganda, Lesotho, Guinea-Bissau, Western Samoa, Mali, Malawi, Upper Volta.

7. The full list is as follows:

Barbados	49,300 metric tons
Fiji	163,600 "
Guyana	157,700 "
Jamaica	118,300 "
Kenya	5,000 "
Madagascar	10,000 "
Malawi	20,000 "
Mauritius	487,200 "
People's Republic of the Congo	10,000 "
Swaziland	116,400 "
Tanzania	10,000 "
Trinidad and Tobago	69,000 "
Uganda	5,000 "

8. As follows:

Barbados	29,600 metric tons
Fiji	25,600 "
Guyana	29,600 "
Jamaica	83,800 "
Madagascar	2,000 "
Mauritius	65,300 "
Swaziland	19,700 "
Trinidad and Tobago	54,200 "

9.   Threshold price is the price fixed for each commodity within the Community under the Common Agricultural Policy.

10. *Telelex African:* No. 2, 9th October 1973, pp. 43-5.

11. Johnson, D. Gale: *World Agriculture in Disarray,* p. 29; London, 1973.

12. Rowe, J.W.F.: *Primary Commodities in International Trade,* p. 121; Cambridge, 1965.

13. *European Development Aid,* an EEC pamphlet published by the Commission for European Communities, p. 21.

14. *Memorandum of the Commission to the Council on the Future Relations between the Community, the present AASM States and the Countries in Africa, the Caribbean, the Indian and Pacific Oceans Referred to in Protocol No. 22 to the Act of Accession, Luxembourg, 4th April 1973,* pp. 12-13.

15. *Daily News,* 29th February 1975.

16. See various reports of the Secretary-General, UNCTAD: TD/B/C.1/166.

17. *Daily News,* 12th February 1975.

18. See 'Report of the Group of Eminent Persons To Study the Impact of Multinational Corporations on Development and on International Relations'. UN document E/5500/Rev./ST/EA/6.

19. *The German Tribune,* Hamburg, 13th February 1975.

ANNEX A
THE 46 ACP STATES

1. AFRICA
West Africa
Dahomey, Guinea, Guinea-Bissau, Mauritania, Mali, The Gambia, Ivory Coast, Niger, Ghana, Liberia, Nigeria, Senegal, Sierra Leone, Togo, Upper Volta.

Central Africa
Cameroon, Congo, Central African Republic, Gabon, Chad, Burundi, Equatorial Guinea, Rwanda, Zaire.

Eastern Africa
Botswana, Ethiopia, Kenya, Lesotho, Madagascar, Malawi, Mauritius, Somalia, Sudan, Swaziland, Tanzania, Uganda, Zambia.

2. THE CARIBBEAN
Bahamas, Barbados, Grenada, Guyana, Jamaica, Trinidad and Tobago.

3. THE PACIFIC
Fiji, Tonga, Western Samoa.

ANNEX B
SUMMARY STATEMENT OF PRINCIPAL EXPORTS WHICH ARE COVERED UNDER THE PRICE STABILISATION SYSTEM

Botswana	leather and hides (9 per cent)
Burundi	coffee (86 per cent), cotton (3 per cent), leather and hides (6 per cent)
Cameroon	cocoa (23 per cent), coffee (26 per cent), timber (12 per cent)
Central African Republic	coffee (23 per cent), timber (12 per cent), cotton (18 per cent)
Chad	cotton (69 per cent)
Congo Peoples' Republic	timber (42 per cent)
Dahomey	palm products (34 per cent)
Ethiopia	coffee (38 per cent), leather and hides (13 per cent)
Fiji	coconut oil (5 per cent)
Gabon	timber (32 per cent)
Gambia	groundnuts, including oil and cattle-cake (94 per cent),
Ghana	cocoa (61 per cent), timber (19 per cent)
Ivory Coast	cocoa (15 per cent), coffee (23 per cent), timber (29 per cent)
Jamaica	bananas (4 per cent)
Kenya	coffee (22 per cent), tea (11 per cent)
Liberia	iron ore (71 per cent)

Madagascar	coffee (30 per cent), sisal (3 per cent)
Malawi	tea (17 per cent), groundnuts (7 per cent)
Mali	cotton (39 per cent), groundnuts (7 per cent)
Mauritania	iron ore (73 per cent)
Niger	groundnuts (15 per cent), groundnut oil (9 per cent)
Rwanda	coffee (61 per cent), raw hides (4 per cent)
Senegal	groundnuts and groundnut oil (35 per cent)
Sierra Leone	iron ore (10 per cent), palm kernel oil (5 per cent)
Somalia	bananas (26 per cent), copra (45 per cent)
Sudan	cotton (56 per cent), groundnuts (9 per cent)
Swaziland	cotton (3 per cent)
Tanzania	coffee (19 per cent), cotton (13 per cent), sisal (9 per cent)
Togo	cocoa beans (26 per cent), coffee (13 per cent)
Tonga	copra (50 per cent)
Uganda	coffee (66 per cent), cotton (15 per cent, tea (5 per cent)
Upper Volta	groundnuts and groundnut oil (8 per cent), cotton (22 per cent)
Western Samoa	cocoa (29 per cent)

Sources: *International Financial Statistics,* Nov. 1974 and statistics.

ANNEX C
EXPORTS OF ACP STATES TO THE EEC (9) IN 1973

	1000, U.A.
Groundnuts (husked)	102,169
Groundnut oil	83,085
Cocoa beans	288,418
Cocoa butter	39,189
Cocoa paste	12,391
Green coffee	350,271
Raw cotton	126,855
Copra	763
Coconut oil	6,716
Palm oil	27,027
Palm-kernel oil	20,685
Palm nuts and kernels	32,029

	1000 U.A.
Ox and cow hides	20,512
Tropical timber (round)	440,111
Tropical timber (sawn)	73,920
Fresh bananas	56,721
Sisal	27,926
Iron ore	275,890
Total	1,984,678

CHAPTER 6
THE WORLD ECONOMIC ORDER— THE OLD AND THE NEW*

I

Since the United Nations General Assembly got involved in the demand for a restructuring of the world economic order, a lot has been written, spoken and negotiated about the need for a new world economic order to replace the 'old' one, which it is agreed is unsuited to the conditions of the crisis in world capitalism today. For a proper understanding of the demand and the 'North-South Dialogue', which is connected with the demand for this new order, it is extremely important to grasp the mechanisms of the old order and its underlying contradictions. It is only in this way that we can understand the limits of what is possible in the new demands and their significance for the struggle against imperialism in general.

It is important to recall that the old order was brought about by the need of the imperialist states, particularly the United States, to refurbish capitalism, which was in crisis at the time, immediately after the second world war. This crisis arose out of the very contradictions inherent in the capitalist mode of production. It is sufficient to point out that when capitalism arose out of the ashes of feudalism it did so as a competitive system, based on the operations of capitalists controlling only a minute part of the market proportionate to the size of their capital, which at this time was very small. This youthful bourgeoisie was very revolutionary, since its drive was to change the old conditions, remove backwardness characteristic of feudal conditions, and establish a rational system of production that did away with a decadent opulence entailing wastage of resources in wars, conspicuous consumption and all the rotten rigmarole of feudal society. For this reason this bourgeoisie was a democratic bourgeoisie, whose interests coincided with those of the broad masses—the dispossessed peasantry now rotting in urban areas, having been put out of production by the enclosure system, the free and tenant peasant still on the land, and the yeoman farmers who had interest in developing production and improving their lot and that of society as a whole. Its push for the abolition of old institutions that inhibited the growth of capital and for letting free those that enabled it to expand was well expressed in the utilitarian philosophy of the time articulated by Jeremy Bentham and others. For Adam Smith production based on capital and free trade, and not the hoarding of gold as a sign of power, was the true path to the wealth of nations.

It was this youthful capitalism, atomistic but rigorous, based on

*Paper prepared for the Panel on the New International Economic Order (North-South Dialogue), Third Biannual Conference of the African Association of Political Science, Rabat, Morocco, 23-27 September 1977.

competition of small capitals for the market which was comprised not only of the goods they sold, but of the goods they bought—raw materials, machinery, buildings and labour-power—that kept the system renovative, revolutionary and generative of a new society. But this new society arose with its own contradictions. As it emerged it survived on the basis of exploiting labour which *produced* new values and at the same time *transferred* old values materialised in the current products into new products and new total values, which the capitalist then realised on the market. Inherent in this phenomenon was a contradiction not only between the *owner of capital,* who at first only supervised but did not produce, and the *worker,* who produced, but also between two aspects of the worker's end-product materialised in his own products which he created. This latter contradiction expressed itself as a contradiction between the past and the future manifesting itself in the present. More concretely, it meant that the worker produced more values that became materialised as capital as the very basis of his exploitation, than the values he realised himself as wages for the replenishment of that part of his labour-power that had been exhausted in the process of production. In short, as he produced more values, a greater part went to the old stock which Marx called *constant capital* and increased, while that part which was paid to him for his consumption, which Marx called *variable capital,* relatively decreased. The effect in totality was that a mass of materialised values came face to face with their producers in a hostile confrontation, since those who owned this mass of values (capital) were the very ones exploiting the labour of the producer. This *objectified power* that was capital stood on the producers' heads like Damocles' sword, with the bourgeoisie and their state as the pole on which the sword was suspended in perpetual threat to the working class. It was the compelling force which subjugated the worker, as a result of his accumulated products and the new values he created, to the new regime of capitalist production. He had to keep on producing, or face starvation. These contradictions propelled the system on, but because of them increasingly brought the new system into irreversible movements.[1]

It is for this reason that while the small capitalist in control of a minor segment of the market operated, he too was subjected to the laws of motion of capitalism that imposed on him an irrevocable system of production behaviour. In order to obtain a greater share of production and the market, he had to keep on renovating, reducing prices and offering his products on the market in ways that made it easier for them to sell. But to do this he also required an increasing amount of capital to stay in the game. That is why he was forced to accumulate all the time a greater part of the product created by labour, leading to the contradiction referred to above. This was not a moral question but a necessity imposed on him by the laws of capitalism if the system was to operate at all. The upshot of this process was the increasing dispossession of the small capitalists who could not renovate and offer better products and lower prices. Just as the small producer under feudalism was dispossessed by this class in order to accumulate for the take-off to capitalism as a system, so too hundreds of the new small owners of capital were being replaced by those with big capital. This was a process of history, a process of the development of capitalism, that Lenin referred to as imperialism,[2] a monopoly stage, a very high stage, indeed the highest. It signalled the crisis that has been referred to in the economic literature as the Great Depression of the 1870s, that set in motion the *complete* colonisation of the precapitalist societies, bringing them into the ambit of capitalist production. Thus the rise of imperialism in the 1880s, based on export of capital, a capital that had obtained a unity of the industrial and financial bourgeoisie, was indeed the 'new economic order' for this stage of capitalism, enabling it to weather out of the crisis that then faced it.

II

But that new order of imperialism carried along with it in an intensified, cumulative way the contradictions of the past. *Pure competition* that led to concentration of capital and imperialism itself was now transformed into *monopolistic competition* as the main force in capitalist production. This new competition implied rivalry over the colonised world among the new super powers which had become the centres of *finance capital.* This new, heightened rivalry could only be contained either by agreements or by war. Thus rivalry in economics implied rivalry in politics and indeed, as Clausewitz had correctly observed,[3] war was the extension of politics by other means. The two wars that were fought in the period 1914-18 and 1939-45 were wars of rivalry over outlets for exports of capital, for raw material bases and for secure markets.

These wars led to a gigantic crisis in imperialism that led to the loss to imperialism of the Soviet Union, one-sixth of the imperialist market. Japan was entering the world market of capitalism as a competitor, and the rivalry in Asia became acute. It is not surprising that the east became the centre of acute struggles of the people against imperialism, in which the people of China, Indochina etc. joined in to challenge French, British, Dutch and Japanese imperialism. These struggles were to have a telling blow at some future time to world imperialism, heightening its crisis ever more.

But that was not all. The contradictions in the world capitalist system that had given rise to these gigantic wars had tremendous effect on the capitalist economy itself. Whereas during the century immediately following the first world war goods moved across national boundaries with relative freedom, the period after that was characterised by tariff wars and other economic offensive and defensive mechanisms. To illustrate, in all trade deals no particular effort was made by the trading nations to achieve a balance in the trade between a pair of countries. As Wilcox has correctly observed: 'Goods and services, loans and investments moved around the circle until accounts were cancelled out.'[4] Under this 'free trade' system, whose financial centre was London, and which was based on the *gold standard,* the currency of one country could be converted freely into another's and because of it the rates of exchange were stable, with any imbalance in trade being settled in gold directly. Under such conditions prices of commodities could easily be adjusted to conform to changes in world demand, and the transfer of real resources in this kind of trade and production was made possible to all the capitalist countries, leading to an overall development. Even prices of primary commodities responded more readily to the market forces. This does not mean to say that the role of the state was non-existent. On the contrary, it was the instrument that enabled class control over production, distribution and exchange within each capitalist country. In general, state diplomacy was concerned with political relationships, a necessary and important part of these trade relations. Its agreements were concerned therefore with bilateral treaties of commerce and navigation. Tariffs were imposed too but mainly for revenue purposes, and at times for defence of certain national production and industries. By 1860 a kind of indirect multilateral trade treaty (the Cobden-Chevalier Treaty) had led to a generalised freedom of trade, but by the 1870s this was breaking down with the entry of the USA and Germany into the world market and with the rise in the productive forces overall.

The first world war, which was a manifestation of increased competition for markets and capital outlets, soon put a stop to this 'luxury'. The German Empire broke up, new states were coming to the scene. The gold standard which had been at the base of this free flow of goods and services was abandoned by Britain in 1914, and in spite of a brief re-encounter with it between 1925 and 1931, it was abandoned entirely in 1931. This led to a chain reaction throughout the capitalist world. Exchange rates could not be made stable, since the currencies now floated according to the demand for the particular currency, which was but a reflection of the competitiveness of that country's goods and services externally. This implied a sharp struggle between the capitalist states to maintain the marketability of their products. In order to maintain its markets Britain devalued her pound sterling, which hitherto had been overvalued relative to gold because of her economic strength. This devaluation set in motion similar devaluations by other states as 'defensive' mechanisms to nullify efforts by Britain to outsell them in their markets. The upshot was the introduction of all kinds of protectionist devices, like multiple rates (different rates of exchange for different types of transaction), fluctuating exchange rates, and direct controls.[5] Tariffs, total prohibitions and bartering arrangements became the order of the day. With counteracting markets, with prices no longer 'determining prices', with production considerably under capacity, productive power had to be destroyed to ensure profitability. Those who could not compete effectively incurred debts to enable them to stay in the market. These developments implied direct intervention by the state into the regulation of the economy in support of the monopolies. Tariffs became a permanent instrument of state action, no longer for defence of one's markets, but more importantly for offence, to enable dumping at lower prices in other markets.

State action at the level of the world order to contain the crisis in the inter-war years proved fruitless. The central point of concern was the removal of trade barriers. It was out of the question to restore the gold standard. The production of gold and its utilisation as money had proved to be a high cost on the whole mode. Efforts to use token money were rational to the extent that it could be converted into gold on demand. The exchange rates around the gold standard proved the only way out, but even this was to prove too costly as well. International conferences—on monetary, trade and financial matters, all intended to revive trade, which was dropping alarmingly—were held in Brussels (1920), Genoa (1922), and Geneva (1923). The latter, since the earlier ones had failed over controls and barriers, restricted itself to simplifying customs formalities. It was clear after the failure of all these conferences that the crisis had come to stay. A World Economic Conference held in May 1927 merely succeeded in producing a 'comprehensive report' outlining a detailed programme for the reform of commercial policies, and recommended a general reduction in tariffs, adoption of non-discrimination as a state policy and the elimination of quantitative restrictions, export subsidies, differential internal taxes, and special privileges to state enterprises.[6] It failed even in these 'limited objectives'. The failure was blamed on lack of political support, since the participants in the conference were bureaucrats. To resolve this failure the League of Nations called a diplomatic conference on the same issue in October 1927. A similar comprehensive treaty was discussed which was to come into force with ratification by eighteen countries. Only seventeen ratified it and it too failed.

The Great Depression of the 1930s found the imperialist countries caught up into ever-increasing rivalry at all levels. Any semblance of 'liberalism' that remained was demolished. With all currencies in a chaotic state, involved in competitive devaluations and subject to state controls, the volume of trade declined further. Unemployment became rampant and all action was directed towards 'recovery'. The tariff wars that had characterised the whole period resulted in other League of Nations conferences all intended to conclude a 'tariff truce'. The first of these 'truce' conferences also failed. The second partially succeeded, by obtaining a one-year truce. Meanwhile the United States, which had in the meantime moved up the stairs and become a net creditor-state, furiously advocating 'free trade' now that she enjoyed a favourable condition, in May 1930 enacted the Hawley-Smoot tariff which raised duties 'to the highest level in its history'. This merely added fuel to the fire and led to another tariff war in other countries. By the end of 1931 twenty-six nations had imposed quantitative restrictions and exchange controls. Britain took her last plunge into protectionism with the Ottawa Agreement in 1932, by which she adopted a general tariff, thus establishing a commonwealth tariff preference system to protect colonial and dominion production and trade against the other imperialist powers.

A further move to settle the international order was made with the Monetary and Economic Conference in London in June 1933, which was aimed at stabilising the currencies. But the United States was in no mood to do this. Caught up in its own 'economic nationalism' to protect its own industry by stimulating domestic prices with a dollar devaluation, it declared it was unable to attend the Conference, thus bringing it to a standstill. The result was to bring into play what Wilcox called 'all the weapons of commercial warfare'—a vicious spiral of restrictionism which produced a further deterioration in world trade.

With this economic nationalism Germany cut itself off from the markets of the world, and instead imposed a tight control over its production and markets. Countries that sold to her were paid in marks that could not be utilised elsewhere in the world. The countries which supplied her raw materials and food were forced to take very highly priced goods made in Germany which were useless to them. In this rather gloomy situation for imperialism only a slight relief was obtained from the US Reciprocal Trade Agreements Act of 1934, under which some twenty agreements were concluded until 1939, with some reduction in tariffs. A Tripartite Agreement which helped stabilise rates of exchange of the dollar, the pound and the franc was concluded in 1936 by the three countries—USA, Britain and France—and was later accepted by Switzerland, Belgium and the Netherlands. But this ray of light was soon extinguished by the second world war, in which Germany, joined by Italy, demanded a redivision of world markets, a return of their colonies and a better order for themselves. This further disrupted any possibility of economic co-operation in the long term. All countries caught in the war were forced to engage in economic warfare to facilitate their war effort. Goods were bought which were not needed, in order to keep them away from the enemy or potential enemy, and were supplied to those who did not need them. All production including all colonial production was geared to war needs, and trade became an instrument of war. The six-year war that ensued destroyed production in many countries. Germany and Italy in particular were put out of action economically. Plant, machinery and equipment were destroyed or under-maintained, transport was disrupted, millions of workers were killed, maimed or deported. As for the US, her production rose sharply. Between 1939 and 1944 it grew by 100 per cent, so that by the end of the war she alone accounted for one-third of world production and for more than half of the world output of manufactured goods. By 1947 she was only taking one-tenth of the world imports while her exports grew:

> Our exports of goods and services amounted to $19 billion. Our export of
> goods, at more than $15 billion, were three times the figures reached during
> the twenties and five times those recorded in the years before the war. Our
> imports, however, ran at only $8 billion. And this means that our exports
> exceeded our imports by $11 billion a year.

This position, although impressive in itself, was also a sign of weakness. With their exports to the US declining or non-existent, the other
imperialist powers could not earn the dollars to buy any more from the
US. Thus the dollar shortage itself was a production shortage—and what
was at issue was crisis in capitalist production. It led to more stringent
controls and restrictions in those dollar-starving countries. This explains
why the US, although strong in her gold reserves, production and
exports, still was weak and vigorously pushed for the establishment of a
new order to revive capitalism. This new order for our purposes is now
the 'old' order, and we shall try to examine it.

III

The underlying forces that led to the crises we have examined in the
previous section—themselves the dialectical result of yet older forces—
still continued to plague, albeit at a higher level of the contradiction,
the capitalist economies and the imperialist system as a whole. While
the second world war was having a telling effect on the economies of
imperialist Europe, the US was trying to reframe the old imperial
order to meet the interests of her bulging monopolies in a new
redivision of the world that had to take into account the shrinking
markets, a reopening of bilateral (colonial and semi-colonial) markets,
and outlets for her expanded capital on the basis of new intensified
monopolistic competition, which she was sure to lead and supervise.
Thus throughout the war years, and particularly beginning in 1943,
the US State Department began to work out proposals in the trade,
monetary and financial fields to revive the system overall, in order to
create an atmosphere conducive to capitalist growth under its
hegemony. Wilcox, who recorded some of these events, has stated:

> These proposals were not prepared in haste; they were developed by a series
> of committees, drawn from various departments and agencies of the
> government, that met continuously in Washington under the chairmanship
> of the Department of State from the spring of 1943 to the autumn of 1945.
> They were built up on experience: they carr[ied] forward policies that have
> been incorporated in our commercial treaties and in our trade agreements
> over many years; they further develop[ed] suggestions that were advanced at
> international economic conferences between the two world wars; they drew
> upon the lessons from history that were set forth by the Economic and
> Financial Committees of the League of Nations in their last reports. The
> *Proposals* were however distinctively American: in substance, if not in

detail—the world that [was] pictured in these proposals [was] the kind of
world that Americans want[ed].

THE GENERAL US POLICY

What were the basic policy positions that underlay these proposals? In
short, the US aimed *first* at the expansion of international trade. It
needed this, according to Wilcox, 'for reasons that are grounded, in
large part, in our interests'. The interests were mainly to push
employment, and to create markets for the mass-production industries
that had emerged and which now exceeded the domestic market, in
order to maintain plant, technology and management, 'essential',
according to the same author, 'to the preservation of our economic
health and even our security'. The US also needed imports of certain
'basic materials' on which it was becoming 'increasingly dependent'.
Secondly, it believed this international trade should be based on
'private enterprise', because this assured that trade would be competitive, efficient, progressive, non-discriminatory and non-political'.
Furthermore, it facilitated buying from the cheapest market and
selling in the dearest one, which would not be the case with state
enterprises. In any case nationalisation could not be stopped, but
where this became inevitable the US would 'demand prompt and
effective compensation—and where loans are requested [we could,
if we choose], refuse to grant them'.

Thirdly, it believed that such trade should be multilateral rather
than bilateral. This was important if the US, with very few colonial
and semi-colonial markets, was to make its entry into those of its
European competitors. The US compared bilateralism to a bartering
arrangement, since the buyers and the sellers were all the time almost
invariably the same, each trying to balance trade with the other.
For this reason, according to the US it limited international trade and
'substituted the judgment of the bureaucrat for the judgment of the
market-place'. Multilateralism placed emphasis on economics and not on
politics. *Fourthly,* the policy of nondiscrimination in trade and
monetary matters was basic to the operation of the new system,
because discrimination obstructed expansion in trade and hence
production. It distorted 'normal relationships' and prevented the most
'desirable division of labour', thus perpetuating itself by 'canalizing'
trade and establishing vested interests and thereby gave rise to
irrationality and 'ill-will'.

Fifthly, the stabilisation of trade in industry had to go hand in hand
and be consistent with the development of agriculture and the relative
policies in international trade. In the pursuit of employment, however,
the producers of 'staple commodities' would have to be afforded 'some
measure of protection' against the sudden impact of 'violent change',
but this had not to be at levels which in the long run could not be
sustained by 'world demand'. *Sixthly* and finally, international co-
operation and consultation were essential to the fulfilment of these

basic policies. Economic warfare led to retaliation. According to President Truman, 'instead of retaining unlimited freedom to commit acts of aggression, its members would adopt a code of economic ethics and agree to live according to its rules'.

These proposals, worked out in detail between 1943 and 1945, had already been generally pronounced on by President Truman in the various declarations of the period, and constituted the basis of policy in the Atlantic Charter and Article VII of the Lend-Lease Agreements in 1942. Under Point IV of the Charter and Article VII of the Agreement, the US insisted that its allies open up their colonial and protected imperial markets. Richard Gardner, writing of the period, observed:

> The First World War did much to stimulate American concern with the political importance of nondiscrimination. An influential body of literature developed which cited unequal opportunity as one of the major causes of the conflict. *Closed trade areas controlled by Imperial powers were held to deny other countries their natural rights [sic!] to the vital raw materials, markets and investment outlets.*[7]

Accordingly Point IV of the Atlantic Charter put the whole problem of multilateral markets as follows:

> They [ie. the US and UK] will endeavour, with due respect for their existing obligations, to further the enjoyment of all states, great or small, victor or vanquished, *of access, on equal terms* to the trade and to the raw materials of the world which are needed for their economic prosperity.

In the same vein, Article VII of the Lend-Lease Agreement between the US and UK expressed the determination of the two parties that their dealings with each other were not to be such as to burden commerce, but to promote mutually advantageous relations between them and the betterment of world-wide economic relations:

> To that end, they shall include provision for agreed action by the United States of America and the United Kingdom, open to participation by all other countries of like mind, directed to the expansion, by appropriate international and domestic measures, of production, employment, and exchange and consumption goods, which are the material foundations of liberty and welfare of all peoples; to the elimination of all forms of discriminatory treatment in international commerce, and to the reduction in tariffs and other trade barriers.

This general declaration was put to thirteen other Lend-Lease recipients of US loans, and was accepted by them, since they also needed assistance from the US.

The US tried to achieve the above objectives by a three-pronged institutional strategy, not to mention the umbrella political system of the post-war period under the UNO which aimed at containing the problems of the cold war and of intra-imperialist rivalries of the multilateral imperialist era. The Havana Charter and its institutional child the ITO got into problems and never came into force. One of the aims of the Atlantic Charter and of the Lend-Lease Agreements as we have seen was a world trading system based on nondiscrimination and free exchange of goods and services. But it was not until 6 December 1945 that the US submitted its proposals.

TRADE
On this basis the US submitted a proposal for the establishment of an International Trade Organisation which, as a specialised agency of the United Nations, would aim at achieving the gradual liberalisation of trade, to combat monopolies, to expand the demand for commodities and to co-ordinate the countercyclical policies of the various countries. As pointed out, this organisation could not take off, as the US Congress did not ratify it. Instead another Agreement—the General Agreement on Trade and Tariffs—was negotiated and concluded. Up to date this agreement has only been ratified by a neocolonial state called Haiti! The US Congress also refused to ratify it on the grounds that it did not incorporate certain key clauses. However, the non-ratification did not prevent the Agreement from being applied, and it is at present being implemented by all the countries under the terms of the Protocol of Provisional Application and the Protocols of Accession.

The United States proposal received opposition from a number of countries. Australia, supported by Britain, pointed out that if there were free trade, the United States would export depressions by such measures as price reductions on the domestic market, which would lead to the stepping up of US exports and the curtailing of her imports. Other countries would then need to be able to protect themselves by increasing import duties. Australia also maintained that the less developed countries should be entitled to avail themselves of the infant-industry protection. This position was also held by India, which among the countries of Asia was the only one represented.

The General Agreement made a distinction between the general aims, which were to be pursued by many other international economic organisations, and specific tasks. The general aims were the improvement of standards of living, the creation of full employment which would lead to 'a large and steadily growing volume of real income and effective demand', and the 'full use of the world's resources and the expansion of production and international trade'. In its specific tasks the GATT planned to contribute to the attainment of these objectives through arrangements directed to the substantial reduction of tariffs and other trade barriers and to the elimination of discrimination. In its policy towards 'less developed countries' it aimed, at least in its declarations in Part IV which was added in 1964, at measures to ensure the stabilisation of commodity prices, better access to the markets of the imperialist countries for processed and manufactured products coming from these neocolonial countries, and the diminution of the burdens which these countries assumed in the interest of their economic development. Article 18 acknowledged the infant-industry protection demanded by Australia and India in a very naive way, and it was the failure to achieve any level of industrialisation that led to new demands for Part IV to the Agreement. But these measures could not solve the basic problem of exploitation of the third world countries by the imperialist countries. After the publication of the Harbeler Report (in 1957), three committees were appointed in November 1958 to examine various aspects of world trade problems, including agricultural protection in the third world countries. These did not result in any concrete achievement.

In May 1963 a programme of action which had been submitted by twenty-one countries was approved by a majority of the contracting parties. According to this programme the imperialist countries would have to refrain from introducing any new trade barriers or restrictions contrary to the General Agreement. Any such barriers and restrictions would have to be suspended within one year. They had of course mushroomed since the inception of GATT against third world industrial products, even in those areas in which, under the 'free trade' myth which the Agreement appeared to subscribe to at least by declaration, they had a 'comparative advantage'. According to the Action Programme the barriers were to be gradually reduced and eliminated. Revenue duties were to cease to operate by 31 December 1965 at the latest.

The EEC countries were unable to agree to these programmes. They considered them to be focused too much on customs duties and quotas, and they thought that more general and 'positive measures' aimed at increasing the export earnings of the third world countries would be more suitable. Other imperialist countries too formulated certain reservations and opted out of the programme. It is these measures which were watered down and incorporated as Part IV to the Agreement, when it became clear that pressures for 'a new organisation' for the 'poor countries' were building up as GATT was increasingly being dubbed a 'rich man's club'. It is these proceedings which explain the rise of UNCTAD.

GATT has been bogged down for the last five years trying to renegotiate a new trade policy under the so-called Tokyo Round. Inaugurated in November 1973, the Tokyo Declaration sought a further reduction in tariffs and removal of non-tariff barriers that had increasingly nullified the effect of previous tariff reductions. But this declaration was before the oil crisis, and since then there has been a resurgence of non-tariff barriers, particularly those against subsidies— mainly offset in the form of countervailing and anti-dumping duties which are a feature of struggle for markets. Furthermore, contrary to GATT principles France is insisting on selective application of the general most-favoured-nation clause, which goes against the very letter and spirit of GATT. As of now 61.2 per cent of semi-processed and processed agricultural products from third world countries have non-tariff barriers of various kinds against them, as compared to 46.9 per cent from other countries. In other words, GATT still is unable under the present monopolistic arrangement to avail markets to a large number of products (duty-free) from many countries of the third world aspiring to develop capitalist economies. As a result the Group of 77 have insisted that the on-going GATT negotiations in the Tokyo Round be shifted to the UN and be dealt with as part of the new order package deal. This has been resisted by the imperialist countries.

Nor is the situation among the imperialist countries all that rosy. Since the oil crisis and other raw material problems they have been undergoing a metamorphosis in their trade policies. New unofficial arrangements behind the rules laid down in GATT have been entered into, creating what a leading business journal has called 'creeping cartelisation':

> The new trend shows up in the 'orderly marketing' agreements being negotiated between importing and exporting countries for a variety of manufactured goods. And it shows up in the proposals for buffer stocks, designed to limit market prices that are currently being discussed for sugar and wheat. This development is a significant departure from the goals of unfettered world trade that were enshrined in the 1948 General Agreement on Trade and Tariffs.[8]

'Orderly or "voluntary" marketing Agreements' (OMAS) is just a different name for market-sharing, and the US, Japan and Europe have entered into these informal arrangements for television sets, shoes, steel, ships, sugar, wheat and even cars. This is a new phenomenon of intensified monopolistic competition that the IMF in its survey of August 1977 describes as the worst since World War II, indicating a new crisis for imperialism.

UNCTAD

As noted UNCTAD, founded as a 'poor man's club', has had a poor record. Its founding in 1964 under a UN General Assembly Resolution was heralded by a number of 'demands' and 'requests' that were characteristic of a petty-bourgeois audience. Having to reform the existing order within itself, the conference drew attention to the decreasing share of the third world in world trade, and to the worsening terms of trade. To remove this 'unfairness' the conference demanded 'compulsory and automatic compensatory measures', which were to be introduced whenever there was a decline in export earnings of these countries. The funds for this purpose were to be provided by 'the rich countries'. Secondly, in order to facilitate the industrialisation of the third world the imperialist countries were to open up their

markets to the manufactured goods of the 'poor countries', and
preference was to be given to their products over those of the rich ones.
This was coupled with demand for more aid to enable this industrialisation to take place, an additional $2,000 to $3,000 million a year. The
imperialist countries were reminded that they would have an economic
interest in bringing 'greater prosperity to the low-income countries',
since their exports to these countries would be stepped up as a result.

Nearly fifteen years since these proposals were made nothing of the
kind has happened to cheer up the 'poor man's club'. The only
achievement, in the form of generalised schemes of preferences, was
nowhere near the demand for preference 'over' the products of the
imperialist countries themselves. On the contrary, the schemes were so
hedged in with safeguards and emergency clauses that no real growth
in markets and industrial production has resulted. Efforts at improving
terms of trade under UNCTAD have also failed.

UNCTAD IV at Nairobi marked the limits of what could be achieved
even then. The conference proposed a 'waiver' of debts for 'the most
seriously affected countries'. This was estimated for the 67 non-oil
producing countries at $8.5 billion in 1973 as compared to $3.5 billion
in 1965. Naturally this proposal was rejected by the investing imperialist
states. A further proposal for the establishment of an integrated
commodity fund of about $7 billion, to finance the purchase of initial
stocks of ten 'core' commodities and seven other commodities, and to
set up buffer stocks and maintain market fluctuations in the prices of
these commodities at 10 per cent range, was also rejected by the US and
other imperialist countries, on the grounds that it was a gigantic 'aid'
programme they could not finance. Negotiations on these and other
'demands' were resumed in Paris. In the meantime the EEC is
resisting textile imports under the schemes on the grounds that they are
creating dangerous competition.

MONEY AND FINANCE

The IMF had its origins and objectives from the same movement, owing
to the currency instability in the majority of European and some Asian
countries. The restoration of international production and trade after
World War II called for considerable capital transfers from the US to
the rest of the world, as we have seen. The US was keen to do this on
conditions that were stipulated.

Discussions on these problems had already been opened during the
war, leading to the simultaneous publication on 7 April 1943 of a
British and an American plan for the establishment of an international
monetary institution.

The British plan, 'Proposals for an International Clearing Union',
was drawn up by J.M. Keynes in collaboration with British Treasury
experts. This plan provided for the founding of an international bank
which would grant credits to the member countries to the extent of
75 per cent of their average imports and exports for the year 1936.

These credits were to be expressed in a new currency unit to be
called the *bancor,* the gold value of which was to be adjusted at regular
intervals to the requirements of monetary circulation. This was
intended to avoid disturbances due to fluctuations in gold production,
to which such value was necessarily tied as a commodity. The national
currencies were to be determined in *bancors.* Any modification would
have required the consent of the International Clearing Union.

These proposals were advantageous to Britain which, with its
considerable foreign trade, would have obtained a high *bancor* quota—
$514 billion, as against $4.1 billion for the US. Furthermore, a proper
economic policy coupled with purchases in the US would have
hastened British industrial recovery. The plan was clearly unacceptable
to the US, since the considerable flow of European orders immediately
after the war would have given rise to inflationary pressure in the US.
Instead the US put forward its own preliminary draft outline of a
proposal for a 'United and Associated Nations Stabilisation Fund',
which had been prepared by a team headed by H.D. White and an
assistant to the Secretary of the Treasury, H. Morgenthau, and which
came to be known as the White Plan. The proposal was based on the
establishment of a fund of at least $5,000 million to which the
member states would transfer a part of their exchange reserve, and in
turn this fund was to serve to grant credit, within certain limits, to the
signatories. The US plan, contrary to the British one, opted for an
international currency unit with a fixed parity to be called the *unitas.*

These two proposals, despite the publication of others by France
and Canada as well as the Soviet Union, formed the basis of an agreement which was published on 21 April 1944, and finally submitted to
the UN Monetary and Financial Conference which met at Bretton
Woods. The UN conference decided to set up two institutions, the
IMF and the IBRD or World Bank. Despite the agreement, the US plan
constituted the bulk of the ideas incorporated into the Articles of
Agreement, which we will examine in a moment.

The Fund and the Bank both came officially into existence on 27
December 1945. The World Bank opened for business on 25 June 1946,
but the Fund started financial operations only in March 1947. On
28 July 1969 an amendment to the Articles of Agreement of the Fund
came into force, establishing a new facility based on special drawing
rights (SDR) and making certain changes in Fund rules and practices.
The objectives were defined in six points. The Fund's real tasks however were spelt out in point 6, namely, to shorten the duration and to
reduce the degree of disequilibrium in balances of payments. This was
to be achieved partly by placing the resources of the Fund, subject to
the necessary guarantees, at the temporary disposal of the member
states, and in that way they were to be afforded the opportunity of
eliminating disequilibria in their payments without taking measures
that would be harmful; and partly by promoting exchange stability,
and to this end measures were to avoid competitive exchange

depreciations.

First and foremost, it was necessary to avoid a return to the repeated devaluation and the floating of currencies by means of which the leading countries had tried in the 1930s to outdo each other in the struggle for markets and outlets for capital exports.

Point 4 of the general objectives prescribed co-operation in the establishment of a multilaterial system of payments in respect of current transactions and in the removal of exchange restrictions that went to hamper the growth of world trade and production. Because of US pressure on this issue, Article 8 providing for the encouragement of multilateral trade was inserted in the Articles of Agreement. This was because the US regarded the restoration of multilateral trade as the main purpose of the Fund. Without the Fund's approval, the intro-duction or maintenance of restrictions on current international trans-actions was prohibited; discriminatory measures *vis-à-vis* the currencies of certain member countries were also ruled out. Though controls necessary to regulate international capital movements were allowed, they were not to restrict payments for current transactions or unduly delay transfers of funds in settlement of commitments. These require-ments were coupled with the need to establish *par value* for each currency tied to gold or the dollar in Article 4.

Despite these provisions, in the period immediately after World War II the majority of countries were unable to fulfil them without jeopardising their balance-of-payments equilibrium. For this reason, Article 14 allowed restrictions on payments, and transfers were allowed provisionally 'in the post-war transitional period'. Nevertheless, although allowed temporary relief (which was assumed would be five years) all those eligible under Article 14 could not introduce new restrictions on current payments without the approval of the Fund under Article 8.

In order to implement currency convertibility, each member was obliged to purchase amounts of its currency held by another member, for gold or that member's currency, if the latter so requested and furnished evidence that this currency had recently been acquired as a result of current transactions, or that it was required in order to pay for operations of the same type (Article 8,4). This had little effect, since it could not be shown easily.

The system was intended to contain the contradictions immanent in monopolistic competition and to revitalise capitalist production. In the short run it worked. But as the US increased capital exports and waged wars of nation repression, and as the other imperialist states underwent reconstruction and intensified competition for markets, monetary stresses followed. Thus in 1966 Britain was forced to devalue her currency in order to assert her position in her existing markets overseas. The elimination of US and UK deficits, while 'good' on the one hand, had adverse effects on reserves. This was the reason behind the creation of SDRs—to substitute for the cessation of reserve increases connected with the UK and US deficit elimination. But before the allocation of the first SDRs, the French franc and the Deutschmark came under pressure, leading to short-term capital flows to Germany. This led to the devaluation of the French franc and the overvaluation of the Deutschmark. In May 1970 floating exchange rates were introduced for the Canadian dollar and Netherlands guilder for one year. On 15 August 1971 came the final blow to the Bretton Woods system, when the US suspended the convertibility of its dollar into gold. This event has been compared in historical significance to the 1931 British decision to suspend the convertibility of sterling.[9]

The result is that since March 1973 the system in operation has been completely different from the Bretton Woods one. Exchange rates are not fixed. All currencies are floating—some independently, others jointly (like the European ones under the 'Snake'), and yet others have pegged rates to the dollar or some other reserve currency including SDRs! The Kingston Accord of the Committee of Twenty agreed, in January 1976, to the amendment of Article IV of the IMF Articles of Agreement to permit countries to apply the exchange arrangement of their choice, subject to supervision by the Fund. The Fund, in order to meet short-term problems created by serious balance of payments problems, set up a Trust Fund from gold sales of the IMF to 'assist' those hard hit. Currently there is proposed another 'multimillion stand-by fund' of $11,000 million to aid ailing currencies. This fund, according to the West Germany newspaper *Diet Zeit,* is being set up by fourteen 'fathers' to assist some 'child' countries. Among those most favoured children are Turkey, Greece, Spain, Portugal and also countries 'on the threshold of development' such as Brazil and Mexico, 'who have covered their foreign exchange requirements by making liberal use of European credit facilities'. This fund is to supplement the IMF fund which was 'too little to live on and too much to die on'! Even then the paper reported that: 'These countries will be required to put their economic houses in order, and the IMF will be watching them carefully to make sure that they do.'[10]

IBRD

The World Bank was envisaged as an instrument for reactivating capital exports from the US particularly to Europe for 'reconstruction' and to the neocolonies for 'development'.

This gave US finance capital through the Marshall Plan a chance to infiltrate into Europe, thus giving US monopolies an easy competitive advantage within the European economic market that was founded in 1957 under the Treaty of Rome. Equally, it enabled US finance capital to gain easy entry into former colonies of the European powers, and became a bridge over which US imperialism introduced itself into the open-door neocolonial world. It has as a result become the greatest creditor institution for imperialist finance capital in the third world. This not only facilitates capital exports from the US, it also enabled the monopolies to have greater access to the resources, including capital and labour, generated in the third world, thus increasingly integrating it into the operations of world capitalism.

At present, 1 per cent in gold and 9 per cent in the national currency are callable from each member country by the Bank. In addition, the Bank obtains funds by selling securities issued or guaranteed by it or in which it has invested part of its resources, the consent of the country where the sale takes place being required. This is the manner in which it is able to be the agent for finance capital in totality.

Lastly, the Bank can borrow currency direct from each member state, provided the country concerned agrees. Unused funds can be applied by the Bank to repurchasing bonds issued or guaranteed by it or in which it has interests, with the consent of the country where the purchase is made. Investments in other securities can be made only from a special reserve, which serves wholly or in part for this purpose, subject to a three-quarters majority decision by the Executive Directors. The Bank's resources are likewise increased when it sells claims or when its previous loans are repaid. Since the Bank lends its funds at rates of interest above those charged by the ordinary commercial banks, it acts as a Bank for all banks for otherwise unused investment funds, thus fulfilling its task as generator of capital exports for all the imperialist world. The Bank also acts as a planner in the neocolonial world, by providing various kinds of experts who examine the profitability and/or viability of various projects which it has to finance. Before a member state makes a formal application for a loan, the project is analysed by the Bank's experts and, if need be, amendments are proposed. In this way the Bank is a data bank for the monopolies on the economies of all the neocolonial world. Working hand in hand with the IMF, it is able to reprimand and discipline all countries that do not act on the advice of the Fund or the reports of the Bank.

As it is not always an easy matter for a new state to submit suitable projects, it has been the practice since 1949 to send general survey missions to certain countries in order to study development prospects. The members of these missions are appointed in co-operation with other international organisations (including FAO, WHO and UNESCO).[11]

In East and West Africa, where the development problems are especially complex, the Bank has established permanent regional missions, primarily to assist the governments in those areas to identify and prepare specific projects for submission to the Bank or the IDA. The offices of these missions are located in Nairobi and Abidjan respectively. At the end of 1968 a resident staff was set up in Indonesia, a country 'in special need of technical assistance'. The Bank is active also in training personnel for the neocolonial states who then act as 'planners'. Government officials from these countries are trained in planning technique at the Economic Development Institute, which was set up by the Bank in January 1956 with the support of the Ford and Rockefeller Foundations. There are also training programmes dealing with the policy of the Bank, development problems and financial administration.

As part of its central role as a multilateral agency for imperialism, the Bank has endeavoured to act as co-ordinator between other multilateral agencies and individual imperialist states who grant aid on a bilateral basis. Thus in 1958 one consortium was set up to help India implement the third five-year plan, and in 1960 another was established to finance part of Pakistan's second five-year plan. In addition to the World Bank and its affiliate the IDA, Canada, France, Japan, the UK, the US and West Germany have participated in both consortia, which have met annually since their inception and have served as vehicles for objective comments on the economic performance and capital requirements of these and other neocolonial states.

For other countries the Bank organises consultative groups of interested capital-exporting imperialist countries. Although they do not engage in annual aid pledges, the groups serve the same purposes as the consortia. Since 1962 consultative groups have been organised for Columbia, Nigeria, Sudan, Tunisia, South Korea, Morocco and East Africa—in each case at the request of the governments receiving aid.

In its role as mediator for international capital, the Bank has encouraged and obtained consent, where other efforts failed, from third world countries to the Convention on the settlement of investment disputes between states and nationals, mainly transnational monopolies of the imperialist states. The Convention, which was sent to member governments in March 1965, came into force on 14 October 1966, and is intended to facilitate the easy flow of private capital to the neocolonies. Under the Convention a Centre for the settlement of investment disputes is maintained at the Bank's headquarters 'near the money', to facilitate settlement of disputes. This is attested to by the fact that an increasing number of investment contracts, bilateral treaties and national laws contain provisions for the submission of disputes to the Centre. Where efforts at drafting an international convention on the minimum standard have failed, the Centre has succeeded, and by developing model clauses and agreements to be used by capital exporters the capital importers, it has helped to bridge the gap between what hitherto was an area of 'vanishing consensus'.[12]

The Bank has also drafted articles of agreement for an international investment insurance agency, to protect investments in the third world countries in order to encourage more capital inflows.

In all these activities the Bank has successfully established itself as a reliable multilateral institution for international capital, and through 'disciplinary measures' of various kinds imposed by the Bank itself and the IMF the economies of all the neocolonial world are becoming ever more integrated into the world capitalist system, despite all the cries for 'fair deal' and 'fair play' in international economic relations.

IV

The new order is no more than a demand—'a toughly worded demand',
according to one international bureaucrat—addressed to the industrialised imperialist countries. The demand came out of the realisation that
the old (existing) order was 'inequitable and unjust'. This petty-
bourgeois outlook, which ignores the real inherent contradictions in
capitalism that alone can help us comprehend imperialist exploitation and domination, is well expressed by the same bureaucrat in the
following passage:

> [T] he present international economic order is a game [*sic!*] in which the rich
> world not only has the good cards but also makes up all the rules. . . They
> [the third world] argue that the world's economic system has still not
> emerged from the colonial era which concentrated wealth and power so over-
> whelmingly in the hands of a few industrialised nations, that to this day they
> can lay down the rules of world trade, regulate the world's monetary system,
> decide what investments will be made where and for what purpose, determine
> the course of science and technology, dominate the economies of the
> developing countries, and organise the international division of labour in their
> own interests. In other words, *the developing nations feel that they are almost
> as dominated and dependent today as they were under direct colonial rule.*
> [Emphasis added] [13]

He goes on to point out that these countries feel, since the prices
of raw materials they sell, the value of foreign currency they use, the
cost of the industrial goods they import, the terms of the investments
they seek, the kind of technology they use, the amount and conditions
of aid they receive, *'are all determined by forces they can little affect'*,
[emphasis added] , 'Third World' countries 'now, want an economic
earthquake to shake [the old order] to its very foundations'. This
'earthquake' is the 'new order' demanded. But when we look at the
'tough demands', we find that the preamble is just a reaffirmation and
declaration of known facts—the usual ceremonious proceedings to a
resolution.

The UN General Assembly resolution 3281 (XXIX) adopted on
12 December 1974 then goes on to 'adopt' a charter of economic
rights and duties of states, in which the 'tough demands' are enumerated.
Firstly, the charter on the 'new order' demands recognition of the right
each state has over its wealth, natural resources and economic activities,
and reaffirms its 'full permanent sovereignty' over them! To this extent
it has a right to regulate foreign investment, supervise monopolies and
rationalise, expropriate, or transfer ownership of foreign-owned
property [Art. 2] . There is nothing new in this since it has always
been so recognised under the principle of sovereign equality of nations.

Secondly, in the field of trade the document restates the principle
of free choice in international relations, reaffirms the right of states to
enter into primary commodity arrangements to ensure 'stable,
remunerative and equitable prices' and calls for the further dismantling

of obstacles to trade, in order to further liberalise and expand world trade. Furthermore it is demanded that, in order to achieve equitable terms of trade, prices of primary commodities should be indexed to those of the manufactured goods [Arts. 4-8, 14-23]. Again, as we have argued before, there is a whole fifteen years' struggle over this issue in the GATT, UNCTAD and IMF, the result of which has shown that no progress is possible under present conditions of production under imperialism. Therefore there is no real departure in these demands. Indeed, the Havana Charter, the GATT and the General Principles of UNCTAD clearly recognise these demands, but in spite of efforts to put them into effect no solution has emerged.

Thirdly, the 'new order' requires all states to recognise that every state has the 'right' to benefit from the advances and developments in science and technology, and hence their transfer should be facilitated, including assistance towards creating an 'indigenous technology' for the benefit of the developing countries. To this end states should 'co-operate in exploring. . . further accepted guidelines or regulations for the transfer of technology' [Arts. 9, 13]. Again here it is important to understand that export of capital of which technology forms part is a preserve of monopolies and is operated by economic laws, although assisted by state action. Technology alone earns these monopolies $16 billion from third world countries alone. Technology is itself already a monopoly 'right' which makes today's imperialism possible, as it is tied to capital exports and skills. 'Guidelines', 'regulations' or 'codes of conduct' cannot deal with this basically economic phenomenon with its own compelling laws.

Fourthly, in order to assist and increase industrialisation of third world countries, imperialist countries should extend, improve and enlarge the system of generalised non-reciprocal, non-discriminatory tariff preferences and agree to the adoption of 'other differential measures' in the field of international economic co-operation 'where it may be feasible' [Arts. 18-19]. At the time of writing these preferences, already extended under the various schemes, are causing havoc in the imperialist countries, and Europe is currently demanding a cut-back in the exports of textiles from the third world countries.

Fifthly, the charter for the 'new order' demands an 'increase [in] official flows of aid from official sources. . . and to improve the terms and conditions thereof' which should include 'economic and technical assistance' [Art. 22]. It is to be noted here that over the last nineteen years, instead of official aid increasing to 1 per cent of the national income of the imperialist countries, as demanded by the Second UNCTAD at New Delhi, it has fallen from 0.52 per cent to 0.3 per cent in 1975. Moreover, the third world at Nairobi UNCTAD IV 'demanded' the cancellation and/or rescheduling of the outstanding $960 billion debt with the monopolies. It is to be noted that, at the current rate, by 1985 the third world will be paying back to the imperialist world more than it is expected to receive in aid. The document further insists that the new monetary system's 'paper gold' be tied to assistance to be given to these countries by channelling through the third world all newly created liquidity before it goes back to the monopolies!

Finally, the 'new order' envisages a fairer share in the invisible earnings from shipping which are currently monopolised by Shipping Conference Lines. This is because it is expected 'national shipping lines' should under the 'new order' be given a more equitable share of the carrying trade. All this is intended to 'increase the foreign exchange earnings' from this source [Art. 27].

These toughly-worded demands did not create any earthquake, or even a ripple over the ocean's waves. On the contrary, the old order continued as before, and relations between the two parts of the system went on with their usual ups and downs. No other voice was heard, with the exception of grumblings here and there and protestations and verbal mudslinging characteristic of the petty bourgeoisie. Neither the UN General Assembly nor the third world (loud majority) could do a thing. The real power lay at the threshold of the financial oligarchies of the imperialist countries. A move was made only when it became necessary to contain prices within the ambit of cartels. When the 'prices' could not determine prices within OPEC, it became necessary for further combined action within OPEC to contain the prices of oil. This is what led to the talks known as the 'North-South Dialogue'.

THE NORTH-SOUTH DIALOGUE

The talks at Kleber Palace Conference Centre in Paris, called by the French President Giscard d'Estaing to discuss matters connected with the oil crisis, later came to be referred to as talks on the new international co-operation. The scope was widened only when the issue warranted widening the terms of reference to include other raw materials prices which had also been rising. The idea was to contain further rises. With eight imperialist countries and nineteen third world countries represented, the conference was not wholly representative of a cross-section of the interests involved. In any case, the issue of the new order which was smuggled in became the major issue of the conference and bogged down the participants in a fruitless eighteen months of dialogue. No new issues were introduced by the third world countries. In the dialogue demand was made for:

1) The adoption of 'suitable principles' and mechanisms in international economic relations to correct and eliminate 'gradually' the 'sources' of the developed countries' 'exploitation' of the developing countries through 'unequal exchange' (non-equivalent trade) and the 'monopolistic position of the developed countries on the world market'.

2) The implementing of a third world proposal for a preferential and non-reciprocal treatment to them for their products and for an 'integrated programme centred around a fund to finance commodity buffer stocks, and to correct the unequitable terms of trade, and

further to establish a system of indexing the prices of manufactured goods in order to protect their purchasing power; and to improve existing compensatory financing under the IMF, as well as 'easing access to modern technology'.

3) The increase in the transfer of financial resources of at least 0.7 per cent of the GNP target set by the UNO by 1980.

4) The restructuring of the world financial and monetary system in order to link new liquidity based on the 'needs' of the third world with the strengthening of their decision—making a role in the IMF which currently accounts for 'a mere' 30 per cent of the votes!

5) The working out of a suitable formula to ease the debt burden mounting to an 'unendurable $180 million'.

It was in the context of these demands that the third world were 'ready and willing' to take up 'the important and complicated problem of world energy including oil'.

The position of the imperialist countries, impervious to such petty threats, was forthright and categoric. In the field of energy, which was their major concern, they rejected tying the issue to other demands and insisted on the principle of 'assured supplies and availability' of this resource—which were in no danger anyway. They rejected demands for protecting purchasing power, easier access to their markets and technology etc. Instead they insisted on the assurance of an adequate investment climate for their private investors (monopolies) and the fullest possible protection of investment, without even being prepared to accede to any 'codes of conduct' for the monopolies, as demanded.

On the other hand they agreed to an increase in 'aid' but did not approve the setting of a target of 0.7 per cent by 1980. A Yugoslav magazine observed:

> The developing countries attempted to orient themselves as much as possible to the import of private capital and the utilisation of the facilities of the IMF and World Bank, but the developed countries wish[ed] to tighten loan conditions further, without corresponding improvements in the position of the developing countries within these financial institutions, particularly in relation to decision-making.[14]

The imperialist countries rejected the demand for 'easing the debt burden', insisting on a country-by-country approach and not a blanket cancellation of all debts. Instead, they were prepared to put aside $1 billion 'aid' for the poorest countries. They agreed to Ministers 'taking up' the matter at a political level over the issue of a common integrated fund to finance commodity buffer stocks, 'with its goals and form to be further discussed in UNCTAD'. They also agreed to further talks on energy 'but not on the institutionalisation of co-operation'; to a $1 billion 'Action Programme'; infrastructures 'for development' in Africa; the Lima 25 per cent demand for industrialisation in third world countries by the year 2000, although it is to be noted that suitable measures for achieving this goal have not been agreed; certain measures regarding transfer of technology; co-operation in agriculture and 'the world food problem'; the stimulation of financial co-operation among developing countries; and steps to 'ease access' to capital markets etc.

The conference agreed to present the results of the Dialogue to the 31st session of the UN General Assembly and to all other relevant UN bodies for the purpose of taking action to implement agreements or to continue the consideration of unresolved questions. When the results were presented at the UN General Assembly, Pakistan, on behalf of the Third World countries, tabled a resolution which called on the Assembly 'to note with great concern and disappointment' the results so far achieved on the new order and called for 'greater efforts' for the establishment of a new international economic order. This is as we put these lines on paper.

V

We began with the theoretical proposition that capital arose and operates on the basis of a contradictory movement specific to it. This contradiction basically is the struggle between the two classes for a greater portion of the product. This struggle heightens competition among the operators, which ultimately leads to monopoly and modern imperialism. The problem of exploitation and domination of the colonial and neocolonial peoples is part of these contradictions of capital, and their fundamental resolution cannot be sought within capital itself.

The demands of the petty bourgeoisie of third world countries are not against exploitation of the producing classes in their countries, but of the domination of their class by monopoly. The demands are therefore for reform—for more credit to enable the petty bourgeois more room *also* to exploit their own labour and extract a greater share of the surplus-value. This is unachievable, for to do so is to negate monopoly—which is an impossible task outside the class struggle. As concentration proceeds on a world scale the demands become even more superfluous as monopoly ever more attracts the socialist revolution.

Nevertheless, one must not underestimate the contradiction inherent in these demands. They represent what the UN bureaucrat referred to as continued 'domination' of the 'Third World' by the West. We have argued that it was the development of monopoly capitalism in the imperialist countries which gave rise to colonialism. It was enhanced by capital exports which went to exploit the cheap labour and resources of the colonial, semi-colonial and neocolonial countries. In the process it also dominated the local exploiting classes with small capital, who were unable to compete against monopolies. To this extent 'national capital' was negated, since the bulk of the surplus-value created was extracted in the form of raw materials, agricultural

products and at times in earnings to the monopolies. This contradiction continues. But in order to succeed, the struggles cannot be
relegated to demands for change at international bodies, mere verbal
protests and parliamentary debates etc. So long as the national
question remains unresolved, the role of the exploited masses remains
crucial in the struggle against neocolonialism. Therefore demands for a
new economic order are made increasingly impossible unless framed in
the general context of a new democratic revolution; the role of the
working class and its allies is crucial to the achievement, in any meaningful way, of a new international economic order.

Without such revolutionary leadership of the working class, failures
at Paris or elsewhere are bound to happen, as indeed the Yugoslav
magazine concluded:

> It is indeed obvious that the Paris conference failed to resolve completely a
> single key question constituting an encumbrance to modern international
> economic relations, nor was any progress made towards the acceptance of the
> developing countries' concept of the new international economic order.[15]

Such will continue to be the case and crisis of imperialism.

NOTES

1.   Marx, K.: *Capital* Vol. I, *op. cit.*
2.   Lenin, V.I.: *Imperialism, the Highest Stage of Capitalism, op. cit.*
3.   Clausewitz, K. von: *On War;* Princeton, 1976.
4.   Wilcox, C., *op. cit.*
5.   Shuster, M.R.: *The Public International Law of Money,* p. 18; Oxford,
      1973.
6.   The following quotes are from Wilcox, C. *op. cit.*, pp. 6-24.
7.   Gardner, R.: *Sterling-Dollar Diplomacy,* Oxford 1956. Emphasis added.
8.   *Business Week — Special Report,* 9 May 1977.
9.   See *The Official History of the IMF.* Vol. 1, Part 5. *Narrative: the system
      under stress.*
10.   *Die Ziet,* 19 August 1977. Reproduced in *The German Tribune* no. 802,
      28 August 1977.
11.   Van Meerhaeghe, M.A.G.: *International Economic Institutions,* London,
      1971. Most of what follows is taken from this work.
12.   Schwarzenberger, G.: *Foreign Investments and International Law,* London,
      1969.
13.   Peter Adamson, consultant to the UNDP, New York, quoted in the
      Daily News, 4 November 1976. Emphasis added.
14.   *Review of International Affairs,* Vol. XXVIII no. 653, Belgrade, 1977.
15.   *Ibid.*

BIBLIOGRAPHY

Alavi, H., 'Imperialism Old and New', in *Socialist Register,* London, 1964.
Amin, Samir, *Accumulation on a World Scale,* New York, 1974.
Austin, J., *The Province of Jurisprudence Determined. Lecture II,* London, 1954.

Banaji, J., 'Nationalism and Socialism' in *Monthly Review,* New York, 1973.
_____, 'Review' in *Economic and Political Weekly* vol. IX, no. 36, 1974.
Baran, P.A. & Sweezy, P.M., *Monopoly Capital,* Harmondsworth, 1968.
Barratt-Brown, M., *After Imperialism,* London, 1967.
_____ , *Economics of Imperialism,* Harmondsworth, 1974.
Beckford, G.L., *Persistent Poverty,* London, 1972.
Bernal, J.D., *Science in History,* Harmondsworth, 1969.
_____ , *The Social Function of Science,* Cambridge, Mass., 1973.

Cairncross, A.K., *Home and Foreign Investments,* Cambridge, 1953.
Caudwell, C., *Studies and Further Studies in a Dying Culture,* New York, 1971.
Clausewitz, K. von, *On War,* Princeton, 1976.
Curzon, G., *Multilateral Commercial Diplomacy,* London, 1965.

Dam, K.W., *The GATT: Law and International Economic Organisation,* Chicago, 1970.
Dell, S., 'An Appraisal of UNCTAD III' in *World Development,* vol. 1, no. 5.
Dutt, Palme, *India Today,* London, 1940.

Economic Commission for Africa, *The Multinational Corporation in Africa,* London, 1972.
Emmanuel, A., *Unequal Exchange,* London, 1972.
_____ , 'White Settler Colonialism and the Myth of Investment Imperialism' in *New Left Review* no. 73, 1972.
Engels, F., *Dialectics of Nature,* Moscow, 1969.
_____ , 'Feuerbach and the End of Classical German Philosophy' in Marx & Engels, *Selected Works, op. cit.*
_____ , *Anti-Dühring,* Moscow, 1969.
_____ , *Peasant War in Germany,* Moscow, 1974.

Fieldhouse, D.K., *The Theory of Capitalist Imperialism,* London, 1967.
Frank, A.G., *Capitalism and Underdevelopment in Latin America,* Harmondsworth, 1971.
_____ , *Latin America, Underdevelopment or Revolution,* New York, 1971.
Frankel, J., *Contemporary International Theory,* Oxford, 1973.

Galtung, J., *The European Community: a superpower in the making,* London, 1973.
Gardner, R., *Sterling-Dollar Diplomacy,* Oxford, 1956.
Giddens, A., *Capitalism and Modern Social Theory,* Cambridge, 1972.
Gosovic, B., *UNCTAD Conflict and Compromise,* Leiden, 1972.
Gouldner, A., *The Coming Crisis in Western Sociology,* New York, 1965.

Hindley, B., 'The UNCTAD Agreement in Preferences', in *Journal of World Trade Law,* vol. 5, no. 6.

Hobson, J.A., *Imperialism: A Study,* London, 1902.

ILO, *Employment, Incomes and Equality in Kenya,* Geneva, 1972.

Jalée, P., *Imperialism in the Seventies,* New York, 1974.

Jenks, L.H., *The Migration of British Capital to 1875,* New York, 1927.

Johnson, D. Gale, *World Agriculture in Disarray,* London, 1973.

Laclau, E., 'Feudalism and Capitalism in Latin America', in *New Left Review,* no. 67, 1970.

Langdon, S., 'Multinational Corporations, Taste Transfer and Underdevelopment: a case study from Kenya', in *Review of African Political Economy* no. 2, 1975.

Le Duan, *The Vietnamese Revolution: Fundamental Problems, Essential Tasks,* Hanoi, 1973.

Lenin, V.I., *Imperialism, the Highest Stage of Capitalism,* Moscow, 1970.

————, 'A Characterisation of Economic Romanticism' in *Collected Works,* Moscow, 1970.

————, *On Literature and Art,* Moscow, 1970.

————, *Critical Remarks on the National Question and the Right of Nations to Self-Determination,* Moscow, 1974.

Lewis, J., *Marx, Weber and Value-Free Sociology,* London, 1975.

Luxemburg, R., *The Accumulation of Capital,* London, 1951.

Mandel, E., *Marxist Economic Theory,* London, 1971.

Mao Tse Tung, 'The Chinese Revolution and the Chinese Communist Party, in *Selected Works, Vol. II,* Peking, 1954.

Marx, K., *Capital Vols. I, II & III,* Moscow, 1968 & 1971.

————, 'Capital, The East India Company, Its History and Results' in Marx and Engels, *On Britain,* Moscow, 1971.

————, *Grundrisse,* Harmondsworth, 1973.

Menshikov, S., *Millionaires and Managers,* Moscow, 1969.

Nabudere, D.W., *Political Economy of Imperialism,* London, 1977.

Novack, G., *The Origins of Materialism,* New York, 1971.

Penrose, E., *The International Patent System,* London, 1951.

Pincus, J., *Trade, Aid and Development,* New York, 1967.

Planck, M., *Where is Science Going?,* London, 1933.

Poulantzas, N., 'Internationalisation of Capitalist Relations and the Nation-State' in *Economy and Society* vol. 3, no. 2, 1974.

Ricardo, D., *Principles of Political Economy and Taxation,* Harmondsworth, 1971.

Rose, H., & Rose, S., *Science and Society,* Harmondsworth, 1961.

Rowe, J.W.F., *Primary Commodities in International Trade,* Cambridge, 1965.

Schumpeter, J.A., *Imperialism and Social Classes,* Oxford, 1951.

Schwarzenberger, G., *Foreign Investments and International Law,* London, 1969.

Semnell, B., *The Rise of Free Trade Imperialism,* Cambridge, 1970.

Shuster, M.R., *The Public International Law of Money,* Oxford, 1973.

Sideri, S., *Trade and Power: Informal Colonialism in Anglo-Portuguese Relations,* Rotterdam, 1970.

Stalin, J.V., 'The October Revolution and the National Question', in *Works* vol. IV.

_____ , 'The National Question Once Again' in *Works,* vol. VII.

_____ , 'Marxism and the National Question' in B. Franklin, *The Essential Stalin,* New York, 1972.

Sweezy, P.M., *The Theory of Capitalist Development,* New York, 1942.

Thomson, G., *The Frist Philosophers,* London, 1972.

UNO, *The Impact of Multinational Corporations on Development and International Relations,* New York, 1974.

Van Meerhaeghe, M.A.G., *International Economic Institutions,* London, 1971.

Vernon, Raymond, *Sovereignty at Bay,* Harmondsworth, 1971.

_____ , *Restrictive Business Practices. The operations of multinational enterprises in developing countries,* New York, 1972.

Wilcox, C., *A Charter for World Trade,* New York, 1972.

Yaffe, D.S., 'The Marxian Theory of Crisis, Capital and the State' in *Economy and Society,* vol. 2, no. 2, 1973.

INDEX

AASM (Associated African and Malagasy States), 123-5
ACP (African, Caribbean and Pacific) States, 123-56
Africa, 58, 62, 83, 92-4, 104-5 *et passim;* classes in, 58, 92 *et passim;* industriali-
sation in, 62; Southern, 65, 92-4, 115
African associated states, 112ff
African Trade Ministers Conference, 127
Algiers Charter, 105
Arusha Declaration, 58
Arusha Group, 98,107ff, 123ff

bananas, 52
banks, 24, 46-8, 50-1, 59
Brasseur Plan, 104
Bretton-Woods System, 29, 172
Brussels Nomenclature (BTN), 106ff, 128 *et passim*

cartels, 21, 23, 26, 30, 68
cash crops, 50, 51 *et passim,* and see individual crops
centre-periphery ideologists, 7, 12, 13, 35, 39-41, 95
China, PR, 2, 91
Churches, 3-4, 83-4
Cobden Chevalier Treaty, 16, 160
cocoa, 101
coffee, 101
Commonwealth Preferences, 113
co-operative societies, 55
copper, 101, 145
Cordemex, 57-8
cotton, 101-2
crises, 9, 18-20, 83, 86
customs duty, 132ff
customs union, 98

DCs, 99-100
Dutch companies, 52

East Africa, 83, 113ff
East African Community, 58
ECOSOC, 102
EDF (European Development Fund), 140
EEC, 51, 98, 105ff, 123-51
EEC Common Agricultural Policy, 126
EFTA, 98
Egemont Palace meeting, 125ff
EIB (European Investment Bank), 140
Engels, 3-4, 5, 74, 87,103

feudal merchant capital, 6
feudal production, 7-8
finance capital, 6, 24-5, 34, 45-63
free trade, 68, 97-120
free trade imperialism, 15-16, 17, 28

GATT, 1, 30, 97-103, 146, 167-8
Generalised schemes of preferences, 97-120

INDEX

Group of Eminent Persons, 148

Harbeler Committee, 100
Havana Charter, 29, 145, 176

IBRD, 30, 58, 170, 172-4
IDA, 47, 54-8
IFC, 47, 54
ILO, 60-1
IMF, 1, 30, 170-2
imperialism, 1, 2, 3, 5, 21, 79 *et passim;* as world system, 26; in history, 6, 67; Lenin's 5 characteristics, 28
import substitution, 103
industrial capital, 6, 46
industrialisation, 62, 99, 102, 130, 168
industry, 99-102
ITO, 29-30
Japan, 30, 58, 101, 104ff, 144, 159
jute, 101

Kenya, 57, 60, 61-2, 83-4, 111, 123, 137; ICFC 60; ILO report on, 61

LDCs, 100ff
Lead, 101
Lenin, 1, 6, 19, 20ff, 65, 85, 87, 89, 90, 91-2
LLDCs, 112ff
Lomé Convention, 123-56
Lusaka Manifesto, 93
Luxemburg, Rosa, 11-12, 14, 20, 28, 38, 91, 92

Mao Tse-Tung, 41, 89
Marshall Plan, 29
Marx, 5, 7, 9, 10, 12, 18ff, 65, 68, 78, 81-2, 83 103
Marxist-Leninist theory, 3, 5, 21, 65, 87 *et passim*
merchant capital, 7, 56
mining, 46, 50, 52
monopolies, 19, 21-5, 26, 27, 31ff, 80-1
most-favoured-nation principle, 97, 128
multilateral imperialism, 2, 29-30, 97

nation states, 87-93
national liberation struggles, 87-95
national question, 41, 65, 85, 87-95
neocolonialism, 2, 36, 48 *et passim;* and education, 84-5, 90-1
neo-Marxists, 1, 31, 35ff, 62, 95
new international economic order, 157ff
Nixon Round, 114
North-South dialogue 157ff, 177ff
Nyerere, President, 90

OECD, 104ff
oil-palm, 52
open door policy, 141ff

patent system, 81, 148
petroleum, 46, 50, 52
plantation economies, 51, 52
product coverage, 107-8, 111

raw materials, 50, 52-3
rubber, 52
rules of origin, 107, 109-11, 112, 127

safeguard measures, 107, 108-9, 112
science, 3-4, 65-6, 78ff, 86
SE Asia, 52
Sears, Roebuck and Co., 48, 49
Self-determination, 91
semi-processed products, 50,52
sisal, 57
soap, 62
socialist countries, 93, 106, 111-2, 117-8
Soviet Union, 2, 91, 93, 102, 106ff
'Stabex', 134-8, 147
Stalin, 41, 88-91
sugar, 52, 145-6

Tanzamex, 57
Tanzania, 54-8, 60, 89, 110, 111, 123; BAT, 56; NDCA, 54ff; Sisal Corporation, 57-8; TDFC, 60; TTB. 55ff
tarriffs, 27-8, 101, 107, 108, 111-2, 127 *et passim*
tea, 52, 101
technology, 35, 50, 54, 78-9, 81, 130 *et passim*
textile industry, 79, 102
timber, 101
tobacco, 54-7, 101
Tokyo Declaration, 116
trade, 6-7, 132-4; terms of, 97-120;
transnational corporation, 2, 31, 45-63, 99; research on, 59-63
Trotskyists, 88, 91, 92
Uganda, 57, 83, 111, 123
UN, 1, 100
UN Economic Commission for Africa, 50
UNCTAD, 1, 97, 103-20, 168-9, 176
under-consumptionist theory, 14, 20-1, 32, 38
unequal exchange, 35, 95
US, 2, 21, 29-30, 34, 46, 51, 52, 58, 79, 83, 93-4, 98, 100, 103 *et passim;* banking in 47-9; transnational corporations in, 45; general policy, 164-6
USSR, see Soviet Union
usury imperialism 26

vegetable oils, 101

World Bank, see IBRD

Yaounde Convention, first, 51, 105ff
Yaounde Group, 98, 107ff, 123ff